HIDEAWAYS HOTELS®

The 100 most Beautiful Hotels and Resorts of the World

KLOCKE PUBLISHING COMPANY

Elounda Gulf Villas
& Suites

DAS DURCHSCHNITTLICHE GIBT DER WELT IHREN BESTAND,
DAS AUSSERGEWÖHNLICHE IHREN WERT.

(OSCAR WILDE)

THE AVERAGE GIVES THE WORLD ITS SUBSTANCE,
THE EXCEPTIONAL ITS VALUE.

(OSCAR WILDE)

Klocke Publishing Company

Louis Vuitton Uhr "Speedy". Automatik Chronograph.
Erhältlich ausschließlich in Louis Vuitton Geschäften. Tel. (0211) 864700 www.louisvuitton.com

EDITORIAL

Auch eine Reise von tausend Meilen
beginnt mit einem Schritt.
(Laotse, chinesischer Philosoph)

Even a journey of a thousand miles
begins with a single step.
(Laotse, Chinese philosopher)

Seit nunmehr zehn Jahren ist unser internationales Reisemagazin HIDEAWAYS zu einer kleinen „Bibel" für Luxusreisende und Connaisseurs auf der ganzen Welt geworden. Wir haben es uns zur Aufgabe gemacht, die einzigartigen, die ganz besonderen Hoteladressen für Sie ausfindig zu machen, die an den atemberaubendsten Destinationen liegen, die sich mit großer Leidenschaft und einem allgegenwärtigen Service dem Wohlgefühl ihrer Gäste widmen und ihnen Interieurs und eine Privatsphäre bieten, die vollkommene Erholung garantieren. Dies müssen nicht ausschließlich Resorts auf einsamen Inseln sein, die Robinson-Crusoe-Feeling deluxe vermitteln, sondern können ebenso hideaways, liebevolle Refugien inmitten von Metropolen sein. Dieses Buch ist eine Zusammenstellung der besten Adressen, die wir entdeckt haben, die wir Ihnen teilweise schon ausführlich in unserem Magazin vorgestellt haben oder Ihnen noch ausführlich präsentieren werden. Wir hoffen, dass die Lektüre dieses Buches vielleicht ein erster Schritt zu zahlreichen Reisen von tausend und noch mehr Meilen sein wird und Sie Urlaubsaufenthalte erleben, die unvergesslich bleiben werden.

Over the last ten years our HIDEAWAYS international travel magazine has established itself as a small "bible" for discerning travellers and connoisseurs across the world. Our objective is to search out the world's very best and most unique hotels for you. Establishments that command impossibly beautiful locations, that are dedicated to looking after the needs of their guests with uncompromising service standards and that offer the kind of privacy and accommodation needed to ensure complete relaxation. And we're not just talking about resorts on far-away desert islands where you can be castaway in the lap of luxury. Our hideaways also include lovingly maintained retreats at the heart of big cities. This book features the very best establishments that we have discovered. Some of these have either already been presented in detail in our magazine or will be in the future. We hope that reading this book will provide you with all the inspiration you need to embark on the first of many wonderful journeys and that you will go on to experience some unforgettably blissful holidays.

Thomas und Martina Klocke
Herausgeber / Publisher

HIDEAWAYS HOTELS
The 100 most Beautiful Hotels and Resorts of the World
2005 / 2006

Klocke Publishing Company
Höfeweg 40
33619 Bielefeld
Germany
Phone: +49 - 5 21 - 9 11 11- 0
Fax: +49 - 5 21 - 9 11 11-12
www.klocke-publishing-company.com
info@klocke-publishing-company.com

Publisher and CEO
Thomas and Martina Klocke

Editor-In-Chief
Thomas Klocke

Marketing Director
Wolfgang Pohl

Photography
Ydo Sol, Klaus Lorke, Martin Bäuml, Jürgen Gutowski,
featured hotels & resorts

Editors
Günter Ned, Gundula Luig-Runge, Sabine Herder,
Bernd Teichgräber, Peter Unger, Jürgen Gutowski

Graphic concept
factory agency, Bielefeld

Graphic design
Sabina Winkelnkemper, Sabine Flöter, Thomas Kacza

Lithography
Klocke Media-Services, Holger Schönfeld, Werner Busch

Production
Claudia Schwarz, Nicole Leermakers

Translation
Twiggs Translation, Zetel-Neuenburg

Printers
Graphischer Betrieb Gieseking GmbH & Co. KG
Bielefeld / Germany
Printed of Optimago from Igepa, made by Burgo

Printed in Germany

ISBN 3-934170-31-5

One&Only Palmilla

DESTINATIONEN / DESTINATIONS

DESTINATIONEN / DESTINATIONS

DEDON®
travel

Discover the spirit of Dedon Island!

Dedon Travel

Marie-Curie-Straße 1

21337 Lüneburg/Germany

Phone: +49 (0) 41 31 40 99 51

Fax: +49 (0) 41 31 40 99 50

info@dedontravel.de

www.dedontravel.de

big's

DESTINATIONEN / DESTINATIONS

«Einmal selbst sehen, ist mehr wert,
als hundert Neuigkeiten hören.»

Japanisches Sprichwort

Erhältlich in jeder Kuoni Reisen-Filiale und in ausgewählten Reisebüros.

BVLGARI

CONTEMPORARY ITALIAN JEWELLERS

THE NEW FRAGRANCE FOR MEN

Komfort à la française: die Air France Business Class l'Espace Affaires
Komfortsessel mit 180° Neigungswinkel, 27 % mehr persönlicher Freiraum, Ablageflächen, 10,4" interaktive Videobildschirme, individueller Service. In Kürze auf allen Langstreckenflügen von Air France.
www.airfrance.de

wo der Himmel am schönsten ist

INHALT A – Z / CONTENTS A – Z

LIVE FROM LONDON

BURBERRY
BRIT

THE FRAGRANCE FOR WOMEN

INHALT A – Z / CONTENTS A – Z

INHALT A – Z / CONTENTS A – Z

Hotel Cipriani, Venedig

traumhaft
Reisen

die schönsten Strände... türkisblaues Meer... die besten Hotels...

STROHBECK
Reisen-Stuttgart

LAUSTRASSE 88   70597 STUTTGART   TELEFON 0711- 46 85 18   FAX 0711- 48 77 68
www.strohbeckreisen.de   e-mail: info@strohbeckreisen.de

AIR MAURITIUS die Partner-Airline von Strohbeck Reisen für Mauritius, Réunion und Südafrika

Indischer Ozean / Indian Ocean
Maldives, Mauritius, Seychelles

Dieser Malediven-Traum liegt am Südende des Baa-Atolls. Dhuni Kolhu ist eine Insel von makelloser, magischer Schönheit, überzogen von üppigster Tropenvegetation, umsäumt von paradiesisch weißen Stränden, eingefasst von einer Lagune in leuchtendem Türkis, mit Korallenbänken, die das Schnorcheln zu einer faszinierenden Begegnung mit der Unterwasserwelt machen. Traumhaft auch die palmstrohgedeckten Villen und Suiten des Resorts. Sie liegen entweder in stiller Abgelegenheit unter Blüten, Farnen und Palmen verborgen auf der Insel oder draußen über der Lagune. Am luxuriösesten erholt man sich in den beiden Lagoon Palace Suiten. Die Baderäume liegen perfekt geschützt im Freien, in das Holzdeck ist ein großer Süßwasserpool eingelassen, von überall hat man einen betörenden Blick über die Lagune, wunderbar die Sonnenuntergänge. Im Herzen des Coco Palm Dhuni Kolhu wartet das Coco Spa mit vier Villen im balinesischen Stil auf Beauty- und Wellnessfans, die die ganzheitliche, naturbezogene asiatische Heilphilosophie schätzen. Man speist maledivische, asiatische, indische und Thai-Cuisine. Romantisch die Inszenierung von Trauungen nach dem Stil der Einheimischen.

This piece of Maldive paradise lies to the south of the Baa Atoll. Dhuni Kolhu is an island of pure magical beauty, covered with fertile tropical beauty and framed by white sand. It is surrounded by a lagoon of bright turquoise with coral banks that make snorkelling a fascinating encounter with the underwater world. The villas and suites of the resorts are heavenly, set as they are among palm trees. They are located either in quiet isolation, hidden by flowers, ferns and palms or out on the lagoon. The most luxurious space for relaxation are the two Lagoon Palace Suites. The bathrooms are situated in complete privacy in the open air. A fresh water pool has been incorporated into the deck that is made of wooden. At every point you will be bewitched by the view of the lagoon and fascinated by wonderful sunsets. In the heart of Coco Palm Dhuni Kolhu the Coco Spa comprising of four villas in Balinese style, awaits beauty and wellness fans. The treatments are based on holistic, natural, Asian healing philosophies. You will enjoy a variety of Maldivian, Asian, Indian and Thai cuisine. You can even engage in a wedding ceremony according to local tradition.

Coco Palm Dhuni Kolhu
General Manager:
Patrick Heuze
Dhuni Kolhu Island
Baa Atoll
Republic of Maldives
Phone: 0 09 60 / 23 00 11
Fax: 0 09 60 / 23 00 22
E-mail: dhunikolhu@
cocopalm.com.mv
Internet: www.cocopalm.com

98 villas and suites
Beach Villa (according to season) from US$ 326 to 536, Deluxe Villa from US$ 386 to 616, Lagoon Villa from US$ 686 to 916, Lagoon Palace Suite from US$ 1,086 to 1,316

Distance from airport:
30 minutes by seaplane

Membership:
Small Luxury Hotels
of the World

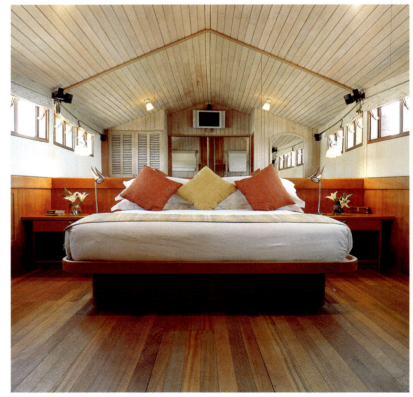

Das Konzept von Dhoni Mighili ist einzigartig. Die Trauminsel auf den Malediven ist gerade mal 1500 Quadratmeter groß. Der Clou des Resorts: Der Hauptwohnsitz der Gäste befindet sich nicht an Land. Wer auf Dhoni Mighili Urlaub macht, lebt auf einem Dhoni. So nennen die Malediver ihre traditionell geformten Holzboote. Versteht sich, dass die sechs Boote, die zur Dhoni-Mighili-Flotte gehören, als Luxusexemplare in der Lagune vor Anker liegen, schwimmende Suiten, perfekt in Hightech und Design, ausgestattet mit allem, was das Herz selbst anspruchsvollster Reisender begehrt. Die Crew ist 24 Stunden pro Tag einsatzbereit, kocht auf Wunsch für die Gäste, freut sich darauf, auch ganz spontane Ausflugswünsche sofort wahr werden zu lassen, ob es zum Tauchen gehen soll, zum Lunch auf eine einsame Insel oder am Abreisetag zurück zum Flughafen von Male. Alle Dhonis haben als Dependance entweder einen Beach Bungalow oder einen Beach Bungalow mit Plunge Pool auf der Insel. Dort gibt es auch ein vorzügliches Restaurant mit multikultureller Gourmet-Cuisine, eine Bar im Dhoni-Design, ein exklusives Sen Spa und alles, was sonst zu einem First-Class-Resort gehört.

Dhoni Mighili's concept is truly unique. This desert island hideaway in the Maldives covers an area of just 1,500 square metres. Just imagine residing in a place that is not on land. Those holidaying on Dhoni Mighili reside on a Dhoni. This is the name that the Maldivians give to their traditionally shaped wooden boats. It goes without saying, of course, that these six boats belonging to the Dhoni-Mighili fleet are incredibly luxurious specimens. At anchor in the lagoon, these boats can best be described as floating luxury suites equipped with everything that even the most discerning of travellers could want. Crew members are available 24 hours a day and are always happy to prepare a meal for guests or embark on a spontaneous trip, whether it's scuba diving, lunch on a deserted island or back to Male Airport when its time to leave. The Dhonis also come with a Bungalow "Residence" on the island. Here on the island you will also find a superb restaurant offering multi-cultural gourmet cuisine, a bar featuring Dhoni design, an exclusive Sen Spa and everything else you would expect from a first-class resort.

Dhoni Mighili
Direction: David and Jacqueline O'Hara
Management: Per Aquum
P.O. Box 2017, North Ari Atoll
Republic of Maldives
Phone: 0 09 60 / 6 66 / 07 51
Fax: 0 09 60 / 6 66 / 07 27
E-mail:
info@dhonimighili.com
Internet:
www.dhonimighili.com

6 Luxury Dhonis with 2 Beach Bungalows and 4 Beach Bungalows with Plunge Pool
Luxury Dhoni with Beach Bungalow from US$ 700 to 1,330, Luxury Dhoni with Beach Bungalow and Plunge Pool from US$ 800 to 1,490 per person per night on Full board basis + 10 % service charge and Government Bed Tax of US$ 8 per person per night

Distance from airport:
30-minute seaplane flight

Das neue Malediven-Resort Huvafen Fushi hält alles, was der Name verspricht – huvafen heißt „Traum" und fushi „Insel". Die zauberhafte Natur dieser Insel im North Male Atoll mischt sich mit Wohnwelten, in denen modernes Design die Akzente setzt. Gäste relaxen hier in 43 Bungalows am Strand oder über dem Wasser, wobei jede Kategorie über ihre eigenen Reize verfügt. Alle Bungalows verfügen über einen eigenen Plunge Pool, der herrliche Erfrischungen beim Sonnenbaden ermöglicht. Schon die Beach Bungalows, direkt am Strand gelegen mit Blick über die Lagune, haben alles, was man sich an zeitgemäßem Luxus wünschen kann, vom Kingsize-Bett bis zum Bose-Surround-System und Plasma-TV. Noch exklusiver sind die Overwater Bungalows, entweder mit Blick auf die Lagune oder auf den Ozean, die von ihrer privaten Terrasse ein unmittelbares Eintauchen in den kristallklaren Ozean ermöglichen. Auf einem exzellenten Niveau präsentiert sich die Cuisine in den drei Restaurants. Das Spektrum reicht von kreativer frischer südostasiatischer Küche über internationale Delikatessen bis hin zur Pizza aus dem Steinofen. Außergewöhnlich ist auch der Aquum Spa, der als weltweit einziger Spa über zwei Unterwasser-Behandlungsräume verfügt. Bestens geschulte Therapeuten verwöhnen hier mit vielseitigen Treatments.

This new resort in the Maldives more than lives up to its name – huvafen means "dream" und fushi "island". It tempts its residents into a world full of beauty. The wonderful environment of this tiny island in the North Male Atoll fits in magnificently with the breathtaking modern design of the living accommodation. Guests to the island live in 43 bungalows either on the beach or over-water. Each of these categories is attractive in its own way. Located directly on the beach with views of the lagoon, the beach bungalows have everything you would expect of contemporary luxury from king-size bed with Frette-sheets and covers to Bose surround-system and plasma screen TV. The over-water villas are even more exclusive, offering views across the lagoon or the ocean. They all have their own plunge-pool on the terrace which grants perfect refreshments for sun-worshippers. If you are looking for excellent cuisine, you will find the island's three restaurants very obliging. Here you can enjoy creative fresh South-East-Asian cuisine and international dishes as well as original stone-oven Italian pizzas. The Aquum Spa with its beautiful over-water and the worlds first under-water treatment rooms, offers a holistically-orientated range of treatments.

Huvafen Fushi
Per Aquum Resorts & Spas
General Manager:
Nick Downing
P.O. Box 2017
North Male Atoll
Phone: 0 09 60 / 6 64 / 42 22
Fax: 0 09 60 / 6 64 / 43 33
E-mail:
info@huvafenfushi.com
Internet:
www.huvafenfushi.com

43 Beach Bungalows
and Over-water Bungalows,
each with private plunge
pool, depending on categroy
and season start from
US$ 660 to 4,800
including breakfast
One Beach Pavilion
with private pool (800 sqm)
from US$ 2,500 to 4,400
Two Ocean Pavilions
with private pool (330 sqm)
from US$ 2,900 to 4,800
All rates are subject to
10 % service charge an
Government Bed Tax of
US$ 8 per person per night

Distance from Airport:
35 minutes by speedboat

HILTON MALDIVES RESORT & SPA, RANGALI ISLAND

FACILITIES

Das exklusive Resort auf dem South Ari Atoll, bestehend aus zwei Inselchen, ist ein spektakulärer Ort, um die Schönheit des Indischen Ozeans zu genießen. Weit verstreut in den tropischen Gärten der Insel Rangalifinolhu zeigen sich 79 bis zu 300 Quadratmeter große Beach Villas als luxuriöse und elegante Oasen der Sinnlichkeit und des Verwöhnens. Direkt am Strand sind die neuen Villas das Beste, was die Malediven an traditioneller Architektur, Design und Atmosphäre zu bieten haben. Wer dem Ozean noch näher sein will, der zieht nach Rangali Island. Fünfzig Water Villas in fünf Kategorien erstrecken sich auf Stelzen errichtet über dem Waser. Zwei große Sunset Water Villas mit Glasboden, Whirlpool, eigenem Butler und Marmorbädern liegen in einem separaten Teil der Lagune. Hinzu kommen 21 neue, über dem Wasser erbaute Spa Water Villas als Teil des atemberaubenden Over Water Spa Village vor Rangalifinolhu. Jede der Villas mit Meerblick verfügt über einen eigenen Behandlungsraum, eine Freiluft-Badewanne und eine Sonnenterrasse. Mit sieben Restaurants und drei Bars verfügt das Hilton Maldives Resort & Spa über die größte kulinarische Vielfalt aller Resorts der Malediven, wobei man im ersten vollverglasten Unterwasserrestaurant der Welt fünf Meter unter der Meeresoberfläche und mitten in einem lebhaften Korallenriff nicht nur lukullische Hochgenüsse, sondern auch herrliche Ausblicke auf die faszinierende Unterwasserwelt genießen kann.

Consisting of two small islands, it's hard to imagine a more pleasing location for enjoying all the beauty of the Indian Ocean than the Hilton Maldives Resort & Spa on the South Ari Atoll. Rangalifinolhu Island's tropical gardens have been used to accommodate 79 generously-proportioned Beach Villas (up to 300 square metres). Here you can look forward to indulging yourself in luxury, style and contentment. Located directly on the beach, the resort's new unparalleled villas ooze traditional architecture, style and atmosphere. If ever there were a place to feel at one with the ocean, then Rangali must surely be it. It offers fifty Water Villas in five categories standing on stilts over the water. Located in a separate part of the lagoon, two large glass-bottomed Sunset Water Villas with their own whirlpool, butler and marble bathroom say to anyone with the eyes to see "Look at us, this is paradise". 21 new Spa Water Villas have been built over the water and form a part of the breathtakingly beautiful Over-Water Spa Village, just off the shores of Rangalifinolhu. All of the villas with a sea view have their very own treatment room, an open-air bath and a sun terrace. No other resort in the Maldives offers more culinary variety than the Hilton Maldives Resort & Spa. It boasts seven restaurants, three bars and something very special indeed. Just imagine dining in the world's very first underwater restaurant at a depth of five metres in the middle of a living coral reef. As well as the delicious food and drink, you can also look forward to marvelling at the breathtakingly beautiful marine life.

Hilton Maldives Resort & Spa
P.O. Box 2034
South Ari Atoll, MV, Maldives
Phone: 0 09 60 / 45 06 29
Fax: 0 09 60 / 45 06 19
At July :
Phone: 0 09 60 / 6 68 06 29
Fax: 0 09 60 / 6 68 06 19
E-mail:
maldives@hilton.com
Internet:
www.hilton.com/
worldwideresorts

150 villas
from US$ 150 to 3,450

Distance from airport:
30 minute seaplane flight
from Male Airport

Membership:
Hilton Worldwide Resorts

Das One&Only Reethi Rah, in ca. 50 Minuten mit der Yacht vom Flughafen in Male zu erreichen, präsentiert sich als neue Spitzen-Destination für anspruchsvollste Inselurlauber. Die Insel selbst zeigt sich als Malediven-Schönheit ersten Ranges mit einer kristallklaren Lagune, mit vielen Buchten und einem Strand, der sage und schreibe sechs Kilometer lang ist. Auf internationalem First-Class-Niveau die Lage, der Schnitt und die Ausstattung der 130 Villen und Suiten. Ob man an Land oder über dem Wasser wohnt, man hat auf Wunsch einen privaten Pool zur Verfügung. Es gibt große Veranden, Sonnendecks, Hängematten über der Lagune, Holzterrassen mit überdachten Ess- und Sitzbereichen, dazu jeden erdenklichen Komfort von Klimaanlage bis zu Plasma-TV, DVD-Player und Surround-Sound-System. Breitgefächert der kulinarische Rahmen: Gäste speisen je nach Restaurant orientalische, mediterrane, zeitgenössische japanische Küche etc. Erstklassig auch das Wellness-, Beauty- und Fitnessprogramm auf über 9 300 Quadratmetern Spa-Fläche an Land und über dem Ozean. Aktivitäten nach Lust und Laune, vom Tiefseefischen und Tauchen bis zum Picknick auf einer einsamen Insel oder einer romantischen Hochzeit am Indischen Ozean.

The new One&Only Reethi Rah, reachable in approx. fifty minutes by yacht from the airport at Male, is a top destination for discerning island holidaymakers. A Maldive treasure of the highest order, this island has a crystal clear lagoon with many beaches including one that is literally six kilometres long. The location, layout and décor of the 130 villas and suites are of the highest international standard. Whether you live on land or on water, you can choose to have a private swimming pool, a large veranda, a sun deck, hammock over water or wooden terrace with shady areas for eating and lounging. On top of this every conceivable comfort is provided from air-conditioning, plasma TV, DVD player and surround-sound system. The culinary programme is diverse. Depending on the restaurant, guests can dine oriental, Mediterranean, Japanese and so on. At the Spa Centre that covers 9,500 square metres above land and sea the agenda for wellness, beauty and sports is exceptional. Some of the other fun activities you can enjoy to your hearts content are deep sea fishing and diving, having a picnic on a desert island and taking part in a romantic wedding on the Indian Ocean.

One&Only Reethi Rah
Republic of Maldives
Phone: 0 09 60 / 44 88 00
Fax: 0 09 60 / 44 88 22
E-mail: reservations@
oneandonlyresorts.com.mv
Internet:
www.oneandonlyresorts.com

130 villas and suites
Beach Villas (according to season and category) from US$ 625 to 1,200, Duplex Villas from US$ 1,250 to 2,700, Grand Beach Villas from US$ 1,590 to 3,600, Water Villas from US$ 920 to 1,700, Grand Water Villa from US$ 1,840 to 3,400

Distance from airport:
50 minutes

Membership:
One&Only Resorts

Einmal auf dem exklusiven Soneva Fushi Resort auf Kunfunadhoo im nördlichen Baa Atoll angekommen, weiß man, dass der Rest der Welt Zeit hat. Den Besucher erwartet außer einem Luxusresort auch ein echtes Naturerlebnis mit Robinson-Crusoe-Feeling, zumal die 65 Bungalows, Suiten und Villen in dem dichten Blätterwald weit verteilt sind. Hinter den Lamellentüren beginnt das First-Class-Wohnen im Urwald mit stilvollen Interieurs aus nachwachsenden Materialien. Soneva Fushi ist ein Resort mit Tischen aus Bambus oder Palmenholz, Wandlampen aus Büffelhaut und Schränken, die sich hinter Bastmatten verbergen. Das Badezimmer mit sonnenhellen Fliesen findet man draußen, abgeschlossen als eigenen Garten, dessen Bananenstauden abends angestrahlt werden. Zu jeder Villa gehört ein Garten, der in einem feinen Sandstrand ausläuft. Die maledivische Küche ist, wie so oft auf entlegenen Inseln, sehr fischreich und dabei der indischen ähnlich. Viele Gemüse- und Salatsorten werden im eigenen Biogarten angebaut und kommen frisch in die Küche. Für jede Art von unmotorisiertem Wassersport bietet Soneva Fushi die besten Voraussetzungen. Ob Surfbrett, Segelboot oder Katamaran, alles kann man hier gleich vom Strand aus zu Wasser lassen. Ganzheitliche Anwendungen im Six Senses Spa ergänzen den Wohlfühlreigen. Seit neuestem bietet das Luxusresort Villen mit eigenen Spa-Suiten an, in denen sich der Gast ganz privat verwöhnen lassen kann. Bei Buchungen dieser Spa-Suiten sind zwei Anwendungen pro Tag im Reservierungspreis enthalten.

When you arrive at the exclusive Soneva Fushi Resort in Kunfunadhoo on the north Baa Atoll, you cannot help feeling that the rest of the world is far, far away. Not only can visitors to the island look forward to enjoying all the comforts of a luxury resort, they can also experience a wonderful natural environment – desert island feel included. This is because its 65 bungalows, suites and villas have been spread out in the thick tropical wood. First-class living begins in style behind your strip tropical forest doors. The interiors are stylish and have been made from renewable materials. Soneva Fushi is a resort with tables made out of bamboo or palm trees, wall lamps out of buffalo hide and wardrobes hidden behind raffia mats. To find the bathroom with its bright tiles, you have to look outside. It's self-contained with its own garden and spot-lit banana trees. Each villa has its own garden that opens out onto a fine sandy beach. Maldivian cuisine draws heavily on fish and is similar to Indian cuisine. A large variety of vegetables and salads are grown in its own organic gardens. Soneva Fushi offers conditions for all kinds of non-motorized water sports. So, whether it's surfing, sailing boat or catamaran, you can launch everything from the beach. This wellbeing experience is rounded off by the Six Senses Spa and its comprehensive range of treatments. Villas with self-contained Spa Suites are a recent addition to this luxury resort, where guests can look forward to indulging themselves in private. Two treatments per day are included in the price when booking the Spa Suites.

Soneva Fushi Resort
General Manager:
Stephen Antram
Kunfunadhoo Island
Baa Atoll
Republic of Maldives
Phone: 0 09 60 / 23 03 04
Fax: 0 09 60 / 23 03 74
E-mail: reservations-fushi@sonevaresorts.com
Internet:
www.six-senses.com

65 villas
from US$ 330 to 5,000

Distance from airport:
35 minute float plane flight

Membership:
Small Luxury Hotels

Wer das Soneva Gili Resort, „Hideaway of the Year 2004", auf einem nur 12 000 Quadratmeter großen Eiland im maledivischen Nord-Atoll betritt, ist am Ziel seiner Inselträume. Ausnahmslos „Water Villas" sind alle 45 Suiten und Residenzen von Soneva Gili, auf Stelzen in die hellblaue Lagune gesetzt. Die außergewöhnlichsten sind die sieben Crusoe-Residenzen und das neue „Private Reserve". Diese Villen erreicht man weder über einen Holzsteg noch mittels einer Straße, sondern nur mit dem eigenen Paddelboot oder mit dem Dhoni, einer kleinen überdachten Fähre. Jede Residenz verschlägt selbst dem weit gereisten Luxus-Traveller mit sofortiger Wirkung den Atem, wenn er sein privates Refugium betritt. Das doppelstöckige, 150 Quadratmeter große Holzhaus ist ein Paradebeispiel für ökologisch-organische Architektur sowie kompromisslosen Luxus. Das Personal präsentiert sich wie im Lehrbuch der Hotellerie: 180 Mitarbeiter kümmern sich hier voll freundlicher Hingabe um die höchstens 90 Gäste des Resorts. Ein weiteres Highlight ist der Six-Senses-Spa-Bereich mit wohltuenden Treatments durch die bestens geschulten Therapeuten. Ob an der Bar oder im Restaurant an Land: die Küche von Soneva Gili lockt mit mediterran-asiatischen Zubereitungen. Jeden Abend steht ein neues leichtes Vier-Gänge-Menü auf der Karte, dazu vegetarische und Spa-Spezialitäten.

Entering the Soneva Gili Resort, "Hideaway of the Year 2004", and stepping onto an island measuring just 12,000 square metres is to fulfil your wildest holiday paradise dreams. All Soneva Gili's 45 suites and residences are Water Villas, that is, they stand on stilts in the turquoise-blue lagoon. The seven Crusoe Residences and the new "Private Reserve" are the most remarkable. Rather than via a wooden landing platform or path, the only way of accessing Crusoe Residences is with your own paddleboat or with the Dhoni, a small covered ferry. All the villas are special enough to take away the breath of even the most experienced of luxury travellers as they enter their very own private retreat. The two-story, 150 square metres wooden building is a shining example of how to draw on organic materials to create environmentally-sound architecture with uncompromising luxury. The island's personnel pride themselves on providing a first-class service. A staff of 180 is on hand to take friendly care of the resort's guests, who never number more than 90. One of the other things that makes this resort so special is its Six Senses Spa, offering wonderful treatments by professionally trained therapists. Regardless of whether you're at the bar or in the restaurant, the cuisine on offer at Soneva Gili is a tempting proposition and draws on Mediterranean and Asian influences. A new light four-course meal is on the menu every evening, as well as vegetarian and healthy speciality options.

Soneva Gili Resort
North Male Atoll
General Manager:
Peter Nilsson
Republic of Maldives
Phone: 0 09 60 / 44 03 04
Fax: 0 09 60 / 44 03 05
E-mail: reservations-gili@
sonevaresorts.com
Internet:
www.sixsenses.com

45 suites and residences
from US$ 740 to 8,000

Distance from airport:
15 minutes speed boat
journey

Membership:
Small Luxury Hotels

Eingebettet in die idyllische Küstenlandschaft der Baie aux Tortues an der Nordwestküste der Insel spricht das Oberoi Mauritius die emotionalen Wünsche einer internationalen Gästeklientel an, die nach exklusiver Privatsphäre, friedvoller Ruhe und regenerierender Entspannung sucht. Optisches Highlight ist ein 12 Meter hoher Aquadukt, der den Eingangsbereich des Resorts bewacht und einen idyllischen Naturteich speist. Rechts neben diesem zentralen Punkt der Anlage gruppieren sich die Gemeinschaftsgebäude im Halbkreis: Hauptrestaurant, Bar, Teepavillon, Shop, Tagungsräume sowie Rezeption. Insgesamt 73 luxuriöse Garten-Villen, mit und ohne Pool sowie als Reihenhäuschen angelegte Luxury Pavilions verteilen sich locker über den bezaubernden Tropenpark. Abtauchen in wohlige Wellness-Welten verspricht „The Oberoi Spa by Banyan Tree", ein Ort, wo Körper, Geist und Seele auf angenehmste Art loslassen und neue Kräfte sammeln können. Zum Topangebot an Massagen, Körper- und Beautyanwendungen kommen noch Sauna, Dampfbad, Fitnesscenter und zwei Flutlicht-Tenniscourts. Exquisit, wie das übrige Ambiente, zeigt sich auch die Gastronomie. Im stilvollen Open-Air-Restaurant diniert man eine vorzügliche Fusion-Cuisine, bestehend aus kreolischen, indischen, orientalischen wie europäischen Komponenten.

Nestled in the idyllic coastal area of the Baie aux Tortues on the north-western coast of the island, The Oberoi Mauritius has clearly been designed to tempt the emotions of international travellers looking for an exclusive private atmosphere, peace, tranquillity and relaxation. You cannot fail to be struck by a 12-metre high aqueduct that stands sentry in front of the resort's entrance area, feeding an idyllic natural pond. The resort's guest-facility buildings are grouped to the right of this, the resort's central aspect. Here you will find the main restaurant, bar, tea pavilion, shop, meeting rooms and reception. All in all, 73 luxurious Garden Villas, with and without pool, and Luxury Pavilions are spaced generously around this breathtakingly beautiful tropical garden. "The Oberoi Spa by Banyan Tree" holds out its hand and invites you to submerge yourself in a world of wellness and wellbeing. Just imagine spending time in a place where you can let your body, soul and spirit go and recharge your batteries – adding some valuable implies a waste of time. In addition to an excellent range of massages, body treatments and beauty treatments, the resort also has a sauna, steam bath, gym and two floodlit tennis courts. Its range of gastronomic delights is just as exquisite as its ambience. You can look forward to dining in a tastefully decorated open-air restaurant to first-rate Fusion cuisine that draws on Creole, Indian, Oriental and European elements.

The Oberoi Mauritius
General Manager:
Markus Engel
Baie aux Tortues
Pointe aux Piments
Mauritius
Phone: 0 02 30 / 2 04 / 36 00
Fax: 0 02 30 / 2 04 / 36 25
E-mail: reservations@
oberoi-mauritius.com
Internet:
www.oberoihotels.com

Luxury Pavilions
Luxury Villa
Luxury Villa with pool
Royal Villa
from Euro 700 to 2,600

Distance from airport:
50 minutes

Memberships:
The Leading Small Hotels
of the World,
SLH – Small Luxury Hotels

The Residence setzte bei seiner Eröffnung im Jahr 1998 ein neues Glanzlicht in die Hotelszene von Mauritius. Großzügigste Architektur, einer der schönsten Strände der Insel, stattliche Zimmer und Suiten, exquisite Cuisine, weite Poollandschaft, ein prachtvoller Garten, und das alles eingewoben in einen Traum aus vergangener Zeit: The Residence lässt den Zauber des legendären kolonialen Lebensstils wieder auferstehen. Wann und wo immer man einem Mitglied der Crew begegnet, der hübsche junge Mann, die schöne junge Frau, in leichte, sandfarbene Leinengewänder gekleidet, verneigen sich und grüßen mit vor der Brust gefalteten Händen, und eine der ersten Bekanntschaften, die man macht, ist der persönliche Butler. Wenn man es wünscht, packt er die Koffer aus, lässt ein Bad ein, bügelt Kleidungsstücke auf. Die 163 Zimmer und Suiten zeigen großzügige Eleganz, vom „einfachen" Garden View Room (54 Quadratmeter) bis zu den Colonial Ocean View Suites (164 Quadratmeter). Die feine Küche zeigt sich von der multikulturellen Exotik der Insel inspiriert. „The Sanctuary", das Spa, verwöhnt seine Gäste u. a. mit La Prairie. Das Schweizer Kosmetik-Label präsentiert seine Linie „The Art of Beauty" bekanntlich nur in den exklusivsten Refugien der Welt.

When it opened its doors in 1998 the Residence became a new highlight in the hotel scene in Mauritius. Stately architecture, one of the loveliest beaches on the island, majestic rooms and suites, exquisite cuisine, an extensive pool landscape and a fabulous garden were all woven into a dream of bygone days. The Residence successfully rekindles the magical lifestyle associated with colonial life. Regardless of when or where you come across one of the Residence's employees, be it one its handsome young men or pretty young women in light sandy-coloured linen garments, you will be greeted with a bow with their hands joined at chest level. One of the first acquaintances you will make will be with your personal butler. If you wish he will unpack your bags, run the bath and iron your clothes. The 163 rooms and suites show an indulgent elegance from the "simple" Garden View Room (54 square metres) to the Colonial Ocean View Suites (164 square metres). The fine restaurant is inspired by the multicultural exoticism of the island. The spa appropriately named "The Sanctuary" will spoil you with the very best products such as La Prairie. Indeed, this Swiss cosmetics company is renowned for reserving its "The Art of Beauty" range for only the most exclusive of establishments.

The Residence Mauritius
Coastal Road, Belle Mare
Mauritius
Hotel Manager:
Frédéric Chrétien
More information and brochures of the hotel are available from the Germay office:
The Residence Mauritius
c/o EuroMarketing Connections
An St. Swidbert 11
D-40489 Düsseldorf
Phone:
00 49 / (0) 2 11 / 4 05 65 04
Fax:
00 49 / (0) 2 11 / 4 05 65 06
think@EuroMarketing
Connections.de

135 rooms und 28 suites
in 4 categories

Available from large tour operators such as airtours, Dertour and/or from specialist operators such as Strohbeck Reisen, Trauminsel Reisen or Treasure Islands with offers starting from Euro 1,635 for flight, 7 nights incl. half board per person in a double room.
Phone: 02 11 / 4 05 85 99
Fax: 02 11 / 4 05 85 27
info@treasure-islands.de

Fotos: fotoseeker

Brandneu auf der Trauminsel im Indischen Ozean: die erste Destination von Elegant Heritage Mauritius. Sie hat den schönen Namen Voile d'Or, Goldsegel (spielt auf die Segelschiffe an, die vor Zeiten mit ihrer Goldfracht hier ankerten) und liegt in Bel Ombre, einer erst jüngst für den gehobenen Tourismus erschlossenen Küstenregion im Südwesten. Erlesen die Atmosphäre des Voile d'Or Resort & Spa. Sie ist spürbar inspiriert von maurischer und portugiesischer Architektur, von englischem Kolonialstil und feiner französischer Lebensart. Paradebeispiel: das Restaurant Le Gavroche des Tropiques – weitgereisten Feinschmeckern dürften da die Ohren klingen, richtig: Der tropische Gourmettreff zaubert seine elegante kreative Cuisine unter der Patronage von Michel Roux jun. auf die Teller, dem Zwei-Sterne-Chef des Le Gavroche in London. Gäste wohnen in 181 luxuriösen Zimmern und Suiten. Attraktiv das Hotel-im-Hotel-Konzept für die Bewohner der Clubzimmer und Suiten: Ihnen steht exklusiv das Colonial Club House zur Verfügung mit eigenem Pool, Restaurant, Business Center etc. Es gibt einen Nightclub, ein exzeptionelles Spa und alles, was den Aufenthalt an einem Traumstrand von Mauritius unvergesslich machen kann.

Brand new on the island paradise in the Indian Ocean: the top destination of Elegant Heritage Mauritius. It was given the name Voile d'Or meaning Sail of Gold (a reference to the sailing ships that anchored here with their gold bullion many years ago) and it lies in Bel Ombre, one of the coastal regions which was recently developed for discerning tourists in the south west. The atmosphere at the Voile d'Or Resort and Spa is exclusive. It was visibly inspired by Moorish and Portuguese architecture, English Colonialism and the fine French way of life. A classic example is offered by Le Gavroche des Tropiques Restaurant where gourmets from far and wide will be carried away by the elegantly creative cuisine that appears as if by magic under the patronage of Michel Roux Junior, the Head of the two star Le Gavroche in London. Guests stay in the 181 luxurious rooms and suites. The concept of hotel-within-hotel will be attractive for guests staying in suites and in rooms attached to the Club: you will have access to the exclusive Colonial Club House with its own pool, restaurant, Business Centre, etc. There is a nightclub, an exceptionally beautiful Spa and everything that will make your stay at a dream beach location in Mauritius an unforgettable experience.

Voile d'Or Resort & Spa
Director:
Jean-Francois Laurant
Allée des Cocotiers
Bel Ombre
Phone: 0 02 30 / 6 23 50 00
Fax: 0 02 30 / 6 23 50 01
E-mail: info@voiledor.com
Internet: www.voiledor.com
Informations:
Representation Voile d'Or
Uferstraße 47
D-55116 Mainz
Phone:
00 49 / 61 31 / 6 27 74-90
Fax:
00 49 / 61 31 / 6 27 74-92
E-mail: nr@voiledor.com
Bookings possible over travel agencies and leading tour operators

181 rooms and suites
Rooms (according to category): Standard rooms from Euro 175 to 285, Club Rooms from Euro 225 to 335, Suites from Euro 335 to 460, Royal Suite Euro 1,500 per person per night incl. half board

Distance from airport:
40 minutes

Für viele Luxustraveller sind die 115 Inseln der Seychellen der Inbegriff romantischer Urlaubsträume und nicht umsonst heiß geliebt bei Hochzeitsreisenden. Rund um die weitläufige Intendance Bucht auf der Hauptinsel Mahé findet junge wie reife Liebe ein Paradies für sinnliches Erleben: das Banyan Tree, Seychelles. Denn wenn es einen Ort gibt, um Körper und Geist wieder in Harmonie zu vereinen, dann diesen. In der Ruhe und Weitläufigkeit dieses geradezu ätherischen Resorts beginnt die Seele ganz von selber zu baumeln. Eine nachhaltige Unterstützung findet der Gast im vielseitigen Massagetherapie-Programm und dem entsprechend hochkarätigen Beautyangebot des grandiosen Banyan Tree Spa und im exklusiven Privatvillen-Konzept. Jede der 47 Villen – ein Traum im viktorianischen Stil; stilvoller Luxus im Tropenparadies mit überdachter Terrasse, eigenem thailändischer Massage-Pavillon und eigenem Pool, großzügigen und eleganten Interieurs und modernstem Komfort. Und da die Liebe bekannterweise durch den Magen geht, bietet das Resort gleich zwei Restaurants, das Gourmetrestaurant „Saffron", das mit original thailändischer Kochkunst bezaubert, und das „Au Jardin d'Epices", das internationale und asiatische Kochkunst offeriert.

For many luxury travellers, the Seychelles represent the ultimate destination for a dream romantic holiday and it is for this very reason that this group of 115 islands is so sought out by honeymooners. Along the great expanse of Intendance Bay on the main island of Mahé, the young and not-so-young alike are certain to find the lovers' paradise they are seeking: Banyan Tree, Seychelles. If there is anywhere on earth that will provide the tranquillity to bring mind and body into harmony again, then this is it. The peaceful surroundings of this sweeping, almost ethereal resort is soul food pure and simple. Guests can maintain this newly-regained balance of mind, body and spirit, by availing themselves of one of the many first-class massage or beauty treatments offered at the fabulous Banyan Tree Spa or in their own private villa. Every single one of its Victorian-style villas is a dream, offering elegance and opulence in the heart of a tropical paradise. Look forward to enjoying a covered patio area, a private Thai massage pavilion, a private pool, generously-dimensioned, elegant interiors and the very latest in modern conveniences. And since a great many aphrodisiacs are of a culinary nature, the resort has not one but two restaurants, "Saffron", for gourmets wishing to be enchanted by original Thai cuisine and "Au Jardin d'Epices", with international and Asian cuisine.

Banyan Tree, Seychelles
General Manager:
Maximilian Lennkh
Anse Intendance
Intendance Road, Mahé
Republic of Seychelles
Phone: 0 02 48 / 3 83 / 5 00
Fax: 0 02 48 / 3 83 / 6 00
E-mail:
seychelles@banyantree.com
Internet:
www.banyantree.com

15 Beach Villas, 5 Intendance
Villas, 6 Rock Pool Villas,
21 Hill Villas.
Rates from
Euro 825 to 1,925
inclusive breakfast

Distance from airport:
30 minutes

Memberships:
The Leading Small Hotels
of the World,
Small Luxury Hotels
of the World

Ursprünglichkeit in ihrer schönsten Form: Das lässt sich auf Cousine Island erleben. Die nur 25 Hektar große Seychellen-Insel ist ein einzigartiges Naturparadies und zählt zu den letzten privaten Naturschutzgebieten dieser Erde. Nur vier elegante Villen streuen sich in die ursprüngliche Natur. Exklusiver kann das Paradies nicht entdeckt werden. Somit ist Cousine Island ein idealer Platz für alle, die Robinson-Crusoe-Feeling suchen, aber auf Luxus nicht verzichten möchten. Nur ein paar Schritte vom Strand entfernt, erstrecken sich die Villen mit eigenem Garten auf über 175 Quadratmetern. Der aufmerksame Service verwöhnt rund um die Uhr. Speisen kann man, wo und wann man will. Zum Lunch und Dinner wird feinste Insel-Cuisine, zugeschnitten auf die Vorlieben der Gäste, serviert. Die größten Kostbarkeiten, die Cousine Island zu bieten hat, sind die zwanzig Riesenschildkröten und die ursprüngliche Natur. Seinen paradiesischen Zustand verdankt Cousine Island einem einzigartigen Naturschutzprogramm, das die Vegetation und die Tierwelt in ihrem für die Seychellen ursprünglichen Zustand erhält. Auf Cousine Island erlebt der Gast eine perfekte Symbiose von Traumurlaub und Naturschutz – und leistet seinen eigenen Beitrag zum Erhalt dieses unberührten Paradieses, denn alle Einnahmen fließen ausschließlich dem Naturschutzprogramm zu, um die Ursprünglichkeit für viele weitere Generationen zu erhalten.

Just imagine enjoying nature at its most natural and most beautiful – you can on Cousine Island. Covering just 25 hectares, this island in the Seychelles is a unique natural paradise and one of the world's last private nature reserves. Just four elegant villas take their place among the island's unspoilt natural environment. Indeed, it's hard to image a more exclusive paradise than this. Make no mistake, Cousine Island is perfect for anyone who would like to enjoy a holiday on a desert island with all the modern luxuries. Located just a few steps from the beach, the island's villas have their own gardens and cover some 175 square metres. The island's attentive service team is on hand to cater for your every need around the clock. You can eat when and where you want. The very finest island cuisine is tailor-made to the guests' own tastes and served for lunch and dinner. But the thing that makes Cousine Island so very special is its 20 giant turtles and its unspoiled natural environment. The island operates a unique nature-protection program that has been carefully conceived to make sure that the island's vegetation and animal world remains just as it has always been in the Seychelles. Guests to Cousine Island can look forward to experiencing a perfect symbiosis between a holiday of a lifetime and environmental protection. Indeed, by visiting the island, you make a real contribution to preserving the beauty of this untouched paradise. This is because all profits flow into the island's nature-protection program.

Cousine Island
Island Manager:
Jock Henwood
P.O. Box 977
Victoria, Mahe, Seychelles
Phone: 0 02 48 / 32 11 07
Fax: 0 02 48 / 32 38 05
E-mail:
cousine@seychelles.net
Internet:
www.cousineisland.com

4 villas
Rates from Euro 1,400 inclusive full board & all beverages

Distance from airport:
15 minutes by helicopter

Nur knapp drei Quadratkilometer klein ist Frégate Island Private, ein behütetes Naturparadies, in dem der Mensch wieder gelernt hat, in Harmonie mit seiner Umwelt zu leben. „Wir möchten unser Paradies mit Menschen teilen, die es zu schätzen wissen, den Luxus eines der letzten Refugien auf diesem Globus mit uns zu teilen", betont General Manager Patrick Brizio, der ein Team von 120 äußerst engagierten Mitarbeitern aus aller Welt um sich versammelt. Stets steht das Denken und Handeln aller im Einklang mit der Ökologie der Insel. Sie zu schützen, Flora und Fauna zu erhalten, ist das vorrangige Ziel. Deshalb beschränkt sich Frégate Island Private freiwillig auf nur 16, je 185 Quadratmeter große Luxus-Villen für maximal vierzig Gäste. Jede Villa verschmilzt mit der sie unmittelbar umgebenden Landschaft und ist so angelegt, dass ihre Gäste sich ungestört fühlen können. Auch die Küche des Resorts setzt auf Ökologie und Produkte aus biologischem Anbau. Die superben Kreationen genießt man im Hauptrestaurant im Frégate House oder im hübsch restaurierten Plantation House in Hafennähe sowie ganz privat in der Villa. Seit einem Jahr relaxen die anspruchsvollen Gäste auch in der magischen Welt des The Rock Spa, das mit sensibler Architektur und raffinierten Treatments aufwartet.

Frégate Private Island has a surface area of just less than three square kilometres and is a protected natural paradise where man has learned once again to live in harmony with his environment. "We want to share our paradise with people who have an appreciation of what it means to share the luxury of one of the last unspoilt refuges on the planet." These are the words of General Manager, Patrick Brizio, who leads a team of 120 highly motivated employees from all over the world. The attitude and behaviour of the people here is always at one with the ecology of the island and it is their number one goal to protect and maintain the flora and fauna. For this reason Frégate Private Island voluntarily limits the number of luxury villas to 16, each of which covers 185 square metres. In total, only forty guests can be catered for on the island at any one time. Every villa blends into its surrounding landscape and is constructed in such a way that the guests can feel completely alone. In the resort restaurant, ecology comes first as only organic produce is used. Superb creations can be enjoyed in the main restaurant in Frégate House, in the beautifully restored Plantation House close to the port or in total privacy in the villa. For the last year, the most discerning guests have been relaxing in the magical world of The Rock Spa and enjoying wonderfully sophisticated treatments designed to pamper in an ambience of sensitive architecture.

Frégate Island Private
Managing Director:
Patrick Brizio
P. O. Box 330, Victoria, Mahé
Republic of Seychelles
Phone: 0 02 48 / 28 22 82
Fax: 0 02 48 / 28 22 85
E-mail: mdir@fregate.com
Internet: www.fregate.com

Reservations:
Sales & Marketing Office
Worldwide, Schwabenstr. 15
D-63263 Neu-Isenburg
Phone: 00 49 / (0) 6102 / 50 13 21
Fax: 00 49 / (0) 6102 / 50 13 22
E-mail: unique.experiences@
debitel.net

16 spacious air conditioned villas with private bedroom area and adjoin lounge sitting room and private sun terrace, daybed and Jacuzzi. Rates per villa, per night, for two people: Euro 1,900 to 2,100 plus 15 % tax & service charge. A minimum stay of 3 nights is required.

Distance to Airport:
Approximate flying time for Helicopter or Twin Otter from Seychelles International Airport (Mahé): 20 minutes

Wer einmal den Weg auf die Seychelleninsel North Island gefunden hat, weiß, dass dieses Archipel ein einzigartiges Fleckchen Erde ist. Fernab vom Alltag genießt der Gast mit allen Sinnen die Schönheit und den Zauber des nur zwei Quadratkilometer großen Seychellen-Eilands und jenen Topkomfort, den weitgereiste Exklusivurlauber zu beanspruchen gewöhnt sind. Elf weiträumige und luftige Villas ziehen sich auf Holzplateaus hin, wurden versteckt zwischen Strand und Granitkliff in die Palmenhaine gesetzt und sind faszinierende Wohnlandschaften, designt mit Großzügigkeit und origineller Phantasie. Raum spielte keine Rolle. Auch verwöhnteste Reisende werden bei ihren Ansprüchen abgeholt und in Ambiancen entführt, deren raffinierter Stil unter die Haut geht: Interior Design auf internationalem Topniveau präsentiert sich mit barfüßigem Robinson-Crusoe-Charme. Serviert wird eine leichte und kreative „Cuisine créole". In spektakulärer Lage lockt ein Spa-Paradies in den Granitfelsen oberhalb des Swimmingpools mit Blick auf die kilometerlange Brandung. Wie die herzliche Zuvorkommenheit des Personals spiegelt auch das umfassende Angebot in drei intimen Villen eine Philosophie wider, die sich die innere und äußere Harmonie des Gastes auf die Fahnen geschrieben hat.

If you have ever found your way to North Island in the Seychelles, you will know what a special part of the world this archipelago is. Far from the hustle and bustle of everyday life, guests here can soak up the beauty and magic of this island with all their senses. The island, which covers a mere two square kilometres, offers the ultimate in comfort expected by globetrotters used to the very exclusive. Eleven spacious, originally designed, airy villas, built on wooden platforms, are completely tucked away in the palm groves between the beach and granite cliffs, offering a fascinating, lavish living space. Space is no obstacle here. The expectations of even the most pampered of travellers are more than met here. Guests will not fail to be seduced by the utter stylishness and ambience of North Island: top quality, world-class interior design mingles here with barefoot Robinson Crusoe charm. The light, creative "Cuisine créole" is served here. A spa paradise beckons from its spectacular location in the granite cliffs above the swimming pool with a view of the surf which stretches for a good kilometre. The courteous service, the many and varied delights offered and the villas designed with privacy and intimacy in mind reflect our philosophy, that of ensuring both inner and outer harmony for our guests.

North Island
Indian Ocean, Seychelles
P.O. Box 1176
Victoria. Mahé
Phone: 0 02 48 / 29 31 00
Fax: 0 02 48 / 29 31 50
Internet:
www.north-island.com

11 villas
from Euro 1,095 to 3,500

Distance from airport:
15 minutes (helicopter)

JUWELEN AUS DEM ERFAHRUNGSSCHATZ VON TREASURE ISLANDS

SOFITEL CENTRAL HUA HIN RESORT ★★★★★

Wie unermesslich kostbar sind die Stunden und Tage, die Sie wunschlos glücklich an einem einzigartigen Ort verbringen. Orten wie der bezaubernden Küstenstadt Hua Hin – der wohl ursprünglichsten Urlaubsdestination Thailands. Um den Traum des vollkommenen Urlaubs Wirklichkeit werden zu lassen, folgt Treasure Islands einer exklusiven Philosophie. Weltweit begeben wir uns persönlich auf die Suche nach einzigartigen Reisezielen, setzen uns aktiv für deren Bewahrung ein und treffen gerne individuelle Urlaubsarrangements für Sie.

Genießen Sie beispielsweise den Luxus des im prächtigen Kolonialstil erbauten 5-Sterne Sofitel Central Hua Hin Resort. Wo in den 30er Jahren des letzten Jahrhunderts die internationale high society residierte, warten heute alle erdenklichen Annehmlichkeiten unserer Zeit auf Sie.

Sprechen Sie mit uns darüber, wo und wie Sie die wertvollsten Stunden des Jahres verbringen möchten. Treasure Islands hat „Schatzinseln" in Asien, Afrika, der Karibik und im Indischen Ozean für Sie entdeckt.

Kaiserswerther Markt 18 | 40489 Düsseldorf
Telefon 0211- 40 585 99 | Fax 0211- 40 585 27
Info@treasure-islands.de | www.treasure-islands.de

TREASURE
ISLANDS
EXKLUSIVES REISEN

Afrika & Mittlerer Osten / Africa & Middle East

Botswana, Namibia, South Africa, Egypt, Dubai, Oman

Das faszinierende Linyanti-Flusssystem im Norden Botswanas gehört zu den Traumzielen jedes Vollblut-Travellers. Luxuriöse Stationen für unvergessliche Safariabenteuer in der ersten Reihe sind dort die Premium Lodges von Wilderness Safaris, deren Engagement mit dem „World Legacy Award", dem Oscar für Öko-Tourismus, ausgezeichnet wurde. Im Kings Pool Camp im 125 000 Hektar großen Linyanti Wildlife Reserve, das vor allem für seine riesige Elefantenpopulation berühmt ist, wohnt man in neun Luxuszelten, die von der freistehenden Badewanne bis zum edlen Interieur keinerlei Komfort vermissen lassen. Hauptattraktion ist die eigene Terrasse – mit Daybed und Privatpool –, von der der Blick auf den Fluss Linyanti und die Kings Pool Lagune geht. In der Trockenzeit zieht es nicht nur Flusspferde und Krokodile an die Lagune, sondern hunderte von Giraffen, Zebras, Büffel, verschiedene Antilopenarten und Elefanten, aber auch Hyänen, afrikanische Wildhunde, Leoparden oder Löwen stillen hier ihren Durst. Nach der nächtlichen Safaritour – die man im Kings Pool auch zu Fuß unternehmen kann – und einem stimmungsvollen Dinner unter dem Sternenzelt wiegt der „Sound of Africa", den man im ganzen Linyanti-Gebiet nicht intensiver erleben kann, in den Schlaf.

The fascinating Linyanti River system in Northern Botswana is a dream destination for any discerning traveller. Wilderness Safaris whose dedication earned them the "World Legacy Award" for Ecological Tourism, provide premium lodges for memorable safari adventures close to the action. Kings Pool Camp is situated on the 310,000 acre Linyanti Wildlife Reserve, famous for its huge population of elephants. There you will sleep in one of nine luxurious tents containing every comfort from fabulous décor to free-standing bathtubs. The highlight is your personal terrace complete with day bed, private pool and a beautiful view of the Linyanti River and the Kings Pool Lagoon. During the dry season hundreds of exotic animals including hippos, crocodiles, giraffes, zebras, buffaloes, various types of antelopes and elephants, hyenas, African wild dogs, leopards and lions make their way to the lagoon to quench their thirst. You will go on foot on a night time safari tour from Kings Pool and enjoy an ambient dinner afterwards under the stars. Returning to your quarters the "Sound of Africa", unsurpassed in any part of the Linyanti area, will lull you to sleep.

Kings Pool Camp
Wilderness Safaris
P.O. Box 5219
Rivonia, Johannesburg 2128
South Africa
Phone: 00 27 / 11 / 8 07 18 00
Fax: 00 27 / 11 / 8 07 21 10
Internet:
www.wilderness-safaris.com
www.kingspool.com

9 luxury tents

Distance from airport
45 minutes per flight

Membership:
A Wilderness Safaris Lodge

Mit den Premier Wilderness Camps präsentiert Wilderness Safaris die First Class seines Portfolios: höchst elegante, stilvolle Destinationen in der wilden Natur, geprägt von exquisitem Design und top-persönlichem Service. Brandneues Beispiel: Vumbura Plains, ein luxuriöses Zeltcamp im privaten Vumbura-Reservat, ganz im Norden des Okavango-Deltas. Gäste leben umgeben von vielfältigen Biotopen und Tierwelten, ausgebreitet auf einem Gebiet von 55 000 Hektar. Vumbura Plains besteht eigentlich aus zwei Camps mit je sieben Wohneinheiten. Gebaut auf erhöhten Holzdecks, hat jede ihren eigenen Dining-Bereich, ihre Lounge, ein komfortables Schlafzimmer, eine „Sala", eine Bar. Auch Außenduschen und Privatpool fehlen nicht. Ausgesucht das Design, großzügig geschnitten die Räume. Das Hauptrestaurant, die Lounge- und Pubszene des Camps sind ebenfalls erhöht;, herrlich der Blick auf die Wasserwelten des Deltas, kühl der Schatten unter uralten Bäumen. Gäste entdecken zu Wasser und zu Land eine einzigartige Naturregion. Mit dem Landrover, mit Booten oder zu Fuß kommen sie den Tieren am Okavango so nahe wie möglich, sehen Löwen, Leoparden, Büffel, Elefanten, Geparden, seltene Vogelarten – erleben Afrika aus spannendsten Perspektiven.

Among the premier wilderness camps, Wilderness Safaris presents first class destinations in its portfolio as highly elegant and stylish set among the wildness of nature while characterised by exquisite design and top class personal service. An example of this is brand new Vumbura Plains, a luxurious camp in the private Vumbura Reserve at the far north of the Okavango Delta. Guests who stay here are surrounded by diverse biotopes and habitats covering an area of 136,000 acres. Vumbura Plains actually consists of two camps, each with seven sleeping quarters. They are built on raised wooden decks and each has its own dining area, lounge, comfortable bedroom, a "sala" and bar. Even outdoor showers and private pools are provided. The main restaurant and the lounge and pub area of the camp are also raised so that the fabulous view of the watery world of the delta can be enjoyed. Under the ancient trees it is cool in the shade. Guests can explore the singular natural environment on water as well as on land. By Land Rover, by boat or on foot they can get as close as possible to the animals of Okavango and see lions, leopards, buffaloes, elephants, cheetahs, unusual species of birds and experience Africa from an exciting perspective.

Vumbura Plains
Wilderness Safaris
P.O. Box 5219
Rivonia, Johannesburg 2128
South Africa
Internet:
www.vumbura.com

14 rooms according to season from Euro 464 to 679 per night, per person sharing

Distance from airport: 20 minutes in an air charter from Maun

Es ist eines der verstecktesten Camps im Süden Afrikas. Serra Cafema liegt im äußersten Nordwesten von Namibia inmitten einer überwältigenden Naturszenerie. Am nördlichen Horizont steigen die Serra-Cafema-Berge auf, direkt am Camp fließt der Kunene-Fluss vorbei – sein Wasser sorgt für eine sattgrüne Oase an den Ufern –, und dann gibt es nur mehr Sand: die Dünenlandschaften einer der trockensten Wüsten der Welt. Das Gebiet gehört den Himba, einem der letzten Nomadenstämme Afrikas. Gäste des Wilderness Serra Cafema Camps leben entsprechend naturnah: Ihr Logis besteht aus acht Zelten, jedes hat sein privates Bad. Im Camp finden sich dazu ein Swimmingpool, ein Restaurant und ein Pub. Man sollte Zeit mitbringen für den Aufenthalt. So sparsam die Beschreibung der Destination ausfällt – es gibt viel zu unternehmen. Nur die Wüste zu sehen ist schon ein Erlebnis – der goldfarbene Sand, immer wieder von Antilopen-, Stauß- und Springbockherden gesprenkelt. Wie spannend erst, mit dem Landrover oder dem Squad-Bike in die Dünenwelt hineinzufahren. Man wandert in den Bergen, fährt im Boot auf dem Fluss zwischen Krokodilen oder lässt sich von den einheimischen Himba ins traditionelle Stammesleben einführen.

As one of the best-hidden camps in southern Africa, Serra Cafema is situated in the most northwesterly tip of Namibia in the middle of an overwhelmingly beautiful natural environment. On the northern horizon the Serra Cafema Mountains rise up. Right beside the camp the Kunene River flows by, its water providing for the luscious green oasis at its banks and beyond that there is sand everywhere – the sand dunes of one of the driest deserts in the world. The region belongs to the Himba, one of the last remaining nomadic tribes in Africa. As such, the guests of Wilderness Serra Cafema Camps live close to nature. Their accommodation consists of eight tents, each one with a private bathroom. In the camp there is a swimming pool, a restaurant and a pub. Travellers should make sure to spend a lot of time here. Brief though the description of the destination may be, there is a lot to do. Just gazing at the desert is an experience in itself, the gold-coloured sand regularly dotted with herds of oryx, springbok and ostriches. How exciting it is to travel through the dunes in a Land Rover or on squad bikes. You can walk in the mountains, go by boat among the crocodiles in the river or learn about the traditional way of life of the local Himba people.

Serra Cafema Camp
Wilderness Safaris
P.O. Box 5219
Rivonia, Johannesburg 2128
South Africa
Internet:
www.serracafema.com

8 tents according to season from Euro 397 to 473 per night, per person sharing

Distance from airport:
3 hours in private charter from Windhoek

Der luxuriöse, 24 000 Quadratmeter große Landsitz im traditionellen Kapstil ist nur fünfzehn Autominuten vom Zentrum Kapstadts entfernt – ein stilles, zur Erholung prädestiniertes Refugium mitten in der Natur. Zum Grundstück gehört ein idyllischer Landschaftspark mit schmuckem Wäldchen, sanft geschwungenen Wiesen, Rosen- und Obstgärten. Allein schon am großen Außenpool zu liegen, den Blick ins Grüne – eine Beschäftigung für lange Mußestunden, umso mehr, als man gewiss sein kann, viel Platz für sich zu haben. Intimität ist hier Trumpf. Das Greenways Hotel bietet Logis nur in siebzehn Luxuszimmern und Executive-Suiten, dort aber mit Feinheit und jedem First-Class-Komfort. Große elegante Bäder, auf Wunsch werden Zimmer mit Balkon reserviert. Im Ashton's Restaurant genießt man eine glückliche „Vermählung" von europäischer und traditioneller Cap-Cuisine, im Winter am knackenden Kaminfeuer, im Sommer auf der geschützten Terrasse mit Blick ins Land. Golfer finden im Umkreis von fünfzehn Kilometern sechs Championship-Kurse. Ans Meer oder nach Robben Island ist es nicht weiter als nach Downtown Kapstadt, und auch für andere Ausflüge ist das Greenways Hotel ein ideales Domizil. Weinfreunde werden sich eine Fahrt in die Stellenbosch-Region (ca. eine Stunde) kaum entgehen lassen.

The luxurious Greenways Mansion (24,000 sqare metres great) represents the traditional architectural style of the Cape and is situated just fifteen minutes drive from the centre of Cape Town. It is best described as an oasis of calm, perfect for relaxation in a natural environment. The grounds contain idyllic scenery with attractive woods, gentle rolling hills, rose gardens and orchards. Just imagine lying at the large outdoor pool, looking into the surrounding greenery for many leisurely hours so that you loose all track of time and space. Intimacy is the essence of this top location. Greenways Hotel offers just 17 luxury rooms and executive suits as accommodation, all stylishly decorated and with every first class comfort. The bathrooms are large and elegant and rooms with balconies can be specially reserved. In Ashton's restaurant you will enjoy a successful marriage of European and traditional Cape cuisine. In Winter you will watch the crackling fire, in summer you will eat on the comfortable terrace with a lovely view of the countryside. Golfers will be delighted with six championship courses in a radius of fifteen kilometres. The seaside and Robben Island are no further away than the centre of Cape Town and Greenways Hotel is an ideal domicile for other day trips. Lovers of wine will not miss the one hour journey to the Stellenbosch Region.

Greenways Hotel
No.1 Torquay Avenue
Upper Claremont /
Bishopscourt
Cape Town 7708
South Africa
Phone: 00 27 / 21 / 7 61 17 92
Fax: 00 27 / 21 / 7 61 08 78
E-mail:
info@greenways.co.za
Internet:
www.greenways.co.za

17 rooms and suites
Luxury Rooms (according to season) from Euro 94 to 118, Executive Suites from Euro 130 to 164 per person, per night inclusive of full breakfast, a selection of softdrinks, wine, spirits, free internet etc.

Distance from airport:
25 minutes

Eine der Traumstrecken Südafrikas, die berühmte Garden Route, hat ein neues Aushängeschild erhalten: Das Pezula Resort Hotel. Das zur exklusiven Southern Sun Collection gehörende Luxusdomizil beeindruckt zum einen durch seine grandiose Lage im beliebten Ferienort Knysna mit Blick auf die Lagune, den Indischen Ozean sowie die Outeniqua-Berge. Zum anderen ist das Fünf-Sterne-Deluxe-Hotel ein echtes Paradies für aktive Gäste – Tennis, Reiten, Wandern, Walbeobachtung und Golf. Der hauseigene Parcours auf den Höhen der Knysna Heads wurde von Roland Fream nach schottischem Vorbild sehr anspruchsvoll gestaltet und bietet spektakuläre Ausblicke. Zurück im Hotel, locken die Annehmlichkeiten des exklusiven Wellness-Centers und Spas oder das erfrischende Nass der Pools. Kreislauf und Muskeln stählt man im topausgestatteten Fitness-Center, bevor es zum Dinner ins elegante Gourmetrestaurant „Zachary's" geht, für dessen ausgezeichnete Küche der international bekannte Geoffrey Murray aus New York verantwortlich ist. Die anspruchsvollen Gäste logieren in 74 großzügigen Suiten – jeweils vier in einer Villa – mit Balkon oder Terrasse oder in einer der beiden Präsidenten-Suiten. Exklusiv wie das Haus auch die Anreise-möglichkeiten mit dem Privatjet, dem Helikopter oder dem hoteleigenen Chauffeur- und Limousinen-Service.

One of South Africa's most beautiful attractions, its famous Garden Route, has recently been given something else to be proud of: The Pezula Resort Hotel. This luxury establishment belongs to the exclusive Southern Sun Collection. It boasts a spectacular location in the popular holiday resort of Knysna with views of the lagoon, the Indian Ocean and the Outeniqua Mountains. This five-star deluxe hotel is also a paradise for active guests – tennis, riding, hilling and walewatching. Its very own course on the Knysna Heads offers spectacular views and was designed by Roland Fream drawing on Scottish influences. Back in the hotel, you can look forward to relaxing in its exclusive wellness centre and spa or taking a dip in the refreshing pool. The hotel's fully equipped gym is perfect for strengthening muscles and improving fitness levels before going for dinner in its elegant "Zachary's" gourmet restaurant. Internationally famous, Geoffrey Murray is the man responsible for its excellent cuisine. Discerning guests either reside in one of its 74 spacious Suites – there are four in each villa – with a balcony or patio area or in one of the hotel's two Presidential Suites. As you would expect from this standard of hotel, it can also cater for arrivals by private jet and helicopter or send out its own chauffeur and limousine service.

Pezula Resort Hotel & Spa
General Manager:
Corinne Harrison
Lagoonview Drive
Sparrebosch, Western Cape
P. O. Box 3327
6570 Knysna, South Africa
Phone: 00 27 / 4 43 02 33 33
Fax: 00 27 / 4 43 02 33 03
E-mail:
reservations@pezula.com
Internet:
www.pezula.com

76 Luxury Suites and
2 Presidential Suites
Prices from Rand 3,150 (Low
Season now till August 31)

Distance from airport:
George Airport 45 minutes
Plettenberg Bay Airport
15 minutes

Memberchips:
Great Hotels of the World,
Southern Sun Collection

Wer erleben will, wie die Oberoi-Gruppe die vielfälti- gen Sphären ägyptischer Kultur in eines ihrer roman- tischsten First-Class-Refugien bannt, der sollte sich nach Hughada locken lassen. Die Hafenstadt mit inter- nationalem Airport, 510 Kilometer von Kairo und 240 Kilometer von Luxor entfernt, hat Sonne das ganze Jahr über, hinreißend schöne Strände und faszinie- rende Unterwasserwelten. The Oberoi, Sahl Hasheesh liegt hautnah an alledem. Die bauliche Anlage scheint aus dem Ehrgeiz heraus entstanden zu sein, die ganze Schönheit arabischer Architektur einzufangen, selbst- verständlich auch in der eigenen Suite – und es stehen im The Oberoi, Sahl Hasheesh ausschließlich Suiten zur Verfügung, 102 im Ganzen. Schon die einfachste Kategorie, die Deluxe Suites, verwöhnt ihre Bewohner auf einer Fläche von 85 Quadratmetern mit elaborier- tem Luxus, und wer im Urlaub gern lebt wie im Mär- chen aus Tausendundeiner Nacht, der sei in die Top- kategorie, in eine der sechs Royal Suiten, geladen. 225 Quadratmeter exklusivste Abgeschiedenheit war- ten auf ihn. Man speist im The Oberoi, Sahl Hasheesh ausgezeichnete internationale und ägyptische Cui- sine. Das Oberoi Spa wird von Banyan Tree gemanagt, Ausweis genug für internationale Topqualität.

To experience just how well the Oberoi Group has managed to capture all the variety of Egyptian cultu- re and integrate it into one of its most romantic first- class establishments, you should seriously consider staying in Hughada. This seaport has an internatio- nal airport, is 510 km away from Cairo, 240 km from Luxor and boasts all-year-round sunshine, impossi- bly beautiful beaches and fascinating marine life. Indeed, The Oberoi, Sahl Hasheesh offers all this and more. As far as the resort's building design is con- cerned, it's almost as though the burning ambition has been to capture all the beauty of Arabian archi- tecture. And this is also true of its suites, of which there are 102 and the only accommodation option in The Oberoi, Sahl Hasheesh. Even the most "basic" Deluxe Suites with their spacious 85 square metres treat their residents to impeccable luxury. But if you want to holiday like in 1001 Arabian Nights, then one of the six top-category Royal Suites is for you. Here you can look forward to 225 square metres of luxu- rious seclusion. The Oberoi, Sahl Hasheesh offers distinguished international and Egyptian cuisine. Banyan Tree is responsible for managing the Oberoi Spa, promising top international standards.

The Oberoi, Sahl Hasheesh
Red Sea, Egypt
Phone: 00 20 65 3440 777
Fax: 00 20 65 3440 788
E-mail:
toshres@oberoi.com.eg
Internet:
www.oberoihotels.com

102 suites
Deluxe Suites (according to season and category) from US$ 250 to 300, Superior De- luxe Suite from US$ 300 to 350, Grand Suite from US$ 475 to 600, Royal Suite from US$ 1,100 to 1,400
All rates are subject to 12 % Service Charge and 13.2 % Government Tax

Distance from airport:
20 minutes

Membership:
The Leading Small Hotels of the World

Die vom Aussterben bedrohten weißen Oryx (Al Maha), eine Antilopenart, gaben dem Ort in der Wüste einst ihren Namen – dem Ort, wo sich der Legende nach eine prächtige Oase befand, deren Quelle von riesigen unterirdischen Seen gespeist wurde. Mit der Eröffnung des Al Maha Resort & Spa im Jahre 1999, Dubais erstem Eco-Tourismus-Projekt, ist diese Legende Wirklichkeit geworden. Denn in der unvergleichlichen Atmosphäre des Luxusresorts erlebt man die Faszination der Wüste aus erster Hand – verwöhnt von ultimativem Luxus, einer hervorragenden und abwechslungsreichen Kulinarik und der sprichwörtlichen Gastlichkeit Arabiens. Kameltrekking, Falknerei-Vorführungen, Bogenschießen, Jeepsafaris oder lehrreiche Naturwanderungen bringen den Gästen die einzigartige Natur und die Traditionen Arabiens näher. Doch auch wer sich dem süßen Nichtstun hingibt, erlebt die Natur der Wüste hautnah. Das vielfach prämierte Angebot der legendären Sechs-Sterne-Luxusoase ist im letzten Jahr um zehn Luxus-Suiten, größere Privatpools in jeder Suite und modernste Tagungsmöglichkeiten erweitert worden. Neuestes Juwel des Wüstenresorts ist das Jamilah Spa: ein luxuriöser Wohlfühltempel, dessen Treatments und natürliche Produkte perfekt zu der harmonischen Ökologie und dem exklusiven Anspruch des gesamten Resorts passen. Neuestes Highlight hierbei: eine von Al Maha in Kooperation mit dem Kosmetikinstitut Barbor entwickelte Kosmetiklinie namens „Timeless", deren Wirkung auf arabischen Datteln und beruhigendem Weihrauch basiert.

This desert location owes its name (Al Maha) to the white oryx, a species of antelope threatened by extinction. This is a place where, according to legend, there was a splendid oasis, springing from enormous subterranean lakes. And this legend indeed became reality in 1999, with the opening of the Al Maha Resort & Spa, Dubai's first ecotourism project. In the inimitable surrounds of this luxury resort, the fascination of the desert can be experienced firsthand. Here, guests are spoilt by the ultimate in opulence, culinary delights equal in both their excellence and variety and, of course, the renowned Arabian hospitality. Camel trekking, displays of falconry, archery, jeep safaris and educational walking tours all give guests a deeper understanding of the unique nature and traditions of the Arab world. And even those who decide simply to relax will experience first-hand the true nature of the desert. This multi award-winning, six-star luxury oasis was expanded last year with the addition of ten luxury suites, even larger private pool in each suite and state-of-the-art conference facilities. The most recent gem to be added is the Jamilah Spa, a luxurious temple of well-being, with treatments and natural products that are in perfect harmony with both the environment and the exclusive nature of the entire resort. Its latest highlight is the 'timeless' range of product. Based on Arabian dates and calming incense, the Al Maha 'timeless' range of product was developed by Al Maha in conjunction with Barbor cosmetics institute.

Al Maha
Desert Resort & Spa
An Emirates Group Hotel
Resident Manager:
Martin Le Roux
P.O. Box 7631, Dubai
United Arab Emirates
Phone reservation:
09 71 / 43 03 42 22
Fax: 09 71 / 43 43 96 96
E-mail:
almaha@emirates.com
Internet: www.al-maha.com

37 Bedouin Suites, 2 Royal
Suites, 1 Emirates Suite
Bedouin Suites:
from US$ 900
Royal Suites:
from US$ 2,000
Emirates Suite:
from US$ 3,000

Distance from airport:
45 km

Memberships:
The Leading Small Hotels
of the World,
Great Hotels of the World

Auf dem Areal des One&Only Royal Mirage Dubai und direkt am schönen Jumeirah Beach zeigt sich das Residence & Spa als Oase für all jene, die grenzenlosen Komfort und Luxus lieben. In der Garden Villa mit privatem Pool, den sechzehn Suiten und zweiunddreißig Prestige Rooms, alle mit Meerblick, Balkon oder Terrasse, taucht man in eine Aura gehobener Wohnkultur, wobei sämtliche Interieurs ein Tribut an die Ausdruckskraft arabischer Architektur sind. Kochkunst und Lebenskultur finden im Dining Room und in der stimmungsvollen Lounge ihren perfekten Rahmen. Das imposante traditionelle orientalische „Hammam & Givenchy Spa" lässt die Schönheits- und Badekultur des Orients wieder auferstehen und verwöhnt mit vielfältigen kosmetischen und therapeutischen Behandlungsmethoden. Exklusiv für den Mittleren Osten bietet die französische Nobelmarke Givenchy ein umfangreiches Programm für gutes Aussehen und Wohlgefühl an, so dass in der entspannenden Atmosphäre dieses Kleinods der Alltag in weite Ferne rückt. Gerne verbringt man den Tag am Pool oder nutzt die Vielzahl der Sport- und Freizeitmöglichkeiten, die das One&Only Royal Mirage Hotel bietet. Wohl zu Recht bezeichnet sich Dubai als die Golfmetropole der Region, denn der Gast des Hauses hat die Wahl zwischen acht 18-Loch-Golfplätzen.

In the grounds of the One&Only Royal Mirage Dubai and directly on beautiful Jumeirah Beach, the Residence & Spa is an oasis for all lovers of limitless comfort and luxury. In the Garden Villa with private pool, the 16 Suites and the 32 Prestige Rooms, all with sea facing and private balcony or terrace, guests are immersed in elegant surroundings evoking true savoir-vivre, with all interiors a tribute to the expressive power of Arabian architecture. Both the culinary arts and the art of elegant living find their perfect expression in the dining room and the special atmosphere of the library lounge. The culture in the Orient of beauty and bathing is brought to life in the traditional Oriental "Hammam and Givenchy Spa", where guests are pampered with a wide range of cosmetic and therapeutic treatments. This is the one place in the Middle East where the French House of Givenchy offers guests an complete beauty and well-being programme. The result is that everyday stresses and strains fade far into the distance in the relaxing surroundings of this Middle Eastern jewel. The day can be spent pleasurably at the poolside or taking advantage of any of the diverse range of sports and leisure opportunities offered by the One&Only Royal Mirage Hotel. Dubai is also known as the golf metropolis of the region, and rightly so, with guests having the choice of eight 18-hole golf courses.

Residence & Spa
One&Only Royal Mirage,
Dubai
Phone: 09 71 / 4 / 3 99 99 99
Fax: 09 71 / 4 / 3 99 99 98
E-mail:
reservations@oneandonly-royalmiragedubai.ae
Internet:
www.oneandonly-royalmirage.com

32 Prestige Rooms, 16 Suites,
1 Garden Villa from Euro 164
to 558

Distance from airport:
20 minutes

Membership:
The Leading Small Hotels
of the World

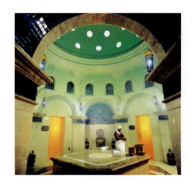

In Oman, am Ostende der Arabischen Halbinsel, hat sich ein erlesenes Beach-Resort innerhalb kürzester Zeit in die internationalen Top-Rankings katapultiert: The Chedi in Muscat – attraktiv unter anderem durch sein raffiniertes Design. Es ist hier gelungen, aus Grundelementen omanischer Architektur Interieurs und Gartenlandschaften entstehen zu lassen, die mit modernster Eleganz arabischen Zauber präsentieren. Bestes Beispiel sind die exklusivsten Wohnszenerien, die 36 Chedi-Club-Suiten. Sie führen, wie das gesamte Resort, eine geometrische Schönheit vor, die es wunderbar versteht, Ruhe, Wohlbehagen und Frieden zu spenden. Es gibt ein Spa, das für seine Pflege- und Beautyprogramme ausschließlich organisch gewonnene Produkte (aus Bali und Australien) verwendet, und „The Restaurant", eine faszinierende architektonische und kulinarische Szenerie. Küchendirektor Enrico Wahl, 34, führt eine Karte mit vier Abteilungen, einer arabischen, einer mediterranen, einer asiatischen und einer indischen. Auch bei längerem Aufenthalt schafft ein Gast kaum all die verführerischen Kombinationen, die da kreuz und quer möglich werden – schönes Bild für die kulturelle Vielfalt eines Resorts, das den Zauber eines ganzes Landes spiegelt.

In Oman, on the eastern side of the Arabian peninsula, a select beach resort has leaped to the top of the international league within a very short space of time: The Chedi in Muscat. It's a highly attractive location for a large number of reasons including its very sophisticated design. The great achievement here has been to draw on basic Oman architectural elements to create interiors and garden landscapes that ooze an aura of highly modern elegance with a sense of Arabic mystery. Its 36 exclusive Chedi Club Suites are the best example of this. As throughout all the resort, these suites have a certain geometric beauty that promotes calm, comfort and peace. At the Spa, only the best organic products from Bali and Australia are used for beauty care and treatments. Under the direction of Enrico Wahl (34) "The Restaurant" exhibits a fascinating architectural and culinary landscape. The menu is divided into four sections with a wide selection of Arabic, Mediterranean, Asian and Indian dishes, so much so, that the guest will find it difficult to try all the different seductive combinations – a pretty allegory for the cultural richness of the resort, reflecting the magic of the country as a whole.

The Chedi
Managing Director:
York Brandes
North Ghubra 232
Way No. 3215, Street No. 46
P.O. Box 964
Postal Code 133 Al Khuwair
Muscat, Sultanate of Oman
Phone: 0 09 68 / 24 52 44 00
Fax: 0 09 68 / 24 49 34 85
Reservation fax:
0 09 68 / 24 49 34 85
E-mail: chedimuscat@
ghmhotels.com
Internet:
www.ghmhotels.com

151 rooms and suites
Superior Room OMR (Omani Rial) 100, Deluxe Room OMR 125, Chedi Club Suite OMR 250 + 17 % tax and service charge (1 Omani Rial approx. US$ 2,60)

Distance from airport:
15 minutes

Membership:
Design Hotels

DER ROLLS ROYCE
UNTER DEN REISEVERANSTALTERN.

Asien / Asia
Indonesia, Thailand, Vietnam

Einfach abtauchen! Das kann man im Matahari Beach Resort an der nahezu unberührten Nordküste der Insel Bali nicht nur im übertragenen Sinne. Denn abtauchen in die prachtvolle Welt der Javasee und des Unterwassernationalparks Bali Barat, eines der schönsten noch unberührten Tauchreviere der Welt, gehört zu den Highlights des einzigen Relais-&-Châteaux-Hauses auf Bali. Weit weg von den gängigen Touristenklischees bieten das außergewöhnliche Resort und die spektakuläre Umgebung nicht nur für Taucher Erlebnisse der besonderen Art. Die Liste der Freizeitmöglichkeiten ist lang und reicht vom Mountainbiken bis Golfen auf dem resorteigenen Pitch- und Putt-Platz. Um vollends aus dem Alltag „abzutauchen" führen die begnadeten Therapeutinnen des Parwathi Spas „starke Geschütze" ins Feld. Nach ultimativen Entspannungskicks wie einer sechshändigen Massage schwebt man wie auf Wolke sieben in die Wirklichkeit zurück. An jedem anderen Ort würde nun Wehmut aufkommen, doch hier steigt man gerne von seiner Wolke, weidet sich an der Traumkulisse des paradiesischen Gartens, der die sechzehn exklusiven Bungalows umgibt, lauscht den Wellen, die an den feinsandigen, dunklen Lavastrand schlagen, oder genießt die phantasievollen Kreationen der exzellenten Küche, die selbst verwöhnteste Gaumen in Verzückung versetzt.

Do you sometimes wish you could leave everything behind and simply melt away? Well now you can do just that and not just metaphorically. The location is the Matahari Beach Resort on the almost untouched north coast of Bali. Letting yourself melt into the deep blue waters of the Java Sea and entering the Bali Barat Underwater National Park is one of the high points of the visit, not least because this is one of the most beautiful and intact diving areas in the world. Far away from the usual tourist strip and surrounded by a spectacular natural environment, the onlyest Relais & Châteaux at Bali offers many special attractions to all patrons including, but not only divers. A long list of leisure activities from mountain biking to golf on the resort's own pitch and putt course yield hours of enjoyment. Meanwhile at the Parwathi Spa talented therapists get extra support to help their clients "melt away" into another world. Using the ultimate relaxation techniques such as a six-handed massage, you are transported to seventh heaven and then brought gently back to reality. Anywhere else the trip back to earth would cause a rude awakening but here you enjoy a soft landing. You can feast your eyes on the idyllic gardens surrounding the 16 exclusive bungalows. You can listen to the sound of the sea washing up on the lava beach with its fine dark sand or you can enjoy the imaginative creations from the restaurant, guaranteed to send even the most discerning palates into ecstasy.

Matahari Beach Resort & Spa
General Manager & Patron:
Johann Paul Herrler
P.O. Box 194
Pemuteran, Bali / Indonesia
Phone: 00 62 / 36 29 23 12
Fax: 00 62 / 36 29 23 13
E-mail:
reservation@m-b-r.com
Internet: www.matahari-beach-resort.com

30 rooms and 2 Deluxe Suites
Garden view rooms from
US$ 186, Deluxe rooms from
US$ 266, Super Deluxe Suite
from US$ 466, rates includes
breakfast

Distance from airport:
120 kilometres

Membership:
Relais & Châteaux

MAYA UBUD RESORT & SPA, BALI

Hoch oben über dem Petanu-River-Tal und unweit von Tjampuhan liegt das Maya Ubud Resort. Eine perfekte Location für das Hideaway, das als Highlight unter den Luxushotels gilt. Die 48 Zimmer im Hauptgebäude bestechen durch elegante und stilvolle Interieurs, Ausblick auf Gärten und Reisfelder und durch alle technischen Raffinessen. In unmittelbaren Einklang mit der Natur lebt man in den Garden-Villen, wie überhaupt sämtliche Luxus-Villen als elegante und königliche Wohnwelten mit eigenem Pool, Garten und großzügigem Residenzraum überzeugen. Der „Spa at Maya" gehört selbst für weitgereiste Luxusglobetrotter zu den schönsten der Welt. Drei Einzelpavillons und zwei Doppellauben stehen zur Verfügung, in denen entspannende balinesische Massagen, natürliche Gesichtsbehandlungen und Body Scrubs sowie Maniküre und Pediküre verabreicht werden – und das alles in einmalig tropischer Umgebung und betreut von fachkundigen und unschlagbar freundlichen asiatischen Fachkräften. Dem Spa gegenüber im River Café oder auch im Fine-Dining-Restaurant „Maya Sari" kommt der Gast in den Genuss einer asiatischen und internationalen Frischeküche auf höchstem Niveau, die durch Vielfalt und hochwertige Qualität feine Gaumen verzaubert.

The Maya Ubud Resort is situated high above the Petanu River valley to the east of Ubud. Indeed, it's hard to imagine a more perfect location for a hideaway that is widely regarded as a gem among luxury hotels. The 48 rooms in the main building boast elegant and stylish interiors, state-of-the-art equipment and raised views across the gardens and rice fields. The garden villas blend in harmoniously with nature, and all luxury villas offer elegant, magnificent surroundings with private pool, garden and generous living quarters. The "Spa at Maya" is one of the most beautiful in the world, even for globetrotters used to travelling in luxury. There are three individual pavilions and two summerhouses, offering relaxing Balinese massage, natural facial treatments, body scrubs, manicures and pedicures. All provided by the superlative, expert local staff, in a unique tropical setting. Opposite the spa, in the River Café or the Fine Dining Restaurant "Maya Sari", guests can enjoy a variety of top Asian and international dishes prepared from the freshest of ingredients, sure to please even the most discerning of palates.

Maya Ubud Resort & Spa
Director: Paul A. Blake
P.O. Box 1001
Ubud / Bali, 80571, Indonesia
Phone: 0 62 / 3 61 / 97 78 88
Fax: 0 62 / 3 61 / 97 75 55
E-mail:
info@mayaubud.com
Internet:
www.mayaubud.com

48 rooms, 23 superior garden villas, 34 deluxe pool villas, 1 Pejeng Duplex Villa, 1 Peliatan Duplex Villa, 1 Petanu Presidential Villa from Euro 180 to 350 plus 21 % service charge and tax

Distance from airport:
55 minutes

Unweit von Ubud nach traditionellen balinesischen Entwürfen gebaut und harmonisch mit der Natur vereint, schmiegt sich das The Royal Pita Maha in die Schönheit der Inselnatur. An einem auserwählten Ort mit spiritueller Aura steht ein Fünf-Sterne-Luxushotel, das wie geschaffen ist, sich verwöhnen zu lassen, zu meditieren und zu entspannen. Die zwölf Hektar des Resorts, das in seinem Erscheinungsbild einem königlichen Dorf ähnelt, sind vollkommen integriert in die ländliche Umgebung mit ihren Reisterrassen, Wildwasserschluchten und tropischen Wäldern. Diese Verschmelzung von Natur und Raum durchdringt das gesamte Anwesen mit einer überwältigenden Atmosphäre von Frieden und Harmonie. Diese Stimmung setzt sich fort in den 75 Pool Villas, den 6 Royal Villas, den 10 Healing Villas sowie im Royal House. Alle Villas stehen auf ihrem eigenen Grundstück, alle bieten einen atemberaubenden Panoramablick auf Schlucht und Fluss und Berge mit tropischem Grün, alle verfügen über einen privaten Garten und Pool. Selbst die „kleinsten" Unterkünfte, die „Pool Villas", bieten 300 Quadratmeter zum Leben und die „Royal Villas" zeigen mit 800 Quadratmetern Residenz-Format. Die beiden Terrassenrestaurants, in dramatischer Lage oberhalb des Wildwassers platziert, garantieren eine kolossale Auswahl an internationalen und lokalen Spezialitäten. Eine Oase für sich ist das exklusive Spa und Wellness-Zentrum (managed by Shiseido).

The Royal Pita Maha, built in traditional Balinese style, nestles snugly a stone's throw away from Ubud, blending in harmoniously with the island's natural beauty. At a select, ethereal location, this five-star luxury hotel is simply made for indulgence, a place to meditate and relax. Despite its stately ambience, the 12-hectare resort blends in seamlessly with the rural surroundings of paddy fields, whitewater ravines and tropical forests. This fusion of raw nature and sweeping expanses imbues the resort with a strong sense of peace and harmony. This ambience is also shared by the 75 Pool Villas, the 6 Royal Villas, the 10 Healing Villas and the Royal House. All villas stand in their own grounds, all command a breathtaking panoramic view of ravines, rivers, mountains and the green hue of the tropics, all have a private garden and pool. Even the "smallest" of the abodes, the Pool Villas, offer 300 square metres of living space, while the 800 square metres Royal Villas are of truly regal proportions. In both of the terrace restaurants, set in a dramatic spot above the whitewater ravine, guests are guaranteed a huge selection of international and local specialities. And the exclusive spa and wellness centre, managed by Shiseido, is an oasis all of its own.

The Royal Pita Maha
Reservation:
The Royal Pita Maha
Desa Kedewatan
P.O. Box 198, Ubud 80571
Bali / Indonesia
Phone: 00 62 / 3 61 / 98 00 22
Fax: 00 62 / 3 61 / 98 00 11
E-mail:
theroyal@indosat.net.id
Internet:
www.royalpitamaha-bali.com

75 Pool Villas, 6 Royal Villas, 10 Healing Villas, 1 Royal House from US$ 400 to 1,500

Distance from airport:
50 minutes

Membership:
Select Hotels & Resorts
International

Am feinsandigen Laguna Beach und von den sanften Wellen des Andamanischen Meers umspült, ist das Banyan Tree an der Westküste der Insel Phuket eine Oase der Ruhe und Entspannung. Das von internationalen Reisemagazinen hochdekorierte tropische Hideaway zeichnet sich durch seine abgeschiedene Lage, exklusivste Ausstattung in elegantem Ambiente und durch die Wärme kultivierter Gastlichkeit aus. Die Villen im offenen Thaistil haben einen kleinen, nicht einsehbaren Gartenbereich und bieten neben luxuriösen Interieurs ein Höchstmaß an Privatsphäre. Seine wohlverdiente Flucht aus dem Alltag genießt man im eigenen Pool, auf der privaten Terrasse, im Jacuzzi oder bei einem Bad unter freiem Himmel. Perfekt verkörpern die Spa-Villen mit Pool und Heilbad die berühmte Banyan-Tree-Philosophie von Romantik, Genuss, Schönheit und gesundem Wohlbefinden. Schönheitsbehandlungen, Massagen, Yoga und Meditationskurse sind Teil des umfangreichen Angebotes für kosmetische und stressreduzierende Maßnahmen. Golfer finden im Laguna Phuket Golfclub ideale Voraussetzungen für ihr Spiel. Auch für Gourmets ist das Banyan Tree Phuket ein Ort des Rundumgenusses. In den fünf Restaurants lüften Meisterköche die Geheimnisse der exotischen asiatischen und internationalen Küche.

Laguna Beach offers fine sands and is lapped by the gentle waves of the Andaman Sea. There you will find Banyan Tree, on the west coast of the island of Phuket, a haven of peace and tranquillity. This tropical hideaway, much-crowned by international travel magazines, is so special because of its secluded location, exclusive facilities, elegant ambience and the hospitality so often found in tropical climes. The villas, which are in the open-plan Thai style, each have a small, secluded garden and offer a combination of luxurious interior with the ultimate in privacy. You can enjoy your well-earned rest from the usual hustle and bustle in your very own pool, on your private terrace, in the jacuzzi or while bathing under an open sky. With their pools and therapeutic baths, the spa villas perfectly embody the famous Banyan Tree philosophy of romance, pleasure, beauty, health and wellbeing. There is a wide range of beauty treatments and stress reduction courses on offer, including massages, yoga and meditation. Golfers will find everything they desire at the Laguna Phuket Golf Club. Banyan Tree Phuket also offers culinary delights for every gourmet's palate. Master chefs reveal the secrets of exotic Asian and international cuisine in the hideaway's five restaurants.

Banyan Tree Phuket
33 Moo 4, Srisoonthorn Road
Cherngtalay, Amphur Talang
Phuket 83110
Thailand
Phone: 00 66 / 76 324 374
Fax: 00 66 / 76 324 375
E-mail:
phuket@banyantree.com
Internet:
www.banyantree.com

121 villas
from US$ 550 to 2,500
per villa per night

Distance from airport:
20 minutes

Memberships:
The Leading Hotels
of the World,
Small Luxury Hotels
of the World

BANYAN TREE, BANGKOK

FACILITIES

Im pulsierenden Herzen des Geschäfts- und Diplomatenviertels liegt das Banyan Tree Bangkok an der noblen South Sathon Road und bietet kurze Anfahrtswege zu den Einkaufszentren der Innenstadt. Für Reisende aus aller Welt ist das Luxushotel ein Ort, um sich zurückzuziehen, zu entspannen und dabei die vielgerühmte thailändische Gastlichkeit mit allen Sinnen zu genießen. Was auch der „Business Traveler" in Großbritannien bestätigt, der das Hotel als eines der „drei weltbesten Business-Hotels" ausgezeichnet hat. Auf der 21. und 22. sowie in der 51. bis 54. Etage mit Blick über Bangkok erleben Wellness-Gourmets den Zauber der ganzheitlichen Banyan-Tree-Spa-Philosophie. Anspruchsvoll gestaltete Räume, das leise Plätschern von Brunnen, angenehm aromatisierte Räume lassen rasch Wohlfühlatmosphäre aufkommen. Es gibt drei elegante Spa Suites mit einer Größe von 120 Quadratmetern die jeweils einen eigenen Spa-Behandlungsraum für absolute Privatsphäre haben. Ein weiteres Highlight des Hauses ist das auf dem Dach in der 61. Etage gelegene Open-Air-Restaurant „Vertigo" mit herrlichem Ausblick auf die 9-Millionen-Metropole. Das „Bai Yun" mit chinesischer Nouvelle Cuisine, das „Saffron" mit thailändisch-internationalen Zubereitungen und das Restaurant „Rom Sai" sind weitere Stationen einer ausgiebigen Aromenreise.

Banyan Tree Bangkok lies on the elegant South Sathon Road at the heart of the city's vibrant commercial and diplomatic quarter, just a short drive from the downtown shopping districts. This luxury hotel is a place for travellers from around the globe to get away from it all, relax and indulge all their senses, soaking up the famed Thai hospitality. Indeed, this view is shared by the UK's Business Traveller Magazine, which voted the hotel one of the top three "Best Business Hotels in the World". On the 21st and 22nd and 51st to 54th floors with a view over Bangkok, wellness aficionados can experience the magic of the hotel's holistic spa approach. The design of the spaces here accommodates the most discerning of tastes, while the gentle trickling of fountains and the fragrantly scented air combine to create a general feeling of wellbeing. There are three elegant spa suites, each covering an area of 120 square metres and each with its own spa treatment room for the ultimate in privacy. Another exclusive feature is "Vertigo", the open-air rooftop restaurant on the 61st floor, offering magnificent views of this city of 9 million. Of course, the traveller can also choose to alight at other culinary destinations: "Bai Yun", offering nouvelle Chinese cuisine, "Saffron" with a mix of Thai and international cuisine or the "Rom Sai" restaurant.

Banyan Tree Bangkok
Senior Vice President
Managing Director – Hotel
Operations
General Manager
Bernold O. Schroeder
21/100 South Sathon Road
Bangkok 10120
Thailand
Phone: 00 66 / 26 79 - 12 00
Fax: 00 66 / 26 79 - 11 99
E-mail:
bangkok@banyantree.com
Internet:
www.banyantree.com

162 suites
from US$ 330 to 2,000

Distance from airport:
30 minutes

Memberships:
The Leading Hotels
of the World,
Small Luxury Hotels
of the World

Ein Hideaway direkt am Golf von Siam, ein Versteck, in dem man alles um sich hat, was den Urlaub traumhaft macht, allen Luxus, alle Schönheit tropischer Natur in einem 41000 Quadratmeter großen Garten Eden. Die 55 Villen sind hell und modern eingerichtet und zeichnen sich durch innovative und elegante Wohnkultur aus. Die „Evason-Hideaway"-Villen sind Residenzen mit riesiger Wohnfläche und verfügen über einen privaten Infinity-Pool, eigenen Garten und einen Butlerservice, der den Gästen jederzeit die Wünsche von den Augen abliest. Der phänomenale Service des Hotels setzt sich fort in den Restaurants des Hideaways. Etwa im „The Beach", dem Open-Air-Restaurant mit Meerblick. In der offenen Showküche werden vorzugsweise Fisch und Meeresfrüchte sowie leichte Salate zubereitet. Im gemütlichen „Living Room Restaurant" genießen die Gäste, umgeben von wunderbaren Lotosteichen, so genannte „Thai-&-Fusion"-Gerichte, asiatische und westliche Spezialitäten, in tropischer Atmosphäre. Auf Entspannung in einer natürlichen Umgebung beruht das ganzheitliche Konzept des Six Senses Spas, das auf eine Mischung aus Verwöhn-Arrangements und Therapien mit Schwerpunkt auf Stressabbau, Gesundheit und Schönheit setzt. Das luxuriöse Hideaway offeriert außerdem Villen mit Spa-Suiten; hier kann sich der Gast ganz privat im eigenen Refugium verwöhnen lassen. Wer mag, kann unbeschwerte Urlaubstage auch mit Trekking oder Segeln verbringen und sich zum Tagesausklang einen stimmungsvollen Barbecue-Abend gönnen.

Located at the Gulf of Siam, this hideaway retreat is holiday paradise personified. It boasts all the luxuries and all the beauty of a tropical Garden of Eden setting covering 41,000 square metres. Its 55 villas are characterized by the innovative and elegant living environment that they offer. The "Evason Hideaway" villas are incredibly spacious with their own private infinity pool, garden and a butler service that is on hand to care of your every whim. And the hotel's phenomenal service doesn't stop there. Its restaurants are incredibly good. Take its "The Beach" open-air restaurant with sea views for example. The open show kitchen prides itself on preparing delicious fish, seafood and light salads. Guests dining in the cosy "Living Room Restaurant" can look forward to enjoying "Thai & Fusion" meals, as well as Asian and Western specialities in a tropical atmosphere surrounded by wonderful lotus ponds. Its holistic Six Senses Spa concept has been designed to provide relaxation in a natural environment and draws on a mixture of pampering treatments and therapies to achieve its objectives of stress reduction, health and beauty. This luxurious hideaway also offers Villas with Spa Suites. Here you can look forward to relaxing and indulging yourself in your own private retreat. And if your idea of a perfect holiday includes trekking, sailing or ending the day with a fantastic barbeque evening, here you'll find more opportunities, more atmosphere and more of everything you're likely to want.

Evason Hideaway at Hua Hin
General Manager:
Frank Wesselhoefft
9/22 Moo 5 Parknampran
Beach
Pranburi Prachuab Khiri
Khan
77220, Thailand
Phone: 00 66 / 32 61 82 00
Fax: 00 66 / 32 61 82 01
E-mail: reservations-hua-hin@evasonhideaways.com
Internet:
www.sixsenses.com

55 Villas from Thai Baht
10,200 to 30,450
(1 Thai Baht
approx. Euro 0,02)

Distance from airport:
30 minutes from Hua Hin

Membership:
Small Luxury Hotels

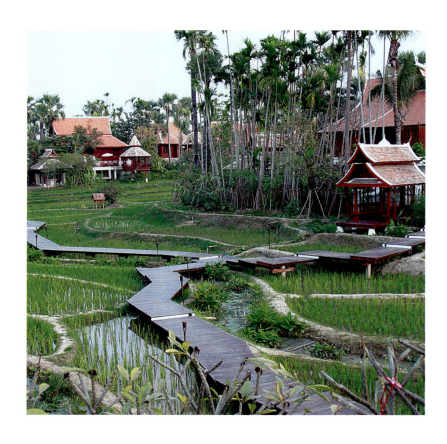

Das Mandarin Oriental Dhara Dhevi Luxury Resort & Spa wurde im Dezember 2004 im thailändischen Chiang Mai eröffnet. Hier sind nicht nur kulturell interessierte Gäste bestens aufgehoben, sondern auch solche, die nach innovativen Wegen suchen, ihre innere Balance wiederzufinden. Schon die Lage zeigt, wie intim das Dhara Dhevi die Atmosphäre des Landes aufnimmt: Die Natur ist ganz nah, malerische Reisfelder, tropische Wälder und exotische Plantagen fassen das Resort ein, und die Architektur schöpft tief aus der Geschichte Nordthailands. Sie zeigt sich überall inspiriert von der Kultur des Lanna-Königreiches. (Die Region wurde durch sie vom Ende des 13. Jahrhunderts an dreihundert Jahre lang geprägt.) Schillernd und facettenreich das Angebot: Man speist in Restaurants mit traditioneller Thai-Küche, mit authentisch chinesischer und klassisch französischer Cuisine; wohnt luxuriös in 80 Colonial Suites, 60 Private Villas mit überdurchschnittlich großen Zimmerschnitten, dazu in vier Themensuiten (Dhara Dhevi Suite, Chiang Mai Suite, Royal Suite, Spa Penthouse Suite). Das Dheva Spa hat das sensationelle Ausmaß von 3 100 Quadratmetern Fläche; es gibt eine „Kulinarische Akademie" und zu allem den gewohnt subtilen, einfühlsamen Mandarin-Oriental-Service.

The Mandarin Oriental Dhara Dhevi Luxury Resort & Spa was opened in December 2004 in Chiang Mai, Thailand. This is a place where those interested in culture will feel just as home as those looking for innovative ways of finding inner balance. Indeed, you only have to look at its location to see how intimately Dhara Dhevi takes in the atmosphere of Thailand. It's hard to imagine being any closer to nature given its picturesque rice fields, tropical forests and exotic plantations. And its architecture draws deeply from North Thailand's past. Wherever you look, the resort has drawn cultural inspiration from the Lanna Kingdom. (The region was influenced by this Kingdom for three centuries from the end of the 13th century.) It offers a dazzlingly rich array of facilities. Its guests dine in restaurants offering traditional Thai cuisine, as well as Chinese and classic French cuisine. Luxurious accommodation is provided by 80 Colonial Suites, 60 Private Villas with larger-than-average proportions and four Theme Suites (Dhara Dhevi Suite, Chiang Mai Suite, Royal Suite, Spa Penthouse Suite). The Dheva Spa boasts proportions of some 3,100 square metres, there is a "Cooking Academy" and, of course, the subtle, sensitive Mandarin Oriental service to which its guests are so accustomed.

Mandarin Oriental
Dhara Dhevi
Chiang Mai
51/4 Chiang Mai–
Sankampaeng Road
Moo 1 T. Tasata A. Muang
Chiang Mai 5000, Thailand
Phone: 00 66 / 53 / 88 88 88
Fax: 00 66 / 53 / 88 89 99
E-mail: mocnx-
reservations@mohg.com
Internet:
www.mandarinoriental.com

80 Colonial Suites, 60 Villas and 4 Theme Suites will become available start 1 November 2005, Villas (according to season and category) from US$ 390 to 2,000 + 10 % service charge, 7 % government tax and 0,8 % provincial tax

Distance from airport:
15 minutes

Membership:
Mandarin Oriental
Hotel Group

SILA EVASON HIDEAWAY & SPA AT SAMUI, THAILAND

Mit seiner spektakulären Lage an der nördlichsten Spitze der thailändischen Ferieninsel Koh Samui, innovativem Design und dem außergewöhnlichen Service eines Six Senses Resorts verwöhnt das Sila Evason Hideaway & Spa at Samui seit Juni 2004 anspruchsvolle Luxustraveller. Das breitgefächerte Angebot des Spas und die hervorragende Küche mit ihrer „East meets West"-Cuisine sind weitere wichtige Zutaten für einen prickelnden Urlaubscocktail, der ganz im Sinne der Company-Philosophie alle Sinne berührt. Das Hideaway verfügt über 66 exklusive, im asiatisch-thailändischen Stil gehaltene Privatvillen, die zwischen 105 und 175 Quadratmeter groß sind, jede einzelne mit herrlichem Panoramablick auf den Golf von Thailand und größtenteils mit eigenem Pool. Die Präsidenten-Suite bietet ultimativen Luxus auf über 514 Quadratmetern inklusive eigenem tropischen Garten, so dass auch hier, wie überall in der Anlage, Ruhe und Privatsphäre garantiert sind. Fernab vom Alltag hält das wunderschön gelegene Spa eine breite Palette von ganzheitlichen Wellness-, Entspannungs- und Verwöhnangeboten für Erholung Suchende bereit. Für sportlich ambitionierte Gäste sind der großzügige Swimmingpool, vielfältige Wassersportmöglichkeiten und der Fitnessbereich genau das Richtige.

Commanding a spectacular position on the most northern tip of the Thai holiday island of Koh Samui, the Sila Evason Hideaway & Spa at Samui boasts innovative design and the kind of exceptional service that you would expect of a Six Senses resort. Indeed, it has been pampering luxury travellers since June 2004. Add to this the wide variety of treatments on offer in the Spa and the resorts excellent East-meets-West cuisine and you have all the ingredients for an exciting holiday cocktail aimed at pleasing all your senses in line with the company's philosophy. The Sila Evason Hideaway comprises 66 exclusive Asian-Thai-styled private villas between 105 and 175 square metres in size. Each and every one of them boasts breathtaking views of the Gulf of Thailand and most have a private pool. The Presidential Suite offers the ultimate in luxury covering 514 square metres – its own tropical garden included. Like everywhere else at the Hideaway, peace and privacy come as standard. Far away from it all, the wonderful located Spa offers a large number of holistic treatments aimed at wellness, relaxation and pure unadulterated pampering. More sport-minded guests can look forward to enjoying the generously-proportioned swimming pool, a wide range of water sports and the resort's own gym.

Sila Evason Hideaway
& Spa at Samui
General Manager:
Eric Hallin
9/ 10 Moo 5
Baan Plai Laem Bophut
Koh Samui Surathani
84320 Thailand
Phone: 00 66 (0) 77 24 56 78
Fax: 00 66 (0) 77 24 56 71
E-mail: reservations-sa-mui@evasonhideaways.com
Internet:
www.sixsenses.com

66 villas from Thai Baht
15,400 to 73,620
(1 Thai Baht
approx. Euro 0,02)

Distance from airport:
10 minutes

Membership:
Small Luxury Hotels

FACILITIES

Dieses Hotel ist eine Legende. Seit über einem Jahrhundert wählen es gekrönte Häupter, Staatsmänner, Künstler und Prominente aus allen Bereichen als ihr Domizil in Bangkok. Direkt am Ufer des Chao Praya Rivers gelegen, wirkt es trotz seiner Größe mit knapp vierhundert Zimmern und dem riesigen Pool im üppig begrünten Innenhof mehr wie ein Resort, wie ein Rückzugsort der Ruhe und des Luxus. Besonders legendär sind die 35 Suiten in der „Author's Residence", die berühmten Schriftstellern gewidmet wurden, die hier gewohnt haben und sich im Oriental zu einigen ihrer bekanntesten Werke inspirieren ließen. Das Serviceniveau der eintausend Mitarbeiter ist legendär, egal ob man in einem der sechs Restaurants Platz nimmt (The Normandie: französische Grande Cuisine; Lord Jim's: Fischspezialitäten, Riverside Terrace: Buffet; Ciao: italienisch; The China House: kantonesische Küche und Dim-Sum; Rin Naam Terrace: thailändische Küche) oder sich mit dem Boot über den Fluss zum Spa zu den wohl besten Treatments der Welt übersetzen lässt, überall wird man sofort mit dem Namen angesprochen. Das Oriental wird seit fast vierzig Jahren von dem charismatischen deutschen General Manager Kurt Wachtveitl geleitet, der von seinen Mitarbeitern wie ein Vater verehrt wird.

This hotel is a legend. For over a century, crowned heads, statesmen, dignitaries, artists and celebrities from all spheres of life have been choosing it as their preferred residence in Bangkok. Located at the shores of the Chao Praya River, it's character with the large pool in the patio seems like a resort, an oasis of tranquility and luxury surrounded by the hustle and bustle of the Thai capital. The accommodation of almost four hundred rooms includes the legendary suites in the "Author's Residence", which are dedicated to famous writers, who have spent time here and been inspired to write some of their best-known works at The Oriental. The service of the one thousand members of staff is legendary, it doesn't matter if you take place in one of the six restaurants (The Normandie: French haute cuisine; Lord Jim's: fish specialities; Riverside Terrace: buffet; Ciao: Italian; The China House: Cantonese dishes and Dim Sum variations; Rin Naam Terrace: original Thai cooking), take the boat shuttle across the river to the Oriental spa, where you can enjoy the world's best treatments, everywhere you are greeted with your name. Charismatic General Manager from Germany, Kurt Wachtveitl, has been managing The Oriental for nearly forty years, he is respected from his staff like a father.

The Oriental Bangkok
General Manager:
Kurt Wachtveitl
48, Oriental Avenue
Bangkok 10500, Thailand
Phone: 00 66 / (2) 6 59 90 00
Fax: 00 66 / (2) 6 59 00 00
E-mail:
orbkk-reservations@
mohg.com
Internet:
www.mandarinoriental.com

358 rooms and 35 suites
Double rooms
from Euro 300,
Executive Suite Euro 450,
De Luxe Suites Euro 750,
Author's Suites
from Euro 900
(+ 10 % service charge
and 7 % government tax)

Distance from airport:
25 minutes

Membership:
The Leading Hotels
of the World

Das Resort The Tongsai Bay auf der thailändischen Ferieninsel Ko Samui macht dem „Land des Lächelns" alle Ehre. Umgeben von tropischer Natur, stilvollem Ambiente und der engagierten Verwöhnphilosophie der Familie Hoontrakul und ihren zweihundert stets lächelnden Mitarbeitern lernt man in der malerischen Tongsai-Bucht den authentischen Zauber Thailands kennen. Dabei fungiert der Prana Spa als effektiver Lotse für den direkten Weg in den siebten Urlaubshimmel. Die ganze Bucht – Strand natürlich inklusive – ist ausschließlich den Gästen des The Tongsai Bay vorbehalten. Das Haupthaus mit luftiger Lobby und dem legendären „Chef Chom's Thai Restaurant" schwebt wie ein Adlerhorst über einem wahrlich paradiesischen Fleckchen Erde. Die 44 Cottage Suiten, die 11 Grand Villen und die 4 Pool Villen ducken sich unter das Grün mächtiger Palmen und üppig blühender Tropenvegetation. Hinzu kommen 24 Beachfront Suiten im Hauptgebäude. Und selbst dieser dreistöckige Trakt unten am großen Seewasserpool fügt sich harmonisch in das naturnahe Gesamtbild ein. Egal ob man im „Chef Chom's Thai Restaurant" authentisch thailändische Küche, im „The Butler's Restaurant" Spezialitäten der europäischen Küche oder im „Floyd's Beach Bistro" internationale Zubereitungen genießt, die hochgesteckten Qualitätsansprüche prägen auch die abwechslungsreiche Kulinarik des Hauses.

The Tongsai Bay Resort on Thailand's holiday island of Ko Samui really does do justice to Thailand's reputation as being the "Land of Smile". Amid a tropical environment, cozy ambience and pampered by the Hoontrakul family and their 200-strong, ever-smiling staff of committed employees, Tongsai Bay really is a wonderful location to discover the true magic of Thailand. Add to this the Prana Spa and what you have is a direct holiday gateway to seventh heaven. The entire bay – including the beach – is reserved exclusively for The Togsai Bay's guests. The resort's main building with its airy lobby and legendary "Chef Chom's Thai Restaurant", hovers above a truly heavenly part of the world like an eagle's nest. It's as if the estate's 44 Cottage Suites, 11 Grand Villas and 4 Pool Villas are crouching down underneath the green leaves of magnificent palm trees and lush tropical vegetation. There are also 24 Beachfront Suites in the main building. Even the three-story wing down below by the large sea-water pool, which houses the Beachfront Suites, fits wonderfully into the natural surroundings. Regardless of whether you choose to enjoy authentic Thai cuisine in "Chef Chom's Thai Restaurant", European gastronomic specialities in "The Butler's Restaurant" or international food at "Floyd's Beach Bistro", the very high quality standards of the entire estate characterizes the varied range of culinary delights on offer.

The Tongsai Bay
General Manager:
Thanakorn Hoontrakul
84 Moo 5, Bo Phut / Ko Samui
Surat Thani 84320 / Thailand
Phone:
00 66 / (0) 77 / 24 54 80
Fax:
00 66 / (0) 77 / 24 56 20
E-mail:
info@tongsaibay.co.th
Internet:
www.tongsaibay.co.th

44 Cottage Suiten, 11 Tongsai Grand Villas, 4 Tongsai Pool Villen from Thai Baht 11,000 to 25,000 (1 Thai Baht approx. Euro 0,02)

Distance from airport:
Ko Samui – 10 minutes

EVASON HIDEAWAY AT ANA MANDARA RESORT & SPA, VIETNAM

FACILITIES

Evason Hideaway ist das exklusive Boutique-Konzept der Six Senses Resorts & Spas, ein Konzept, das die Natur in verstärktem Maße mit einbindet. Die Lage des Evason Hideaway an der abgeschiedenen Ninh-Van-Bucht ist einzigartig und sehr beeindruckend. Man ist umgeben vom Dschungel und von plätschernden Bergflüssen, hat einen weißen feinen Sandstrand vor sich, der weit hinaus ins Meer führt, und auch ein vorgelagertes Korallenriff. Die Serviceleistungen des Resorts ermöglichen es dem Gast, in absoluter Abgeschiedenheit zurück zu sich selbst zu finden. Gäste logieren in 54 luxuriösen Villen, die mal am Strand, mal über dem Wasser oder auf den Felsen erbaut sind, alle mit viel Freiraum und privatem Pool. Das hohe Serviceniveau dokumentiert sich u. a. durch einen aufmerksamen Pool-Butler für die Gäste. Die Küche des Hauses offeriert regionale wie internationale Spezialitäten sowie eine beeindruckende Auswahl an Weinen aus aller Welt. Das Six Senses Spa, ein Schlüsselelement eines jeden Evason Hideaway, liegt eingebettet in eine imposante Fluss- und Wasserfalllandschaft. Es bietet Gästen ein maßgeschneidertes Behandlungs- und Regenerationsprogramm durch ein internationales Therapeuten-Team. Zum Freizeitprogramm des Hotels gehören u. a. Tennis, Tauchen und zahlreiche andere Wassersportarten, Wandern sowie ein Fitnessstudio.

Evason Hideaway identifies the boutique category of Evason. Attention to detail, the creation of memorable guest experiences and a focused commitment to the environment are driving forces. The site of the Evason Hideaway at Ana Mandara on dramatic Ninh Van Bay is quite unique, taking full advantage of the setting. Impressive rock formations, the coral reef, white sand beach, a playful stream and towering mountains to the rear, all add to the sense of being luxuriously at one with nature. Accommodations comprise 54 villas with private pools. The villas are set on the beachfront, over rocks or over water, providing generous personal space and present an uncompromised standard of luxury. Service levels are very high, with pool butlers exemplifying the personal attention offered to every guest. Dining and refreshment services cover international and locally-inspired cuisine and an impressive selection of vintages from around the world. The Six Senses Spa, a key component of each Evason Hideaway, compliments the rockscape beside a gentle waterfall. It provides signature treatments together with individual rejuvenation specialties of the region and of the international therapists. Evason Hideaway activities include tennis, water sports and dive facilities, gymnasium, and trekking and nature trails that take advantage of the unique location of the Hideaway.

Evason Hideaway
at Ana Mandara Resort & Spa
Beachside Tran Phu Blvd.
Nha Trang – Khanh Hoa
Phone: 00 84 / 58 52 47 05
Fax: 00 84 / 58 52 47 04
E-mail:
reservations-anamandara
@evasonhideaways.com
Internet:
www.sixsenses.com/
hideaway-anamandara

Distance from airport:
30 minutes by van,
15 minutes by speedboat

Membership:
Six Senses
Hotels, Resorts & Spas

The Beach House, Barbuda

1492 wollte Kolumbus nach Indien und entdeckte die Karibik

1982 wollten wir in die Karibik und entdeckten ein

neues Lebensgefühl

Unzählige, einzigartige, kleine Inseln zwischen Florida und Venezuela, Inseln vulkanischen Ursprungs oder aus Korallensand bieten eine Natur von unberührter Schönheit, unendlich weite Strände, tiefgrüne Regenwälder mit Wasserfällen, einsame verträumte Badebuchten und gastfreundliche Menschen, die Sie willkommen heißen.

Ob Karibik oder more, immer nach der Maxime – individuell und maßgeschneidert.

Wenn auch Sie Karibik & more entdecken möchten, nehmen wir uns gerne Zeit für Sie. Sagen Sie uns einfach Ihre Wünsche und wir stellen Ihnen Ihre Reise ganz nach Ihren Vorstellungen zusammen.

Michaela Jaudszims   Raimund Weber

Karibik & more

Der Spezialist für die Karibik * www.Karibik-and-more.de

Neuffener Straße 3/1, 72581 Dettingen
Tel.: 0 71 23 / 97 68 76, Fax: 0 71 23 / 97 68 75
Karibik_and_more@t-online.de
www.Karibik-and-more.de

Amerika & Karibik / America & Caribbean
Florida, Mexico, Barbados, Jamaica, Virgin Islands

Direkt am feinsandigen Strand von South Beach, dem pulsierenden Herz der quirligen Boomtown Miami, entführt das luxuriöse The Setai in die Welt feinster Wohn- und Hotelkultur und vermittelt einen zuverlässigen Eindruck vom ungezwungenen Lifestyle der exotischen Metropole. An der angesagten „Oceanfront" führt General Manager und Vice President der GHM-Hotels Manvinder Puri ein „Leading Hotel of the World", in dem sich ein Höchstmaß an Privatsphäre mit vorbildlichem Service-Niveau vereint. In sämtlichen 75 Hotelzimmern und in den 50 Suiten des vierzig Stockwerke hohen Residential Tower (Wohnen mit Hotelservice) stellen sich Entspannung und Wohlgefühl im Handumdrehen ein. Highlight ist das über 900 Quadratmeter große Penthouse mit Pool auf der Dachterrasse und herrlichem Blick auf das Meer. Drei Swimmingpools, umgeben von einem tropischen Gartenareal, der eigene Beach Club und das Spa sorgen für Entspannung und aktive Erholung rund um „fun & sun". Wem es beliebt, der bringt sich mit Wassersport, Golf, Tennis oder im Fitness-Center rasch in Höchstform. Für kulinarische Streicheleinheiten sorgt die „Trans-Ethnic-Cuisine", während Gourmets in der edlen „Champagner, Crustacean and Caviar-Bar" auf ihre Kosten kommen.

Located right on the sandy shores of Miami's vibrant heart, South Beach, The Setai reaches out its hand and invites you to enter into a luxurious world of fine accommodation. Once inside you are instantly struck by the apparent ease with which the unforced lifestyle of this exotic metropolis seems to pervade the entire building. On the fashionable Ocean Front, its General Manager and Vice President of GHM Hotels, Manvinder Puri, presides over a "Leading Hotel of the World". It's a place that combines extremely high privacy standards with an exemplary service. In all 75 rooms and 50 suites located inside the hotel's forty-floor-high Residential Tower (accommodation with hotel service), you are instantly struck by an overwhelming sense of relaxation and well-being. Pièce de résistance is the hotel's 900 square metre Penthouse featuring a roof pool and breathtaking views of the ocean. Its three swimming pools in a tropical garden setting, its own beach club and health spa ensure that all its guests can look forward to keeping in shape and relaxing under the Florida sunshine. If water sports, golf, tennis or the gym are your thing, you'll find ample opportunity to stretch your wings here. When it comes to pampering of the culinary variety, it offers trans-ethnic cuisine. Gourmets can indulge themselves in the very refined Champagne, Crustacean and Caviar Bar.

The Setai
General Manager:
Manvinder Puri
2001 Collins Avenue
Miami Beach, Florida 33139
USA
Phone: 0 01 / 305 / 520 / 60 00
Fax: 0 01 / 305 / 520 / 66 00
Internet: www.setai.com
www.ghmhotels.com

Residental Tower: 50 suites
Hotel: 75 rooms
from US$ 900 (Studio Suite, City) to 6,000
(3 Bedroom Suite and Den, Ocean Front, Balcony)

Distance from airport:
30 minutes

Membership:
The Leading Hotels
of the World

An der Südspitze der Baja California, zwischen den Städten San Jose del Cabo im Osten und Cabo San Lucas im Westen, liegt Mexicos Mekka des Luxustourismus, die Region Los Cabos. Ihr Prachtstück: Las Ventanas al Paraiso, für viele First-Class-Weltenbummler das schönste Hotel-Resort der Welt. Las Ventanas al Paraiso heißt übersetzt: Die Fenster zum Paradies – dabei präsentiert sich die Traumadresse am Kap von Mexiko schon selbst als Garten Eden. Sie erscheint so gar nicht als Hotel, eher als eleganter Pueblo. Zwischen den Villen blühen zauberhafte Gärten. Wasserläufe ziehen sich durchs Resort. „The Restaurant" bietet leichte feine Mittelmeer-Cuisine mit spektakulärem Poolblick. Der „Sea Grill" wartet mit moderner mexikanischer Küche auf, ein kulinarisches Highlight auch die „Tequila & Ceviche Bar". Die 61 Gästewohnungen bestehen ausschließlich aus Suiten, so großzügig angelegt, dass sie selbst verwöhnteste Ansprüche zufriedenstellen. Kunstvoll ins Flair gewebt: viel erlesene lokale Handwerkskunst. Das Spa bietet nicht weniger als zwölf verschiedene Wirkungsbereiche mit einem Gesamtmenü von zirka achtzig Anwendungen. Der Robert-Trent-Jones-II-Golfkurs liegt unmittelbar neben dem Resort. Und wenn sie sich paaren, springen vor der Küste die Wale.

Dramatically located at the tip of the Baja California Peninsula, Los Cabos is Mexico's Mecca of luxury tourism. And Las Ventanas al Paraiso is the jewel in the crown. The prestigious Andrew Harper's Hideaway Report proclaimed it the "Number One International Resort of 2004". Translated, Las Ventanas al Paraiso means "The Windows to Paradise", and this dream resort delights in presenting itself as a Garden of Eden. The blooming gardens throughout the resort echo the natural landscape of the surrounding desert. A network of infinity-edge pools winds down to the sand's edge. "The Restaurant" prepares unique, mouth-watering Baja-Mediterranean cuisine. If it's Mexican specialties you're looking for, enjoy Contemporary Mexican Cuisine at the Sea Grill to the soothing sounds of the waves. The Tequila & Ceviche Bar, with its innovative ceviches and world's-best Margaritas, is another dining delight. The 61 suites are so spacious and ultra-luxurious that they will meet with the approval of the most discerning travelers. Particularly charming is the hand-done Mexican artisanry that has been woven into the character of the suites and throughout the resort. The Spa offers both indoor and garden areas to experience an incredible array of treatments and therapies from around the world, as well as Las Ventanas' signature Baja Desert treatments. A Robert Trent Jones II golf course wraps around the resort. You can tee off on the 15th hole by the water to the magnificent sight of pods of whales passing by during their annual migrations.

Las Ventanas al Paraiso
Rosewood Hotels & Resorts
Director: Luis Fernandes
Km 19,5 Carretera Transpeninsular Cabo San Lucas –
San Jose del Cabo, Baja California Sur, 23400 Mexico
Phone: 00 52 / 62 41 44 03 00
Fax: 00 52 / 62 41 44 03 01
E-mail: lasventanas@
rosewoodhotels.com
Internet:
www.lasventanas.com

61 suites
Junior Suites (according to season) from US$ 450 to 1,150, Ocean View Suite from US$ 1,800 to 2,600, Ocean Front Suite from US$ 2,000 to 2,900, Three Bedroom Luxury Suite from US$ 3,800 to 4,500 + 12 % tax and 15 % service charge

Distance from airport:
15 minutes

Memberships:
Rosewood Hotels & Resorts,
The Leading Hotels
of the World

An der Südspitze der sonnigen Halbinsel Baja California serviert das Luxusresort One&Only Palmilla einen prickelnden Urlaubscocktail für alle Sinne: landschaftliche Schönheit und Naturerlebnisse ebenso wie die Eleganz eines First-Class-Domizils, die Wärme mexikanischer Gastfreundschaft und kleine kulinarische Träume. Eingebettet in ein tropisches Areal gruppieren sich zahlreiche exklusive Villen um das Hauptgebäude im Hacienda-Stil. Geschwungene Natursteinwege führen zwischen leuchtenden Blütenmeeren zu sattgrünen Rasenflächen und schattigen Innenhöfen mit plätschernden Brunnen, begleiten weiß getünchte Wände und Mauern aus Sandstein, die hier und da mit den Farben der Natur sowie dem Blau der Pools und des Meeres kontrastieren. Dreizehn abgeschirmte und exklusive Spa-Villen mit intimer Privatsphäre entführen in eine meditativ besinnliche Welt aus natürlichen Materialien, Farben, Licht und betörenden Düften. Zurück im Hotel findet man in den 172 Zimmern und Suiten mit Terrasse, Meerblick und 24-Stunden-Roomservice allen erdenklichen Komfort. Ob im offenen „Agua"-Restaurant mit „mexiterranen" Gerichten, auf der Terrasse des „Breeze" oder im trendigen Gourmetrestaurants „C" – feine Zungen dürfen sich auf erstklassige Darbietungen aus Küche und Keller freuen.

On the southern tip of the sunny peninsula of Baja California, the luxury resort of One&Only Palmilla serves a holiday cocktail to make all the senses tingle: scenic beauty and the experience of nature mixed in equal measure with the elegance of a first-class residence, warm Mexican hospitality and small culinary delights. Nestled in tropical surroundings, numerous exclusive villas are arranged around the main, hacienda-style building. Meandering natural stone trails lead between seas of brightly-coloured flowers to lush green lawns and shady inner courtyards with gently splashing fountains and run alongside whitewashed sandstone walls that lending a touch of contrast here and there with the colours of nature, the blue of the pool and the sea. The guest will be charmed by any of the thirteen screened, exclusive spa villas, offering privacy in the perfect setting for meditative contemplation, surrounded by natural materials, colour, light and beguiling scents. Back at the hotel, the guest will find every imaginable comfort in each of the 172 rooms and suites with terrace, sea view and round-the-clock room service. Whether in the open-air "Agua" Restaurant with "Mexiterranean" dishes, on the terrace of the "Breeze" or in the fashionable "C" restaurant for gourmet cuisine, first-class wines and Epicurean delights await the most discerning of palates.

One&Only Palmilla
Managing Director:
Edward T. Steiner
Km 7.5
Carretera Transpeninsular
San Jose Del Cabo
BCS, CP 23400 Mexico
Phone: 0052 / 624 / 146 / 70 00
Fax: 0052 / 624 / 146 / 70 01
Internet:
oneandonlypalmilla.com

172 rooms and suites
from US$ 325 to 1,450

Distance from airport:
20 minutes

Membership:
The Leading Hotels
of the World

An der mexikanischen Pazifikküste im romantischen Fischerdorf Zihuatanejo macht das luxuriöse Resort Villa del Sol – das Sonnenhaus – seinem Namen alle Ehre: Postkartenidylle mit Palmen, 180 Meter bestens gepflegter Privatstrand und spektakuläre Sonnenuntergänge. Aber auch glitzernde Pools und plätschernde Brunnen, üppige Gärten und warmherzige Gastlichkeit, fröhliche Menschen und vollkommene Harmonie machen den Aufenthalt zum Erlebnis. Nicht umsonst zieren die Historie des mexikanischen Luxusresorts unzählige Auszeichnungen und vorderste Rangplätze auf der renommierten Condé-Nast-Gold-Liste. Der Reisende erlebt eine außergewöhnliche Dienstleistungsphilosophie, die ihn von der ersten bis zur letzten Minute in den Mittelpunkt stellt. Die Gäste haben die Wahl zwischen 35 Suiten (alle mit eigenem Pool) und 35 Zimmern. Eine Wahl, die im Sonnenhaus durchaus nicht leicht fällt, denn keine Suite gleicht der anderen und jede ist ein farbenprächtiges Schmuckkästchen für mexikanische Handwerkskunst. Neben den elf luxuriösen Beach Suiten mit Meerblick bieten besonders die Lagoon Penthouse Suite oder die Presidential Suite mit Privatpool sinnliche Wohnerlebnisse der Extraklasse. Neben den erwähnten Privatpools gibt es fünf weitere Pools im Garten. Adäquat ist das Angebot rund um unbeschwerte Sport-, Wellness- und Beautytage. Einen Besuch der beiden Restaurants mit mexikanischer und internationaler Küche sollte man auf keinen Fall versäumen.

On the Pacific coast of Mexico in the romantic fishing village of Zihuatanejo, the luxurious resort of Villa del Sol – House of the Sun – more than lives up to its name: Simply imagine a picture-postcard setting with palm trees, a 180-metre white sandy beach and spectacular sunsets. Add to this shimmering pools, gently splashing fountains, lush gardens, warm hospitality, the cheerful disposition of the local population, and this is a true experience of utter harmony. It is no coincidence that this luxury resort has received countless awards and top rankings in the famous Condé Nast Gold List. It takes the comfort and wellbeing of its guests to a higher level, with an exceptional, guest-centred service philosophy that places the visitor's needs first from the very outset. Guests can choose from among 35 suites (all with their own pools) and 35 rooms. Not a very easy choice in this "house of the sun", since no suite is alike, each an individual, splendidly-coloured treasure trove of Mexican craftsmanship. In addition to the eleven luxurious Beach Suites with sea view, the Lagoon Penthouse Suite and the Presidential Suite with private pool offer an experience to awaken the senses. There are five other pools in the garden in addition to the private pools already mentioned. The hotel also offers a good number of relaxation, sports, wellness and beauty specials. And a visit to one of the two restaurants, with Mexican and international cuisine, should definitely not be missed.

Villa del Sol
Director: Helmut Leins
Playa La Ropa
P.O. Box 84
Zihuatanejo, Gro. 40880
Mexico
Phone: 00 52 / 7 55 / 5 55 00
Fax: 00 52 / 7 55 / 4 27 58
E-mail:
res@hotelvilladelsol.com
Internet:
www.hotelvilladelsol.com

35 rooms and 35 suites
from US$ 270 to 1,350

Distance from airport Ixtapa-Zihuatanejo International:
12 minutes

Membership:
Small Luxury Hotels
of the World

Das kleine Barbados präsentiert sich als eine der schönsten und friedlichsten Inseln der Karibik. Die exklusivste und außergewöhnlichste Art, die beschauliche Inselidylle in vollen Zügen zu genießen, ist das Leading Hotel Sandy Lane direkt am nahezu endlosen St. James Beach. Um für die Ansprüche der Luxus-Traveller des 21. Jahrhunderts gerüstet zu sein, wurde das gesamte Resort zur Jahrhundertwende komplett restauriert und mit einem neuen Servicekonzept versehen. Dieses Resort glänzt mit mehr als fünf Sternen und macht dem erlauchten Kreis der Preferred Hotels & Resorts wirklich alle Ehre. Denn es sind nicht nur der perfekte Service, die hervorragende Küche, die einmalige Lage und die wunderschöne Architektur, die den Ruhm der legendären Adresse begründen. Das breitgefächerte Angebot für sportlich aktive und wellnessorientierte Urlauber sucht in der Karibik seinesgleichen. Drei (!) hoteleigene Golfplätze, ein professionelles Wassersportzentrum und ein riesiges Spa-Center bieten wahrhaft märchenhafte Möglichkeiten.

The small island of Barbados is one of the most beautiful and peaceful islands in the Caribbean. The "Leading Hotel" of Sandy Lane, directly on the seemingly endless St James' Beach, offers one of the most exclusive and exceptional ways of enjoying the tranquil island idyll to the full. To accommodate the requirements of the luxury traveller in the 21st century, the resort was completely renovated at the turn of the millennium, including the introduction of a new service philosophy. The result is a resort that plainly offers more than a gleaming five stars and is indeed a credit to the illustrious group of Preferred Hotels & Resorts. Yet it is not simply the superlative service, excellent cuisine, unique location and beautiful architecture to which this legendary establishment owes its name. The wide range of activities and treatments we offer to sporting and wellness enthusiasts is unbeatable in the Caribbean. The fact that the hotel has no less than three golf courses, along with a professional water sports centre and a huge spa centre, means the possibilities are truly out of this world.

Sandy Lane
General Manager:
Colm Hannon
St. James, Barbados
West Indies
Phone: 00 12 46 / 4 44 20 00
Fax: 00 12 46 / 4 44 22 22
E-mail:
mail@sandylane.com
Internet:
www.sandylane.com
Attractive packages
available at:
Strohbeck Reisen
Laustraße 88
D-70597 Stuttgart
Phone:
00 49 / (0) 7 11 / 46 85 18
info@strohbeckreisen.de
www.strohbeckreisen.de

112 rooms and suites
Double rooms from US$ 800,
Suites from US$ 1,300,
The Villa from US$ 8,000

Distance from airport:
29 kilometres

Membership:
Preferred Hotels & Resorts

ROUND HILL HOTEL & VILLAS, MONTEGO BAY

FACILITIES

Das exklusive Domizil Round Hill Hotel & Villas auf Jamaika ist nicht nur einfach ein Hotel. Das erste wirkliche Luxusresort der Karibik ist mehr. Fast schon eine Legende, die seit der Eröffnung 1953 Maßstäbe in der Nobelhotellerie gesetzt hat und deren Gästebuch sich wie ein Who's who der Finanz- und Filmwelt liest. Die 27 Villen, die sich rund um die hoteleigene Bucht an den sanft ansteigenden Hügel schmiegen, befinden sich alle in Privatbesitz. Ganz nach dem Geschmack des jeweiligen Besitzers eingerichtet, glänzen sie mit einer stilvollen Individualität und eigenem Pool. An der Konzeption des Round Hill Hotel & Villas hat sich in all den Jahren nichts wirklich Entscheidendes geändert. Von Anfang an vermittelten die Villen das Gefühl, bei Freunden zu Gast zu sein und die Hausangestellten, die bis heute ein fester Bestandteil der Round-Hill-Philosophie sind, sorgten sich um das Wohl der anspruchsvollen Gäste. Direkt auf dem Strand liegt das Pineapple House, dessen Zimmer gerade erst vom renommierten Designer Ralph Lauren – der selbst zwei der Round Villen besitzt – komplett neu gestaltet wurden. Seine lichten Interpretationen von luxuriösem „beach living" setzen dem service-orientierten Angebot mit Wellness Center, Kid's Club, Gourmetrestaurant und Wassersportzentrum das letzte i-Tüpfelchen auf.

The exclusive Round Hill Hotel & Villas resort in Jamaica is not only a hotel. No, the Caribbean's first real luxury resort is much more. It's all but legendary and has been setting new luxury hotel standards since opening in 1953. Its guestbook reads like a who's who of the world of finance and film. 27 privately owned villas nestle gently onto the slopes surrounding the hotel's very own bay. Decorated according to their owners' tastes, the villas boast stylish individuality and their own pool. As the years have passed very little has changed to the Round Hill Hotel & Villas' concept. Right from the outset, the villas have always had the ability to make you feel as if you were staying with friends. And the staff, who remain a firm part of the Round Hill Philosophy, have always made sure that the needs of its very discerning residents are perfectly catered for. The Pineapple House is located right on the beach. Its rooms have just been completely redesigned and renovated by the famous designer, Ralph Lauren, who owns two of the Round Villas himself. His clear interpretation of how luxury beach living should be puts the icing on the cake of a wonderfully service-orientated location with wellness centre, kid's club, gourmet restaurant and water sports centre.

Round Hill Hotel & Villas
Managing Director:
Josef F. Fortmayr
P.O. Box 64
Montego Bay, Jamaica W.I.
Phone: 0 01 / 8 76 / 9 56 70 50
Fax: 0 01 / 8 76 / 9 56 75 05
E-mail:
roundhill@cwjamaica.com
Internet:
www.roundhilljamaica.com
Attractive packages
available at:
Strohbeck Reisen
Laustraße 88
D-70597 Stuttgart
Phone:
00 49 / (0) 7 11 / 46 85 18
info@strohbeckreisen.de
www.strohbeckreisen.de

27 Private Villas with
74 suites, 36 rooms in the
Pineapple House
Superior room from US$ 260
Villa Suite from US$ 380

Distance from airport:
20 minutes

Memberships:
Elegant Resorts International,
Fine Hotels, Resorts and Spas,
Green Globe 21 certified

Strahlend weiß und puderzuckerfein schwingen sich die beiden Privatstrände an der Riviera Ocho Rios zu Füßen einer der exklusivsten Hotel-Ikonen Jamaikas: dem Royal Plantation – über Jahrzehnte berühmt geworden als elegante Anlaufstätte für anspruchsvolle Traveller. Das Resort knüpft nach millionenteurer Sanierung an die Glanzzeiten vergangener Jahre an und hat sich ganz auf die Bedürfnisse anspruchsvoller Luxus-Traveller eingestellt. Eingebettet in einen herrlichen Tropengarten offeriert das Resort 74 wundervolle Suiten mit phantastischem Meerblick sowie die Villa Plantana mit drei Schlafzimmern für alle, denen Privatsphäre und luxuriöse Abgeschiedenheit besonders wichtig sind. Für Gourmets ist in den vier Spezialitätenrestaurants mit ausgezeichneter kreativer Küche gesorgt, und anschließend geht es in die für Jamaika einzigartige C-Bar, einer Fusion aus iranischem Kaviar und Champagner Veuve Clicquot. Für einen unvergesslichen Urlaub sorgen Annehmlichkeiten wie der mit zwei zusätzlichen Whirlpools ausgestattete Swimmingpool sowie ein adäquates Angebot an Wassersportarten wie Kanu, Kajak, Paddelboot, Tauchen, Windsurfen und Segeln. Der ganz in der Nähe gelegene Upton Country Club bietet Tennis rund um die Uhr, auch mit Flutlichtbeleuchtung, sowie Tennisunterricht und einen Golfplatz. Wellness ist Wohlfühlen – dem Körper und der Seele ein paar Tage der Entspannung gönnen im Royal Spa, mit einem umfangreichen Angebot an Behandlungen und Anwendungen aus internationalen sowie vor Ort gewonnenen Ingredienzen.

Quietly elegant and nestled above two white sandy beaches on the Ocho Rios Riviera, Royal Plantation is the epitome of refined and glamorous Jamaican hospitality. Since 1957, discerning travellers from all around the world have passed through the elegant portals of this famous hotel. There are seventy-four beautifully styled ocean facing suites and nestled within the lush tropical gardens is the three-bedroom Villa Plantana affording the ultimate in privacy and seclusion. Four speciality restaurants offer creative and innovative cuisine and unique in Jamaica is the C-Bar, a fusion of Iranian caviar and Veuve Clicquot champagne. The swimming pool is complemented with two whirlpools and nautical sports include canoeing, kayaking, paddle-boats, scuba diving, windsurfing and sailing. There are tennis courts, lit for night playing and with instruction and golf is available nearby at Upton Country Club. The Royal Spa offers a complete range of treatments and applications combining international and locally sourced ingredients.

Royal Plantation, Ocho Rios
General Manager:
Peter Fraser
P. O. Box 2
Ocho Rios
St. Ann, Jamaica, W.I.
Phone: 00 18 76 / 9 57 / 44 08
Fax: 00 18 76 / 9 57 / 43 73
Internet:
www.royalplantation.com

74 comfortable suites
in seven categories
Suites from US$ 430,
Villa Plantana with private
butler US$ 3,100
Rates all inclusive

Distance from airport:
90 minutes

Memberships:
The Leading Small Hotels
of the World,
Leading Spa of the World,
Elegant Resorts
International

Virgin Gorda ist ein karibisches Stück vom Paradies. Rund ums Jahr klettern rote, gelbe, rosa Bougainvilleen; strahlend weiße, makellos reine Frangipaniblüten duften betörend in der Sommerluft. Im Rosewood Resort Little Dix Bay pflegt ein Heer von Gärtnern eine gigantische Zahl von Pflanzen, Stauden, Blumen und tropischen Gewächsen. Natur pur auch in den 96 Zimmern und Suiten. Sie wurden erst kürzlich mit Multi-Millionenaufwand renoviert – die komplette Fertigstellung der Bäder ist in 2006 abgeschlossen. Helle Pastell- und Naturfarben schaffen eine unprätentiöse, lauschig-elegante Atmosphäre. Exklusiv der Komfort. Gewaltige Aussichten ins Blaue genießt man praktisch von jedem Ort des Anwesens, auch von den Tischen der drei Restaurants. Die „Sugar Mill" – tatsächlich eine ehemalige Zuckermühle – ist das Hauptkulinarium an der Little Dix Bay, spezialisiert auf leichte italienische Gerichte, gegrillte Meeresfrüchte und Fleischgerichte, die mit lokalen Zutaten akzentuiert werden. Ein Traum sind die Strände: einer vor der Haustür, kilometerlang, weiß und in weitem Bogen, teilweise beschattet von Palmen; dreizehn weitere sind leicht per Wassertaxi erreichbar. Man segelt, paddelt, fährt Wasserski, taucht oder schnorchelt – und das alles in wahrlich paradiesischen Gewässern.

Virgin Gorda is a piece of Caribbean paradise. Here you will find red, yellow and pink bougainvillea climbing all year round and some of the whitest, most perfectly formed frangipani flowers filling the summer air with their scent. An army of gardeners has been charged with tending to Little Dix Bay's huge number of shrubs, flowers and tropical plants. Its 96 rooms and suites couldn't be closer to nature. Indeed, they have been finished completed following a multi-million renovation package – a carefully executed enhancement project to update and upgrade all bathrooms will be completetd in 2006. Pale pastels and natural colours conspire to create an unpretentious and quietly elegant atmosphere. They offer wonderfully exclusive comfort. Magnificent views of the sea can be enjoyed from virtually every part of the resort, even from the tables of its three restaurants. Formally a sugar mill, the Sugar Mill restaurant is Little Dix Bay's main culinary centre of excellence. It specializes in light Italian dishes, grilled seafood and meat dishes accentuated with local ingredients. Its beaches are a real dream. The one on the doorstep is miles long, white, sandy, curved and partially shaded by palm trees. The other thirteen beaches can be easily reached by water taxi. Here you can look forward to sailing, paddling, water skiing, diving or snorkelling in truly paradisiacal waters.

Little Dix Bay,
A Rosewood Resort
Managing Director:
Martein van Wagenberg
P.O. Box 70, Virgin Gorda
British Virgin Islands
Phone: 0 02 84 / 4 95 / 55 55
Fax: 0 02 84 / 4 95 / 56 61
E-mail: littledixbay@
rosewoodhotels.com
Internet:
www.littledixbay.com

96 rooms and suites
Ocean View Room (according to season) from US$ 325 to 495, Premium Room from US$ 495 to 595, Beach Front Cottage from US$ 575 to 695, Rosewood Junior Suite from US$ 700 to 1,000, One-Bedroom Suite US$ 900 to 1,200, Villas from US$ 1,800 to 3,300 + 7 % tax and 10 % room surcharge
For rates 2006 please look: www.littledixbay.com

Distance from airport:
15 minutes by luxury boat launch

Membership:
Rosewood Hotels & Resorts

CANEEL BAY, A ROSEWOOD RESORT, U.S. VIRGIN ISLANDS

FACILITIES

Das Rosewood Resort Caneel Bay ist umgeben von sieben feinen Sandstränden, kristallklarem Wasser, Korallenriffen und einer phantastischen Unterwasserwelt. Die Karibische See umspült das Anwesen auf St. John, US-Jungferninseln, von drei Seiten. Alle 166 Zimmer haben eine Veranda mit Aussicht auf mindestens einen der sieben Strände oder auf die zauberhaften Szenerien des Virgin Islands National Parks. Jedes Logis wurde großzügig gestaltet, karibisches Flair durchdringt alle Interieurs. Auch die vier Restaurants des Resorts schöpfen aus der Ursprünglichkeit des Ortes, komponieren ihre Menüs aus fangfrischem Fisch und Meeresfrüchten oder anderen Inselprodukten, verfeinern sie mit den pikanten Gewürzen und exotischen Aromen der Karibik. Wöchentliche Attraktion: die traditionelle Rum-Probe in der ehemaligen Zuckerplantage. Ein umfangreiches Aktivitätenprogramm sorgt für den sportlichen Ausgleich. Im „Self Centre" regenerieren Körper und Geist. Kinder sind in „Turtle Town" bestens aufgehoben. Wichtig: Caneel Bay ist eine echte „Zuflucht", wie das Resort unterstreicht: „absichtlich ferngehalten vom modernen Glitter, von digitalen Ablenkungen und vom rasanten Tempo der Welt zu Hause".

Caneel Bay, a Rosewood Resort, is surrounded by seven beaches of fine sand, crystal clear water, coral reefs and a fantastic underwater world. The Caribbean Sea washes against the hotel grounds on three sides. All 166 rooms have a veranda with a view of a least one of the seven beaches or the magical scenery of the Virgin Islands National Parks. All rooms are spacious and Caribbean flair characterises their interiors. In addition, the four restaurants of the resort take their inspiration from the origins of the area. The menus are composed of freshly caught fish and sea food or other produce of the island and are perfected with the spicy herbs and exotic aromas of the Caribbean. The weekly attraction is the traditional rum sampling on the former plantation. An extensive programme of activities provides the appropriate counterbalance for exercise. In the "Self Centre", body and soul can regenerate. Children are in good hands in "Turtle Town". Most importantly Caneel Bay is a true place of refuge. The resort emphasises that it is "intentionally kept away from modern glitter, digital distractions and the fast pace of life at home".

Caneel Bay
A Rosewood Resort
Managing Director: Rik Blyth
P.O. Box 720, St. John, U.S.V.I.
00831-0720
Phone: 3 40 / 7 76 / 61 11
Fax: 3 40 / 6 93 / 82 80
E-mail:
caneel@rosewoodhotels.com
Internet.
www.caneelbay.com

166 rooms
Rates according to season:
Courtside from US$ 350 to 450, Garden View from US$ 425 to 625, Ocean View from US$ 475 to 725, Beach Front from US$ 525 to 850, Premium Ocean View from US$ 550 to 875, Premium Beach Front from US$ 625 to 925, Cottage 7 from US$ 875 to 1,350

Distance from airport:
45 minutes

Membership:
Rosewood Resorts

REISEN UND MEHR...
Unser Name ist Programm!

Sie haben Träume, Wünsche oder Vorstellungen?
Zumindest beim Reisen können wir Ihnen helfen.
Wir entführen Sie an die schönsten Orte,
in die romantischsten Hotels und Resorts,
die herrlichsten Spa und Wellness Center,
auf private Jachten, in Urwaldcamps oder
zu exklusiven Golfplätzen, organisieren
außergewöhnliche Rundreisen und Spritztouren,
einfach: was Sie sich wünschen.
Unsere Reisedesigner kennen die Welt.
Lassen Sie sich inspirieren, das Buch gibt Anregungen,
wir führen sie aus, individuell, maßgeschneidert
und zuverlässig.

www.prestigeres.com

Prestige Resorts GmbH
Berthold Graf Stauffenberg
Salvatorstraße 2, Im Theatinerhof, 80333 München
Telefon: 00 49 / (0) 89 / 24 22 77 70
Telefax: 00 49 / (0) 89 / 24 22 77 77
info@prestigeres.com

Albergo Giardino

airportclub

Der Airport Club ist einer der bedeutendsten Business-Clubs in Europa, seine Mitglieder sind weltweit in ausgewählten Clubs willkommen. Es ist eine der exklusivsten Adressen, die Frankfurt zu bieten hat – ideal für Arbeitstreffen sowie hochkarätige kulturelle und gesellschaftliche Veranstaltungen. Persönlichkeiten aus dem In- und Ausland, aus Wirtschaft, Kultur und Politik nutzen die Mitgliedschaft zum Meinungs- und Erfahrungsaustausch.

Konferenzen, Kultur & Kulinarisches

1988 von der Deutschen Bank und der Deutschen Lufthansa gegründet, bietet der Airport Club nicht nur alle Annehmlichkeiten und den perfekten Service eines großen Conference Centers, sondern auch die diskrete Atmosphäre und den anspruchsvollen Stil eines außergewöhnlichen Privatclubs.

Ausstattung und Lage
- 29 klimatisierte Konferenzräume
- Wireless LAN-Zugang ins Internet
- Modernste Konferenztechnik
- Zentrale Lage im 9. Stock des Frankfurt Airport Center 1, zwischen Terminal 1 und ICE-Bahnhof

Kulturelles und Kulinarisches
Zu Gast bei Veranstaltungen im Airport Club waren bereits so bedeutende und faszinierende Persönlichkeiten wie Marcel Reich-Ranicki, Lothar Späth, Helmut Maucher, Mario Adorf und viele weitere. Einen Abend lang verwöhnte Drei-Sterne-Koch Dieter Müller mit einer Selektion aus seinem Amuse bouche-Menü, ein anderes Mal diskutierten der ehemalige Deutsche Bank-Chef Hilmar Kopper, der Kunst- und Theaterkritiker Peter Iden und der Maler und Bildhauer Markus Lüpertz über Kunst und Kommerz.

Sie haben Interesse an einer Mitgliedschaft? Wir informieren Sie gerne:

AIRPORT CLUB

Airport Club für International Executives GmbH
Direktion Mitgliedschaften:
Kerstin Gluth, Claudia Fleischmann
Tel.: 069 – 69 70 71 21
E-Mail: info@airportclub.de
www.airportclub.de

Vila Joya

(Einzige Armbanduhr mit Viertelstundenrepetition)

CR
CHRONOSWISS
Faszination der Mechanik

Gerd-R. Lang, Uhrmachermeister
und Gründer der Chronoswiss

„Manche Uhren machen viel von sich reden – von dieser hier werden Sie auch noch einiges hören." Schenken Sie der Zeit ruhig einmal etwas Gehör. Denn sie hat jetzt einen wunderschönen Klang. Zwei winzig kleine Hämmerchen bringen auf Knopfdruck Tonfedern zum Schwingen und lassen für Stunden und Viertelstunden jeweils eine Melodie erklingen. Und wer nicht hören will, der kann immer noch fühlen. Oder sich am Anblick des Zifferblatts aus massivem Sterlingsilber erfreuen. Mehr über meine neue Klangskulptu(h)r und Chronoswiss finden Sie im „Buch mit dem Tick", das ich Ihnen auf Wunsch gerne zusende.

Chronoswiss, Elly-Staegmeyr-Str. 12, 80999 München, Tel. +49 (0) 89 89 26 07-0, Fax +49 (0) 89 8 12 12 35, www.chronoswiss.de

Grecotel Mykonos Blue

BRENNER'S PARK-HOTEL & SPA, BADEN-BADEN

FACILITIES

Seit mehr als 130 Jahren ist Brenner's Park-Hotel & Spa das führende Hotel in Baden-Baden. Als vor fünf Jahren Frank Marrenbach das Haus als Geschäftsführender Direktor übernahm, gab er ihm eine neue Maxime: „Ein Grandhotel wird jünger." Natürlich ist das Brenner's nach wie vor ein elegantes Luxushotel und natürlich ist das Publikum, das hier logiert, entsprechend kultiviert und gut situiert. Aber überall spürt man die gelungene Verjüngungskur, die der sympathische Direktor dem Haus verordnet hat. Der architektonische Umbau ist abgeschlossen, es gibt zwei Beauty Spas, im „Kanebo Harmonising & Care" arbeitet man exklusiv mit Produkten von Kanebo, im anderen wählt man zwischen Kosmetik von Futuresse, Bvlgari, Sisley und Brenner's hauseigener Marke Spirit of Jaipur. Im Medical Spa findet man fachärztliche Betreuung, eine Privatpraxis für Zahnheilkunde, ein Physio-Spa, Ernährungscoaching sowie ein Institut für Präventivmedizin. Drei Restaurants erfüllen alle kulinarischen Wünsche, der Salon Lichtental bittet zum exquisiten Frühstück, der Wintergarten mit der Parkterrasse ist sowohl im Sommer als auch im Winter ein Gedicht und im Park-Restaurant tischt man eine ambitionierte Gourmet-Cuisine auf.

Since more than 130 years Brenner's Park-Hotel & Spa is the leading hotel in Baden-Baden. As Frank Marrenbach took over the management of the hotel as Managing Director five years ago, he restored the lasting beauty of a hotel with youthful charm. His first objective and belief was that "a Grand hotel becomes younger". That's not to say, of course, that the Brenner's has lost any of its grand hotel elegance or that its guests are any less refined or well-to-do. But in all areas you will feel the results of a very successful and sensitive rejuvenation cure. The architectural refurbishment project has now been finsihed, there are two beauty spas: The Kanebo Harmonising & Care draws exclusively on Kanebo products, in the other beauty spa you can choose between cosmetic products by Futuresse, Bvlgari, Sisley and Brenner's very own Spirit of Jaipur brand. In the Medical Spa you will find a team of medical specialists for consulting, medical treatments and for individual health check-ups and also dentistry. Three restaurants fullfill all your culinary desires, the Salon Lichtental offers an exquisite breakfast, the Wintergarten with the Park-Terrace is not only during the summertime an amazing place for fine dining and in the Park-Restaurant you can enjoy an ambitious gourmet cuisine.

Brenner's Park-Hotel & Spa
Managing Director:
Frank Marrenbach
Schillerstraße 4–6
D-76530 Baden-Baden
Phone: 00 49 / 72 21 / 90 00
Fax: 00 49 / 72 21 / 3 87 72
E-mail:
information@brenners.com
Internet:
www.brenners.com

100 rooms, junior suites
and suites
from Euro 215 to 1,200
Presidential Suite
on request

Distance from airport:
90 minutes from Frankfurt
International Airport

Memberships:
The Leading Hotels
of the World,
Selektion Deutscher
Luxushotels

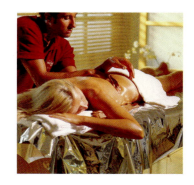

Nur eine Autostunde von München entfernt – an der schönsten Stelle des Tegernsees, der Egerner Bucht, umgeben von der traumhaften Kulisse der Bayerischen Alpen – erwartet Reisende ein spektakuläres Fünf-Sterne-Luxusdomizil. Die Gäste logieren in 135 Zimmern und 53 Suiten mit feinsten Interieurs aus edlen Materialien, u. a. Marmor, Seide, Kristall, erlesene Hölzer und handgewebte Teppiche. Vielfältig erweist sich die gastronomische Palette des Seehotels. Rustikal kommt die „Bayernstube" mit einer Auswahl an deftigen Klassikern der Region und Neuschöpfungen daher, während im Restaurant „Egerner Bucht" mit Brasserie eine schnörkellose, leichte und mediterrane Küche serviert wird – selbstverständlich mit Grundprodukten von Topqualität. Eine exquisite Auswahl von Weinen aus aller Welt bietet die Gewölbe-Vinothek. Gesundes Wohlbefinden vermitteln nicht nur Küche und Keller des Hauses, sondern auch der mit 2000 Quadratmetern sehr großzügige Royal-Spa-Bereich. Dazu gehören internationale Saunavarianten von finnisch bis japanisch, ein Sports Center mit Individualtraining und einer der modernsten Beauty-Salons Deutschlands mit Produkten von Shiseido und Ligne St. Barth. Als weltweit einziges Hotel ist das Seehotel Überfahrt autorisiert, die exklusiven Produkte der französischen Luxusmarke Cle de peau Beauté zu führen und anzuwenden.

Situated just an hour's drive from Munich and boasting one of the most beautiful spots on Tegernsee Lake, Egerner Bay, the Dorint Seehotel Überfahrt offers its guests magnificent views of the Bavarian Alps and all the comforts of a spectacular 5-star luxury hotel. Its guests reside in one of 135 rooms and 53 suites featuring wonderfully elegant interiors and the finest materials, incl. marble, silk, fine woods and hand-woven carpets. The hotel also offers plenty of variety when it comes to delicious cuisine. While the "Bayernstube" restaurant prides itself on offering a fine selection of hearty regional favourites and new creations, the "Egerner Bucht" restaurant with Brasserie enjoys serving light Mediterranean cuisine without the frills made from the very best produce. Its arched-cellar wine bar offers a selection of fine wines from across the world. Yet for all this, it's not only the hotel's restaurants and wine cellars that promote an atmosphere of healthy wellbeing. It also has wonderfully large Royal Spa health facilities covering some 2,000 square metres. Here you will find international sauna variations from Finish to Japanese, a sports centre offering individual training sessions and one of Germany's most up-to-date beauty salons with products from Shiseido and Ligne St. Barth. Indeed, the Dorint Seehotel Überfahrt is the only hotel in the world that is authorized to stock and apply the French luxury brand of Cle de peau Beauté.

Seehotel Überfahrt
Dorint Sofitel
General Manager:
Chris H. Muth
Überfahrtstraße 10
D-83700 Rottach-Egern
Phone:
00 49 / (0) 80 22 / 66 90
Fax:
00 49 / (0) 80 22 / 6 69 10 00
E-mail:
info.mucteg@dorint.com
Internet:
www.dorint.de/tegernsee

188 rooms including
53 suites. Rates depending
on saison and category
from Euro 195 to 345

Distance from airport:
Munich Airport
60 minutes drive by car

Natürlich ist der Sommer die schönste Jahreszeit, um die Schönheiten der deutschen Nordseeinsel Sylt zu genießen. Doch im Söl'ring Hof grenzt es fast an Verschwendung, die Zeit unter freiem Himmel zu verbringen. Denn die individuelle Atmosphäre und die vorbildliche Gastlichkeit von Johannes King und Claudia Reichelt sollte man von der ersten bis zur letzten Minute in vollen Zügen genießen. Wohin man auch schaut, alle Aufmerksamkeiten und Details verströmen Hingabe und integrieren sich in eine Philosophie, wo die persönliche und individuelle Betreuung den Ton angibt. Das kleine Fünf-Sterne- Refugium liegt umgeben von nichts als Dünen und Meer in ausgewählt ruhiger Lage. Berauschend im wahrsten Sinne des Wortes sind die luxuriös gestalteten Zimmer und Suiten mit einzigartigem Strandpanorama. Wie im ganzen Haus liegt das gewisse Etwas im Detail: die Inklusive-Minibar oder die Badaccessoires von Hermès stehen für exklusive Gastlichkeit. Stürmische Zeiten überstehen die Gäste am besten in der kleinen wunderbaren Wellnessoase mit Sauna, Dampfbad, Solarium, Muschelduschen, Eisbrunnen mit Fußreflexzonenbereich, beheizten Porzellanliegestühlen und Massagebereich. Die hohe Schule der Kochkunst erlebt man im exklusiven Restaurant. Dort zelebriert Johannes King eine feine klassische Küche mit leichter Ausrichtung, die von zwei Michelin-Sternen gekrönt wird.

While the summer months might the best time of year to enjoy all that Germany's North Sea island of Sylt has to offer, spending your time outside would almost be a crime when it comes to staying at the Söl'ring Hof. That's because the individual atmosphere and exemplary hospitality that Johannes King and Claudia Reichelt offer should be enjoyed in all its splendour from the first to the very last minute in the hotel. No matter where you look, you cannot fail to be struck by the attention to detail and the hotel's philosophy which sets great store by looking after its guests personally and taking care of their individual needs. This small five-star refuge is surrounded entirely by dunes and sea and commands a wonderfully quiet location. Its luxurious rooms and suites with their unique beach panorama are breathtaking in every sense of the word. Just like the rest of the hotel, the secret is in the detail. Take, for instance, the inclusive mini bar or the bath accessories by Hermès, which underline its commitment to exclusive hospitality. When it's stormy outside, guests can look forward to relaxing in the hotel's absolutely fabulous small wellness oasis with a sauna, steam bath, solarium, shell shower, ice fountain with foot-reflex zone, heated porcelain deckchairs and massaging area. High class cuisine is on offer in the exclusive restaurant. Here Johannes King celebrates fine traditional cuisine with an orientation on lightness. Indeed, it has been awarded two Michelin Stars.

Dorint Sofitel
Söl'ring Hof, Sylt
Hosts: Johannes King
and Claudia Reichelt
Am Sandwall 1
D-25980 Rantum
Phone:
00 49 / (0) 46 51 / 83 62 00
Fax:
00 49 / (0) 46 51 / 8 36 20 20
E-mail:
info.GWTRAT@dorint.com
Internet:
www.dorint.com
www.sofitel.com

15 rooms and suites
Double room from Euro 295
Suite from Euro 550

Distance from Airport:
15 minutes

Seit mehr als 140 Jahren hat sich das Excelsior Hotel Ernst den hohen Ruf eines Hotels erworben, das als gesellschaftlicher Mittelpunkt der Rheinmetropole gilt und seine internationalen Gäste in die Welt gehobener Wohn- und Genusskultur entführt. Damals wie heute schätzen Besucher den exklusiven Rahmen dieses Hauses, in dem überall Individualität, wohltuend persönlicher Service und klassische Eleganz in stilvollem Rahmen blühen. Dank seiner exponierten Lage vis-à-vis des Kölner Doms und unweit von Hauptbahnhof und Flughafen, sind alle Sehenswürdigkeiten der Domstadt bequem zu Fuß zu erreichen. Tradition und Moderne werden in den 152 luxuriösen Gästezimmern und Suiten miteinander verbunden, die jeweils individuell ausgestattet sind und durch ihre eleganten Interieurs den Charme eines Grandhotels vermitteln. Mit dem hohen Standard des Hotels korrespondiert die kreative und innovative Küche in der bekannten „Hanse Stube", während das Restaurant „taku" bundesweit zu den Topadressen für asiatische Genüsse zählt. Zeitgemäßen Komfort bieten auch die zehn exklusiven Bankettsalons für bis zu zweihundert Personen mit technisch modernster Ausstattung. Im stilvollen und noblen Ambiente der Beautyfarm lässt das ganzheitliche Relax- und Pflegeangebot für Damen und Herren keine Wünsche offen.

For over 140 years, the Excelsior Hotel Ernst has enjoyed a high reputation, both as a centre of social life in the metropolis of Cologne on the Rhine and as an establishment that offers international guests all the allure of a world of luxury and indulgence. Visitors today continue to treasure the exclusivity of this hotel, which fosters a stylish atmosphere of individuality, friendly, personal service and traditional elegance. Thanks to its open outlook and location opposite Cologne Cathedral and a short distance from the airport and main railway station, all visitor attractions in this cathedral city can be easily reached on foot. In each of the individual interiors of the hotel's 152 luxurious guest rooms and suites, tradition sits easily with modernity, while overall the ambience is one of Grand Hotel elegance. The high standards found throughout the hotel are maintained in both the creative, innovative cuisine of the renowned "Hanse Stube" and in "taku", one of Germany's top restaurants for those seeking Asian delights. State-of-the art, modern comfort is also offered by the ten exclusive banqueting halls, which can accommodate up to two hundred. In the stylish, elegant ambience of the beauty and wellness centre, our all-round relaxation and bodycare programme is sure to meet the individual needs of any lady or gentleman guest.

Excelsior Hotel Ernst
Director: Wilhelm Luxem
Domplatz
D-50667 Köln
Phone: 00 49 / 2 21 / 27 01
Fax: 00 49 / 2 21 / 2 70 33 33
E-mail:
info@excelsior-hotel-ernst.de
Internet:
www.excelsior-hotel-ernst.de

152 rooms and suites
from Euro 220 to 1,700

Distance from airport:
15 minutes

Membership:
The Leading Hotels
of the World

Das Schauspiel ist legendär. Wer auf dem Obersalzberg vor die Berge tritt, erlebt ein überwältigendes Naturspektakel. Deutschlands erstes Mountain Resort – das InterContinental Berchtesgaden – liegt auf eintausend Metern Höhe, und es macht sein Gebirgspanorama zum inspirierenden Grundmotiv für die ganze Anlage: So schön, wie man hier das Salzburger Land und das Watzmann-Massiv vor Augen hat – das kann einem den Atem nehmen. Gäste haben den Blick von überall: von der Lobby aus mit ihrer sieben Meter hohen Natursteinwand; in der Lounge sogar durchs Kaminfeuer hindurch; selbstverständlich bei den Mahlzeiten (360°-Restaurant & Grill mit spannender Showküche, Le Ciel mit kreativer Gourmet-Cuisine); im Spa auf 1400 Quadratmetern (es zeigt alle Facetten moderner Beauty- und Wellnesskultur) und in allen 138 Zimmern und Suiten. Ein Erlebnis für sich, in einer der luxuriösen Duplex-Suiten (154 Quadratmeter Fläche ziehen sich über zwei Etagen) auf der weiten Terrasse zu sitzen, die phantastische Bergwelt zum Greifen nahe. Die Zimmer zeigen wie alle anderen Interieurs eine Innenarchitektur, die sich zur Naturkulisse kongenial verhält: Kostbare Naturmaterialien und minimalistisches Design bilden raffinierte Innenwelten.

The spectacle is legendary. Anyone who stands at Obersalzberg facing the mountains will experience an overwhelming view of the natural environment. Germany's top mountain resort, the InterContinental Berchtesgaden, lies 1,000 metres high and has made the mountain panorama the inspiring Leitmotif for the entire complex. It is so beautiful to gaze at the Salzburg region and the Watzmann-Massiv that it can take your breath away. Guests can enjoy the stunning view from every location; from the lobby with its seven-metre-high natural stone wall, in the lounge even through the fireplace, during meals in a 360° Restaurant & Grill with an intriguing kitchen visible to the guests, or in Le Ciel with creative gourmet food, from the 1400 square metres large spa that offers all aspects of contemporary beauty treatments and wellness therapies as well as from the every one of the 138 rooms and suites. It is a unique treat to sit on the terrace of one of the luxurious duplex suites (154 square metres on two levels) with the fantastic mountain range almost at your fingertips. All rooms and indeed all interiors exhibit an architectural style that is based on the same theme as the panoramic backdrop: precious natural materials and minimalist design.

InterContinental Resort Berchtesgaden
Director: Jörg T. Böckeler
Hintereck 1
D-83471 Berchtesgaden
Germany
Phone:
00 49 / 86 52 / 9 75 50
Fax:
00 49 / 86 52 / 97 55 99
E-mail:
berchtesgaden@
ichotelsgroup.com
Internet:
www.berchtesgaden.inter-continental.com

138 rooms and suites
Standard Deluxe from Euro 279 to 339, Executive Studio from Euro 299 to 359, Panorama Suite from Euro 409 to 359, Duplex Suite from Euro 999 to 1.830, Presidential Suite Euro 2.500

Distance from airport:
35 minutes

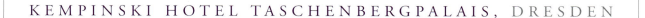

KEMPINSKI HOTEL TASCHENBERGPALAIS, DRESDEN

Der Aufenthalt im Kempinski Hotel Taschenbergpalais gehört auf jeden Fall zu den Dingen, die einen Aufenthalt in Dresden zu etwas Besonderem machen. Seit der Eröffnung des Domizils vor zehn Jahren ist es zu einer der ersten Adressen in den neuen Bundesländern avanciert und gilt heute als eine der schönsten Perlen der Hotelgruppe Kempinski. Die Lage des Palais könnte nicht privilegierter sein: es liegt unmittelbar neben dem Schloss gegenüber dem Zwinger und nur wenige Schritte entfernt von Semperoper, Frauenkirche und Brühlscher Terrasse. Mit Ronald in 't Veld leitet ein kosmopolitischer Gastgeber das Hotel, der unter dem Dach der fünf Sterne stilvolle Eleganz mit höherer Kulinarik und der Wärme kultivierter Gastlichkeit zu einem harmonischen Ganzen verbindet. Wer durch das Portal ins Innere tritt, taucht ein in eine Ambiance von ausgesuchter Finesse. Den anspruchsvollen Gast erwarten 182 elegante Zimmer und 32 luxuriöse Suiten. Kulinarisch wird er mit einer feinen Cuisine in zahlreichen Restaurants versorgt. Für Freunde gehobener Genusskultur und Lebensart bietet sich die Classic American Bar „Karl May" an, die nach einem New Yorker Vorbild entstand. Frische Kraft und Energie schöpft der Kempinski-Gast im Wellnessbereich unter dem Dach.

A stay in the Kempinski Hotel Taschenbergpalais will certainly make any visit to Dresden something very special. Since its opening ten years ago, it has risen to become one of the premier addresses in the former East Germany, another sparkling jewel in the crown of the Kempinski hotel group. It could not be in a more well-appointed location, directly by Dresden Castle opposite the famous Rococo-style Zwinger building and only a few steps from the Semper Opera House, the "Frauenkirche" and the "Brühlsche Terrassen". The hotel has a cosmopolitan leader in Ronald in 't Veld, who knows how to combine style with haute cuisine and warm, courteous hospitality under one five-star roof. Those passing through the grand entrance will find themselves immersed in a world of discerning elegance. A range of 182 rooms and 32 luxurious suites awaits the sophisticated traveller, as do fine culinary delights in an array of restaurants. For bons vivants who enjoy the very best things in life, there is the "Karl May", a classic New York style bar. And for those wishing to recharge their depleted batteries, there is no better place than the top-floor spa and fitness centre.

Kempinski Hotel
Taschenbergpalais Dresden
Managing Director:
Ronald in 't Veld
Taschenberg 3
D-01067 Dresden
Phone:
00 49 / (0) 3 51 / 49 12-0
Fax:
00 49 / (0) 3 51 / 49 12-8 12
E-mail:
reservations.taschenberg
palais@kempinski.com
Internet:
www.kempinski-dresden.de

182 rooms and 32 suites
from Euro 152 to 2,800

Distance from airport:
30 minutes

Membership:
The Leading Hotels
of the World

Nur dreißig Autominuten von Freiburg, der Metropole des Schwarzwaldes, entfernt, schmiegt sich das Parkhotel Adler in Hinterzarten in die wunderschöne Naturlandschaft des Südschwarzwaldes. Ob im Winter zum Skifahren oder im Frühling und Sommer zum Wandern oder einfach nur zum Entspannen und Erholen – das ehrwürdige Parkhotel Adler ist bis heute familiengeführt und traditionsbewusst geblieben. Mit seinen 78 luxuriösen Zimmern und Suiten, umgeben von einem weitläufigen Privatpark mit Wildgehege und Hubschrauberlandeplatz, entführt das Anwesen in die Welt feiner Ländlichkeit. Mit dem eleganten Gourmetrestaurant Adler und dem Adlerwirtshaus ist das Domizil zugleich ein Ort kulinarischer Vergnüglichkeiten für lustvolle Genießer. Das ganze Jahr locken attraktive Freizeitmöglichkeiten von Ballonfahren über Golfspielen bis zum Rafting. Powervoll beginnt ein Verwöhntag im Spa im Park, der sich mit einem einmaligen Angebot für Fitness, Schönheit und Gesundheit präsentiert. Hier finden stressgeplagte Geister unter fachkundiger Anleitung ein abwechslungsreiches Verwöhnprogramm für Leib und Seele. Von Thalasso-Kuranwendungen über Ayurveda bis hin zu maßgeschneiderten Beauty-Programmen ist man in den Händen des geschulten Wellness-Teams bestens aufgehoben.

Only thirty minutes' drive from the Black forest city of Freiburg, the Parkhotel Adler in Hinterzarten can be found nestling in the beautiful natural setting of the southern Black Forest. Whether for winter skiing or spring or summertime hiking or simply for relaxing and recharging batteries, the distinguished Parkhotel Adler has remained family-run and in keeping with tradition to this day. This residence transports the guest to the world of fine country living with its 78 luxurious rooms and suites, surrounded by sweeping private parkland with game reserve and helicopter landing pad. The establishment also offers culinary delights for passionate bons vivants, in the elegant Adler restaurant and the country-style inn. Attractive leisure activities are on offer the whole year round, from ballooning to golf to rafting. Guests can start a day of pampering energetically in the Park Spa, which offers a unique array of fitness, beauty and wellness treatments and activities. Here, those seeking to de-stress will find a multitude of solutions for body and soul, all under expert supervision. You will certainly be in the best of hands with the qualified wellness team, whether you choose Thalasso treatments, Ayurveda or your own personalised beauty programme.

Parkhotel Adler
Direction: Katja Trescher,
James Newman
Adlerplatz 3
D-79856 Hinterzarten
Phone:
00 49 / (0) 76 52 / 127 - 0
Fax:
00 49 / (0) 76 52 / 1 27 - 7 17
E-mail:
info@parkhoteladler.de
Internet:
www.parkhoteladler.de

78 rooms and suites
from Euro 100 to 530

Distance from airport Basel:
60 minutes
Distance from airport Zurich:
80 minutes

Membership:
The Leading Small Hotels
of the World

Eine ehemalige Posthalterstation aus dem Jahr 1707 verwandelte sich in einen Ort des Rundumgenusses, in einen Hotel-Traum des 21. Jahrhunderts. Pflaums Posthotel Pegnitz, das ist ein Hotel der neuen Art. PPP, das bedeutet: Luxus als Erlebnis, als Reise, im Restaurant, Spa und Beauty. Luxus als Ausflug in die Natur des PPP. Für Erlebnisverwöhnte und Erlebnissüchtige. Wer viele Erlebnisse hat, lebt kein banales Leben. Im PPP genießt er eine Atmosphäre der „Entschleunigung". Culture unlimited. PPP schafft ein grenzenloses kulturelles Erlebnis. Gastgeber Andreas Pflaum: „Die zukünftige Vision von Luxus wird das inszenierte Erlebnis, von der Kunst mitgenommen zu werden, das sie nur hier und im Moment erfüllt. Wenn diese Intensität eintritt, wenn die Wangen rot werden oder das Herz schneller schlägt, dann spüren Sie das PPP-Erlebnis. Erlebnis hat viel mit Menschen zu tun, mit Gastfreundschaft, mit Vitalität. Das PPP ist mit seinem prickelnden Angebot auf einem sehr guten Weg, die Vision einzulösen. Die Zeit der Privathotellerie ist gekommen. Gäste wünschen sich sehnlichst Individualität, Authentizität, Persönlichkeit, neue Erfahrungen. Das PPP nimmt diese Sehnsüchte wahr, gestützt auf 298 Jahre Erfahrung."

A postmaster station built in 1707 has been transformed into a place of total pleasure – into a 21st century dream hotel. Pflaum's Posthotel Pegnitz is a hotel of the new order. PPP stands for luxury as an experience, as a holiday, in the restaurant, the spa and in the beauty parlour. Stepping out into the natural environment of the PPP is also a luxurious experience for those both used to and addicted to experiencing new things. If your life is full, you don't get bored. And at the PPP, you can look forward to enjoying an atmosphere of deceleration, of culture unlimited. PPP creates an unlimited cultural experience. According to hotelier Andreas Pflaum "orchestrated events will form the future vision of luxury, that is, the art of being carried away by what fulfils you at that moment. When this intensity occurs, when your cheeks burn or your heart beats faster, then you know you're experiencing all that PPP has to offer. The experience has a lot to do with people, with hospitality, with vitality. With this exciting concept, PPP is on the best road to making its vision become reality. The time of the private hotelier has arrived. Guests want nothing more than individuality, authenticity, personality, and new experiences. PPP makes these desires come true, based on 298 years of experience."

Pflaums Posthotel Pegnitz
Wellness-Spa-Golfhotel
Direction: Andreas Pflaum
Nürnberger Straße 8–16
D-91257 Pegnitz /
Fränkische Schweiz
Phone: 00 49 / 92 41 / 72 50
Fax: 00 49 / 92 41 / 8 04 04
E-mail: info@ppp.com
Internet: www.ppp.com

25 rooms, 25 suites,
rooms from Euro 75 to 200,
suites from Euro 200
(Napoleon Suite) to Euro 495
(Laura Ashley Suite)

Distance from airport:
30 minutes

Private hoteliers since 1707

Am geschichtsträchtigen Potsdamer Platz lässt The Ritz-Carlton Berlin die Welt des Grandhotels wieder blühen. Highlights: beziehungsreiche Architektur, Gourmetcuisine und der legendäre Ritz-Carlton-Service. Als Teil des Beisheim Centers kontert das Ritz-Carlton Jahns himmelstürmende Glas- und Stahlarchitektur mit dem Stil jener Art-déco-Hochhäuser, wie sie in den Golden Twenties die Stadtbilder von New York und Chicago prägten. Gut aus der Geschichte des Ortes begründet das Interior Design: Es spielt mit dem Spät-Empire, wie Karl Friedrich Schinkel es liebte. Doch so stilvoll-elegant und mit leichtem Retroblick auf damals die 302 Zimmer und Suiten ihre Gäste auch aufnehmen, niemand muss auf luxuriösesten Gegenwartskomfort verzichten. Perfekt kombiniert das kulinarische Profil. Direktor Rainer J. Bürkle und der legendäre César Ritz haben eines gemeinsam: Sie kommen aus der Gastronomie. Kein Wunder also, dass das Grandhotel am Potsdamer Platz 3 auch eine erstklassige Destination für Gourmets ist. Thomas Kellermanns Cuisine im Gourmetrestaurant Vitrum präsentiert sich mit modernster Kreativität. Als Erlebnis-Kleinod tritt die Brasserie Debrosses auf – sie kam im Originalzustand aus Frankreich.

At its historical location of Potsdamer Platz, the Ritz-Carlton Berlin revives the heyday of the Grand Hotel. Main attractions include a rich interplay of architectural notes, gourmet cuisine and the legendary Ritz-Carlton service. As an integral part of the Beisheim Center complex, the Ritz-Carlton serves as a counterpoint to Helmut Jahn's high-rise steel and glass Sony Center. The hotel is in the Art Déco style so typical of the New York and Chicago of the golden era of the 1920s. The interior design takes its inspiration from artefacts from the history of the location, playing with the time of the Late Empire as beloved by the renowned painter and architect Karl Friedrich Schinkel. Yet despite being received in such style and elegance in the 302 rooms and suites, which cast a gentle glance back to this era, guests need renounce no luxury or modern comfort. And the hotel's cuisine offers the perfect complement to all of this. General Manager Rainer J. Bürkle and the legendary César Ritz have one thing in common: they both have backgrounds in gastronomy. It should come as no surprise, then, that this Grand Hotel at Potsdamer Platz 3 is also a top destination for gourmets. Thomas Kellermann's cuisine in the Vitrum gourmet restaurant combines a modern approach with creative verve. The Brasserie Debrosses, an authentic eatery spirited here all the way from France, also offers a culinary experience to treasure.

The Ritz-Carlton Berlin
General Manager:
Rainer J. Bürkle
Potsdamer Platz 3
D-10785 Berlin
Phone:
00 49 / (0) 30 / 33 77 77
Fax:
00 49 / (0) 30 / 3 37 77 55 55
E-mail:
berlin@ritzcarlton.com
Internet:
www.ritzcarlton.com

302 rooms and suites
Double Rooms from Euro 250 to 410, Junior Suite Euro 450, Suites from Euro 500 to 700, Grand Suite Euro 2,500, The Ritz-Carlton Suite Euro 5,000

FACILITIES

Ein feiner englischer Rasen, uralte Bäume und viele lauschige Plätze – inmitten einer prächtigen Parkanlage liegt märchenhaft schön das efeubewachsene Schloss Lerbach, das seit 1992 als exklusives Hotel auch den anspruchsvollsten Reisenden zum Schwärmen verleitet. Die Individualität der Gastfreundschaft entspricht dem Anspruch der Althoff Hotels & Residences des Kölner Hoteliers Thomas H. Althoff. Die 52 Zimmer und Suiten, die im Jahre 2004 komplett renoviert worden sind, präsentieren sich mehr denn je als wahre Wohnträume und vermitteln das Flair eines Landhauses von unaufdringlicher Eleganz. Hauptanziehungspunkt für Feinschmecker ist das gleichnamige renommierte Restaurant von Drei-Sterne-Koch Dieter Müller, in dem der Spitzencuisinier mit einem engagierten Team eine aromenbetonte und leichte feine Küche zubereitet – zu lernen auch für Hobbyköche: in der Kochschule Lerbach unter Dieter Müllers Patronat. Neben den kulinarischen Freuden sorgen vielfältige Anwendungen sowie Beauty- und Spa-Behandlungen für die ganz persönliche „Flucht aus dem Alltag". Relaxt wird im Schwimmbad, in der Sauna oder im Solarium. Spezialprodukte von La Prairie, Lancaster oder Decleor versprechen auf der Beautyfarm bestmögliche Resultate für das Aussehen und das Wohlbefinden. Die Freunde des grünen Sports kommen im Golfclub „Bergerhöhe" voll auf ihre Kosten.

Boasting lush green lawns, ancient trees, some impossibly lovely quiet spots and situated in the middle of magnificent gardens, Schloss Lerbach is an exclusive ivy-covered hotel that has been impressing the most discerning of travellers since 1992. The individuality of its hospitality reflects the philosophy of Althoff Hotels & Residences, belonging to Thomas H. Althoff from Cologne. Its 52 rooms and suites are nothing less than a dream, oozing all the flair of a country house with unobtrusive elegance. As far as gourmets are concerned, the main attraction is its famous restaurant. Bearing his name, the restaurant is run by Dieter Müller who is a Three-Star Chef. Here, together with his committed team, this top chef prides himself on preparing light and fine cuisine with an emphasis on flavour. Budding cooks will also be delighted to hear that he also holds lessons in the Lerbach cookery school. In addition to all its culinary delights, the hotel also offers a wide range of beauty and health-spa treatments designed to let you "escape completely from everyday life". Look forward to relaxing in the steam bath, sauna or solarium. Drawing on special products by La Prairie, Lancaster and Decleor, its beauty farm promises the best possible results for both appearance and wellbeing. Lovers of golf can play to their heart's content at the "Bergerhöhe" Golf Club.

Schlosshotel Lerbach
Managing Director:
Bernd Maesse
Lerbacher Weg
D-51465 Bergisch Gladbach
Phone:
00 49 / (0) 22 02 / 20 40
Fax:
00 49 / (0) 22 02 / 20 49 40
E-mail: info@
schlosshotel-lerbach.com
Internet: www.schlosshotel-
lerbach.com
www.alacarte.de

52 rooms and suites
from Euro 200 to 1,350

Distance from airport:
30 minutes

Membership:
Relais & Châteaux

Inmitten einer einzigartigen Parklandschaft liegt das Renaissance-Schloss Münchhausen. Nach einer grundlegenden Renovierung im Jahre 2004 als Hotel eröffnet, bietet das historische Anwesen seinen Gästen in 66 Zimmern und Suiten nicht nur den modernen Luxus eines Fünf-Sterne-Hauses, sondern ist gleichzeitig eine Oase für Menschen, die Ruhe suchen und Freude am Genuss haben – oder beides in einer exklusiven Business-Tagung verbinden möchten. Das Schlosshotel Münchhausen bietet vielfältige Möglichkeiten, den schönen Seiten des Lebens auf die Spur zu kommen, sei es bei einem Spaziergang im ausgedehnten Schlosspark oder während der Traumhochzeit in der alten Schlosskapelle. Im modernen Wellness- und Spa-Bereich findet der Gast ausreichend Möglichkeiten zum Entspannen und Relaxen. Zwei unmittelbar an das Schloss angrenzende 18-Loch-Plätze machen Münchhausen auch für Golfer attraktiv. Natürlich kommen auch die Gaumenfreuden im Schlosshotel nicht zu kurz. Regionale Spezialitäten und bodenständige Klassiker werden täglich frisch im stimmungsvollen Schlosskeller serviert. Kulinarische Highlights à la française mit mediterranen Zwischentönen garantiert Chefkoch Achim Schwekendiek seinen Gästen im Gourmetrestaurant. Wer einfach nur die Sonne und Kuchen aus der Schlossbackstube genießen möchte, der findet auf der gemütlichen Seeterrasse den richtigen Platz.

The Renaissance Castle Münchhausen lies in a unique parkland setting. Opened as a hotel after thorough renovation work in 2004, this historic residence, with 66 rooms and suites, offers guests not only the modern luxuries of a five-star hotel, but is also a true oasis for those seeking tranquillity and the enjoyment of life's pleasures. Both of these aspects can also be combined with an exclusive business conference. Indeed, the Schlossotel Münchhausen offers a wide range of possibilities for discovering the finer side of life, whether this takes the form of a relaxed walk through the sweeping castle grounds, or a dream wedding in the old castle chapel. Guests will also find plenty of wellness and spa offerings to aid relaxation. Münchhausen also attracts golfers with the two 18-hole courses directly adjoining the castle. Of course, gourmet palates will not be disappointed either in the Castle Hotel, with regional specialities and traditional German dishes served daily from the freshest of ingredients in the lively atmosphere of the castle cellar. Head chef Achim Schwekendiek ensures that guests in the Gourmet Restaurant are regaled with culinary delights à la française with a slightly Mediterranean flavour. And for those simply wishing to enjoy the sun along with some cake from the castle bakehouse, the cosy lake terrace is the right spot.

Schlosshotel Münchhausen
Director: Karsten Wierig
Schwöbber 9
D-31855 Aerzen / Hameln
Phone:
00 49 / (0) 51 54 / 70 60 - 0
Fax:
00 49 / (0) 51 54 / 70 60 - 130
E-mail: info@schlosshotel-muenchhausen.com
Internet: www.schlosshotel-muenchhausen.com

66 rooms and suites
from Euro 145 to 650

Distance from airport:
60 minutes

Im Herzen des brandenburgischen Oberspreewaldes liegt Burg, das touristische Zentrum des Biosphären-reservates Spreewald. Eingebettet in diese faszinie-rende Urlandschaft aus Kanälen und Flüsschen liegt eines der außergewöhnlichsten Wellness-Hotels Europas: das Resort & Spa Zur Bleiche. Zu jeder Jahreszeit ein Ort der Zuflucht für Menschen, die sich nach Erholung, Ruhe und Entspannung sehnen. Entscheidendes Element dabei: die 4 200 Quadratmeter große Landtherme, eine kuschelige wie inspirative Wellness-Landschaft, die zu Recht als „Well-Nest" bezeichnet wird. Ein „Nest", in dessen phantasievoller Welt sich asiatische wie heimatbezogene Denkansätze zu einem kraftvoll harmonischen Ganzen verbinden. Doch nicht nur die Landtherme der Bleiche fällt aus dem Rahmen. Auch die neunzig Zimmer und Suiten, die sich auf mehrere Gebäude verteilen, bieten unvergleichliches Flair. Wie jeder Bereich des Hauses tragen sie die stilsichere Handschrift der engagierten Gastgeber Christine und Heinrich Michael Clausing, die ehrgeizig und mit viel Liebe zum Detail eine stimmige Harmonie geschaffen haben. Außergewöhnlich auch die hochdekorierte Küche des Hauses. Gleich sieben (!) individuell gestaltete Restaurants sorgen für kulinarische Abwechslung.

In the heart of the Brandenburg Upper Spree Valley lies Burg, the tourist centre of the Spreewald Biosphere Reserve. Nestled in a fascinating primordial landscape of canals and brooks lies one of Europe's most exceptional wellness hotels: the Zur Bleiche Resort & Spa. A place of retreat the whole year round for those seeking peace and relaxation. The central attraction here is the 4,200 square metres thermal baths, a wellness landscape that is both cosy and inspirational, which has aptly been called a "wellnest". In the imaginative world of this "nest", both Asian and indigenous approaches are combined to create a powerful, harmonious whole. But it is not only the thermal baths that are unique. The ninety rooms and suites, divided among several buildings, offer incomparable flair. As everywhere in the establishment, they bear the effortlessly stylish signature of hosts Christine and Heinrich Michael Clausing, who have imbued the surroundings with their passion and unswerving dedication right down to the very detail, creating balance and harmony. Exceptional too is the hotel's multi award-winning cuisine. Indeed, the guest is spoilt for choice with no fewer than seven restaurants, each with its own unique atmosphere.

Resort & Spa Zur Bleiche
Owner: Christine and
Heinrich Michael Clausing
Bleichestraße 16
D-03096 Burg / Spreewald
Phone:
00 49 / (0) 3 56 03 / 6 20
Fax:
00 49 / (0) 3 56 03 / 6 02 92
E-Mail: reservierung@hotel-zur-bleiche.com
Internet:
www.hotel-zur-bleiche.com

81 rooms and 9 suites
Double room from Euro 120
Suites from Euro 225
Rates inclusive half board

Distance from airport:
70 minutes

Memberships:
Slow Food e.V.,
L'Ordre des Coteaux
de Champagne,
Chaîne des Rôtisseurs

Kenner sind sich einig: Das Château de Bagnols ist nicht nur eines der bedeutendsten historischen Baudenkmäler Frankreichs, es ist zugleich eines der schönsten Schlosshotels auf Fünf-Sterne-Niveau. Seine prachtvolle Wiedergeburt verdankt das Château der britischen Verlegergattin Helen Hamlyn. Sie leitete den Wiederaufbau. Vierhundert Handwerker und Restauratoren arbeiteten vier Jahre lang daran. Dabei gewann das Château de Bagnols nicht nur seine architektonische Gestalt, seine prachtvollen Interieurs zurück. Unter der Inspiration der heutigen Besitzerin erblühte auch die gesellschaftliche Atmosphäre neu. Stil, Charme und Schönheit sind wieder eingezogen. Die Cuvier ist zu einem stimmungsvollen Ort für Konzerte, für private Feiern oder Empfänge geworden. Der Weinkeller darunter führt erstklassige Tropfen französischer Anbaugebiete (mit Schwerpunkt auf Burgund und Beaujolais) – vorzügliche Begleitungen für die kreative Cuisine française, die Gäste in der Salle des Gardes vor dem größten gotischen Kamin Frankreichs genießen oder auf der Terrasse unter den Lindenbäumen. Die Wohnsphären der 21 Zimmer und Suiten sind schlicht einzigartig. Reizvolle Ausflugsziele im Beaujolais und im nahen Lyon.

Experts all agree on one thing. That not only is Château de Bagnols one of France's most important historical monuments, but that it is also one of the finest Five-star Château hotels. Lady Helen Hamlyn is the woman responsible for the Château's magnificent rebirth. She oversaw all its renovations. Four hundred craftsmen and restorers worked on the project for four years. And it was during this time that the Château de Bagnols began to take shape architecturally and was given its magnificent interior. Inspired by its owner, the whole atmosphere of the building was also transformed into a wonderful social setting. Style, charm and beauty once again grace its floors. Its Cuvier has been made into a location full of atmosphere for concerts, private events and receptions. Its wine cellar boasts first-class French wines (with an emphasis on Burgundy and Beaujolais). These wines go absolutely perfectly with its creative Cuisine française, which guests can look forward to enjoying in the Salle des Gardes in front of the large Gothic fireplace or on the patio underneath the lime trees. Its 21 rooms and suites are simply unequalled. It also offers exciting local attractions in Beaujolais and Lyon.

Château de Bagnols
Director: Franco Mora
F-69620 Bagnols-en-Beaujolais
Phone: 00 33 / 4 74 71 40 00
Fax: 00 33 / 4 74 71 40 49
E-mail: info@bagnols.com
Internet: www.roccofortehotels.com

21 rooms and suites
Traditional Rooms Euro 425,
Deluxe Rooms Euro 520,
Junior Suites Euro 615,
Château Suites Euro 805,
Residence Suite Euro 2,200

Distance from airport:
45 minutes

Membership:
The Leading Small Hotels
of the World

VILLA BELROSE, GASSIN / ST. TROPEZ

FACILITIES

Die Villa Belrose ist ein faszinierendes Domizil für den Traumurlaub an der Côte d'Azur, ein stilles, luxuriöses Refugium hoch über dem Hafen von Saint-Tropez. Vom 7000 Quadratmeter großen Grundstück mit seinen Gärten und Pinienhainen aus genießen Gäste das hinreißende Panorama des Golfs von Saint-Tropez, sehen St. Maxime, den Hafen, die Burg, Ramatuelle und Cap Camarat. Das idyllisch gelegene Landhaus verwöhnt sein Publikum mit vierzig Doppelzimmern und Suiten – alle individuell und anspruchsvoll im klassizistisch-provenzalischen Stil eingerichtet. Von der Terrasse oder den Balkonen eines jeden Raumes hat man ebenfalls einen atemberaubenden Ausblick auf die Region. Wer es locker angehen lässt, genießt das Dolce Vita am 200 Quadratmeter großen Pool oder begibt sich im Fitnessraum und Beauty-Spa in sachkundige Hände. Im Gourmetrestaurant des Hauses verwöhnt Sternekoch Thierry Thiercelin mit traditionell mediterraner Küche. In den täglich wechselnden Menüs findet man z. B. eine Auswahl der hiesigen Mittelmeerfische wie St. Pierre oder Loup de Mer, die in ihrer Komposition mit frischen Kräutern und provenzalischen Beilagen so angenehm duften und schmecken, dass man die Nähe zum Meer – auch ohne den wunderbaren Blick aus dem Restaurant über den Golf – intensiv spürt.

Villa Belrose is a fascinating domicile for a dream holiday on the Côte d'Azur. It is a quiet, luxurious refuge, high above the port of Saint Tropez. From the large grounds covering 7,000 square metres with its gardens and groves of pine trees, those staying here can look forward to enjoying the splendid panorama of the Gulf of Saint Tropez, St. Maxime, the port, the castle, Ramatuelle and Cape Camarat. At this idyllically situated country house the residents live in great style in the forty double rooms and suites all of which are individually decorated to a high standard in the classical provençal style. From the terrace or balcony of each room there is also a breathtaking view of the region. For relaxation one can enjoy the dolce vita around the 200 square metres pool or visit the gym and beauty spa for expert treatment. Star Chef Thierry Thiercelin delights in treating his guests to traditional Mediterranean cuisine in his gourmet restaurant. The menu changes on a daily basis and you can look forward to finding a fine selection of local Mediterranean fish such as St. Pierre or Loup de Mer. Indeed, together with fresh herbs and Provencial side dishes, they smell and taste so good that you would feel close to the sea even without the restaurant's breathtaking views over the Gulf.

Villa Belrose
Managing Director:
Robert-Jan van Straaten
Boulevard des Crêtes
F-83580 Gassin / Saint Tropez
Phone: 00 33 / 4 94 / 55 97 97
Fax: 00 33 / 4 94 / 55 97 98
E-mail:
belrose@relaischateaux.com
Internet:
www.villabelrose.com

40 rooms and suites
from Euro 230 to 2,600

Distance from airport:
1 hour 30 minutes

Membership:
Relais & Châteaux

HIDEAWAYS HOTELS

151

Das beschauliche Fischerdörfchen Elounda hat sich in den letzten Jahren zu einem der modernsten griechischen Urlaubsorte entwickelt. Darum verwundert es auch kaum, dass man hier eines der exklusivsten Hotels von ganz Griechenland findet, die Elounda Gulf Villas. Ein hochdekorierter Geheimtipp, dessen vierzehn luxuriöse Villen mit privaten Pools und zehn sehr geschmackvolle Suiten wie auf einem Logenplatz mit herrlichem Panoramablick oberhalb der Mirabello-Bucht thronen. Für all jene, die einfach für ein paar Tage abschalten möchten, ist dieses von der Eigentümerfamilie Kadianakis sehr liebevoll geführte Haus ein wahres Geschenk der Götter. Die privaten Pools mit integriertem Jacuzzi sind nahezu uneinsehbar und garantieren höchste Privatsphäre. Genau wie die luxuriös eingerichteten Villen und Suiten, die mit Kitchenette, wunderschönen Bädern, viel Platz und teilweise sogar mit privatem Pool und Sauna sowie türkischem Dampfbad glänzen. Das liebevoll servierte Frühstück und ein paar Snacks und Salate für den kleinen Hunger zwischendurch bringt der Butlerservice. Das Restaurant Argo verwöhnt mit mediterraner und internationaler Küche. Wer sich sportlich betätigen möchte, findet in der Elixir Fitness Gallery modernste Geräte, eine Sauna, ein Dampfbad, einen beheizbaren Outdoor-Jacuzzi sowie einen Massageraum.

The tranquil fishing village of Elounda has been quietly developing into one of Greece's most fashionable holiday resorts over the past few years. So it will come as no surprise to find out that Elounda is also home to one of the most exclusive hotels in Greece, the Elounda Gulf Villas. Its 14 luxury villas with private pools and ten very tasteful suites sit high in solitary splendour over Mirabello Bay. When it comes to insider tips, this one offers a seriously special location and breathtaking panoramic views. Just imagine getting away from it all and spending a few wonderful days in this lovingly run family establishment that is a gift from the gods in every sense. The private pools featuring integrated Jacuzzis are all but completely hidden and offer the ultimate in privacy. So, too, do the luxuriously furnished villas and suites. These come complete with a kitchenette, a lovely bathroom, plenty of room and even your own private pool, sauna and Turkish steam bath in some cases. There is also a butler service on hand to serve breakfast and small snacks and salads for between meals. Look forward to enjoying Mediterranean and international cuisine in the Argo Restaurant. If you're interested in exercise, you'll find the very latest equipment in the Elixir Fitness Gallery, as well as a sauna, steam bath, outdoor heated Jacuzzi and a massage room.

Elounda Gulf Villas & Suites
General Manager:
Anna Papakaliatis-
Kadianakis
GR-72053 Elounda / Crete
Phone: 00 30 / 2 84 10 / 9 03 00
Fax: 00 30 / 2 84 10 / 4 22 74
E-mail:
info@eloundavillas.com
Internet:
www.eloundavillas.com

14 villas with private pools
and 10 suites
Double room from Euro 200,
villas from Euro 500

Distance from airport:
60 minutes

Memberships:
Small Luxury Hotels
of the World,
Great Hotels of the World

ELOUNDA MARE HOTEL, CRETE

FACILITIES

Eine stille Bucht mit kristallklarem Wasser ist der perfekte Rahmen des elounda mare, Mitglied von Relais & Châteaux® seit 1988. Luxus ist in diesem Familienunternehmen durch Kultur gekennzeichnet: antikes Kunsthandwerk, vereint mit traditionellen architektonischen Stilelementen, ist in allen Ecken des Hotels anzutreffen. Hier kann man die Sonne in der Abgeschiedenheit eines privaten Bungalows, in einem nicht einsehbaren Winkel des verwunschenen Gartens oder am ruhigen privaten Strand genießen. Auf Schritt und Tritt ist der Betrachter von dem behaglich lauschigen Charakter des elounda mare verzaubert. elounda mare ist berühmt für seinen höflichen und aufmerksamen Service, der in drei der apartesten Restaurants mit der wohl feinsten Küche des östlichen Mittelmeerraumes anzutreffen ist. Wassersport wie Wasserski, Scuba-Tauchen und Segeln wird angeboten und ergänzt durch zwei Kunstrasen-Tennisplätze und einen Fitnessraum. Ein privater 9-Loch-Golfplatz kann zu Fuß erreicht werden und ein 18-Loch-Platz befindet sich nur eine halbe Autostunde entfernt. Das weltberühmte Six Senses Spas™ bietet seine einzigartigen ganzheitlichen Behandlungen in elounda mares privatem Spa an.

A quiet cove with crystal clear waters provides the perfect setting for the elounda mare, member of the Relais & Châteaux® since 1988. Luxury in this family-owned establishment is of the cultured kind, with antique pieces of folk art adorning every corner and traditional architectural themes incorporated throughout. Here you can enjoy the sun in the seclusion of a private-pool bungalow, in an isolated corner of the lush gardens, or by the calm sandy beach. One never ceases to be enchanted by the incomparably intimate character of the elounda mare. Renowned for its courteous people and attentive service, it offers three magnificent settings for some of the finest dining in the Eastern Mediterranean. Sea sports like ski, scuba diving and sailing are offered, in addition to two green-set tennis courts and a gymnasium. A private 9-hole golf course is at walking distance while an 18-hole course is a mere half-hour drive away. The world-renowned Six Senses Spas™ offer their signature treatments at the elounda mare's private spa.

Elounda Mare Hotel
Owner:
Spyros and Eliana Kokotos
GR-72053 Elounda / Crete
Phone:
00 30 / 2 84 10 / 4 11 02-3
Fax:
00 30 / 2 84 10 / 4 13 07
E-mail:
mare@elounda-sa.com
Internet:
www.eloundamare.com

74 units
from Euro 107 to 550

Distance from airport:
60 minutes

Membership:
Relais & Châteaux

Errichtet auf einer erhöhten vorgelagerten Halbinsel, umgeben vom Meer, verspricht das elounda peninsula ALL SUITE HOTEL zauberhafte Ausblicke und Abgeschiedenheit. Unverwechselbar – das einzige ALL SUITE Hotel in Griechenland, das unmittelbar am Meer gelegen ist. Es verfügt über einen privaten 9-Loch-Golfplatz im benachbarten Schwesterhotel, ein privates Kino, ein privates Spa mit Six Senses Spas™-Behandlungen und über die wohl erlesenste Gastronomie des ganzen Landes. Das Außergewöhnliche des elounda peninsula ALL SUITE HOTEL liegt begründet in der unvergleichlichen Tradition exzellenten Service, der größtmögliche Aufmerksamkeit eines jeden Mitarbeiters garantiert, egal ob es sich dabei um ein privates Dinner, den persönlichen Fitnesstrainer, die privaten Spa-Behandlungen oder die 24-stündige Beaufsichtigung der Kinder handelt. Die Suiten im elounda peninsula ALL SUITE HOTEL werden unterschieden in Collection Suites auf zwei Ebenen mit Zugang von der eigenen Terrasse zu vorgelagerten Pools, in Junior Suiten mit privaten Pools und direktem Zugang zum Meer und finden ihren krönenden Abschluss in der Grande Suite, einem Zwei-Schlafzimmer-Komplex mit privatem Hallenbad und Außenpool, nicht zu vergessen der private Bootsanlager mit Zugang zum Meer. Das hoteleigene Gourmetrestaurant mit seinem privaten Weinkeller hat inzwischen internationale Auszeichnungen erhalten und die neue Bar, direkt oberhalb des Meeresspiegels, ist einfach überwältigend.

Situated on an elevated peninsula surrounded by the sea, the elounda peninsula ALL SUITE HOTEL enjoys magnificent sea views and seclusion. Unique for being the only all-suite seaside hotel in Greece, it also boasts a private 9-hole golf course at the sister-resort next door, a private cinema theatre, a private spa with Six Senses Spas™ treatments, and some of the country's finest dining. The elounda peninsula ALL SUITE HOTEL is founded on an unparalleled tradition of excellence in service and it ensures that guests receive the utmost attention of every staff member, whether catering to en-suite dining, personal gym training, private spa treatments, or children's 24-hour care and recreation. Suites at the elounda peninsula ALL SUITE HOTEL start from the Collection Suites on two levels with terrace-accessed swimming pools, then continue to the junior suites with private swimming pools and sea access, and culminate at the Grande Suite, a two-bedroom complex that includes an indoor and an outdoor swimming pool as well as a private jetty on the sea. The hotel's own gourmet restaurant with its private wine cellar has received international honours since first opening, while the new waterfront bar, literally over the waves, is absolutely astonishing.

Elounda Peninsula
ALL SUITE HOTEL
Owner:
Spyros and Eliana Kokotos
GR-72053 Elounda / Crete
Phone:
00 30 / 2 84 10 / 6 82 50
Fax:
00 30 / 2 84 10 / 4 18 89
E-mail: eloundapeninsula@
elounda-sa.com
Internet:
www.eloundapeninsula.com

28 suites and 10 Presidential
Suites from Euro 420 to 8,500

Distance from airport:
60 minutes

Einer der imposantesten und schönsten Ausblicke ganz Kretas ist der Panoramablick auf die Bucht von Elounda, wo sich das porto elounda DE LUXE RESORT, das einzige Golf- und Spa-Resort in Griechenland befindet. Der 9-Loch-Golfplatz ist eine Herausforderung in sich, während der 18-Loch-Platz nur eine halbe Autostunde entfernt ist. Die weltberühmten Six Senses Spas™-Behandlungen werden seit Frühjahr 2005 in speziell hierfür entworfenen Bereichen des Hotels angeboten. Eine neue 2000 Quadratmeter umfassende Six Senses Spas™-Einrichtung inmitten des Resorts – ein echtes Wunder an Design – wird ab Frühjahr 2006 die einzigartigen ganzheitlichen Behandlungen anbieten. Die Auswahl der unterschiedlichen Unterkunftsarten ist umfangreich und reicht von unvergleichlichen Poolzimmern, die sich durch privaten Zugang zu großen vorgelagerten Schwimmbädern kennzeichnen, über die sehr beliebten Familien-Strand-Villen mit privatem Pool und Garten bis hin zu den Seafront Bungalows, die unmittelbar am Meer gelegen sind. Unterhaltung für Kinder wird ganztägig geboten, ob am hoteleigenen privaten Sandstrand oder im speziell eingerichteten Kinderclub „Childrens Ark", einer außergewöhnlichen modernen Spieleinrichtung, die ihresgleichen sucht. Weiterhin ist eine große Auswahl an Restaurants anzutreffen, ebenso Wassersport, Tennisplätze, ein Hallenbad, ein Fitnessraum, eben alles, was man von einem echten Weltklasse-Luxusresort erwarten darf. porto elounda DE LUXE RESORT ist ein wunderbares Refugium für Familien und Gruppen.

One of the loveliest sights on the whole of Crete is the panoramic view of the bay of Elounda, where the porto elounda DE LUXE RESORT, the only golf-and-spa resort in Greece, is to be found. The 9-hole golf course is challenging in itself, while an 18-hole course is a mere half-hour drive away. The world-renowned Six Senses Spas™ signature treatments will be offered as of spring 2005 in specially designed areas in the hotel. A new, 2,000 square metres Six Senses Spas™ facility within the resort, a true marvel of design, will host the treatments beginning Spring 2006. The choice of accommodation is very wide and ranges from the unique pool-rooms that offer private direct access to large seawater swimming pools, to the very popular family beach-side villas with private pools and gardens, to the ideal-for-couples seafront bungalows. Entertainment for children is available throughout the day, both by the resort's private sandy beach and at the dedicated childcare facility, the Children's Ark, a magnificent modern play area like no other. Then there is a large choice of restaurants, water sports, tennis courts, indoor pool, gymnasium and everything one expects in a truly world-class luxury resort, ideal for families and groups of friends looking for recreation and relaxation.

Porto Elounda
DE LUXE RESORT
Owner:
Spyros and Eliana Kokotos
GR-72053 Elounda / Crete
Phone:
00 30 / 2 84 10 / 6 80 00
Fax:
00 30 / 2 84 10 / 4 18 89
E-mail:
porto@elounda-sa.com
Internet:
www.portoelounda.com

53 bungalows and villas,
104 units from Euro 145
to 1,700

Distance from airport:
60 minutes

Membership:
Preferred Hotels & Resorts
Worldwide

Schon immer ließen sich die griechischen Götter dort nieder, wo die Natur am schönsten war. Auch Kap Sounion im Süden des attischen Festlandes gehörte zu ihren bevorzugten Stätten, wie der berühmte Poseidon-Tempel hoch oben über dem Saronischen Golf beweist. Auf diesem heiligen Fleckchen Erde unmittelbar neben dem Tempelbezirk entstand das neue Grecotel Cape Sounio. Ein Hotelresort im Einklang mit der Natur, in Harmonie mit seinen Baumaterialien Stein, Bronze und Ton – Rohstoffe aus der Erde. Inspiriert von der stets lebendigen Geschichte Hellas', gleicht die Architektur des Cape Sounio einem klassischen Amphitheater. 149 Bungalows, Suiten und Villen, luxuriös und individuell in der Ausstattung, verschmelzen mit ihren terracottafarbenen Außenwänden mit der prächtigen Gartenlandschaft. Reichlich Unterstützung, um „neue Kraft zu tanken", finden die Gäste im luxuriösen Spa Elixir 007 – ein achteckiges Gebäude mit Spiegelglaswänden und Lagunen-Atmosphäre. Schönste Badefreuden erlebt man an den geschützten Meeresbuchten der beiden hoteleigenen Strände. Ganz den Göttern würdig erweist sich die vorzügliche Cape Cuisine, dargereicht im Feinschmeckerrestaurant des Hauptgebäudes oder auf dessen weitläufiger Terrasse. Griechische und internationale Köstlichkeiten sowie die reichen Früchte des Meeres versprechen Gaumenfreuden für jeden Geschmack.

The Greek gods have always presided over the most beautiful natural settings. Located in the south of the Attican mainland, Cape Sounio was also one of their elect resting places, as evidenced by the imposing presence of the renowned Temple of Poseidon high above the Saronic Gulf. And it was here on this revered piece of earth that the decision was taken to develop the new Grecotel Cape Sounioa right alongside the temple grounds. This hotel resort co-exists harmoniously with nature and this is even reflected in its construction materials of stone, bronze and clay – all raw materials from the earth. Inspired by the ever-vibrant Hellenic tradition, the architectural style of the Cape Sounio emulates a classical amphitheatre. 149 luxurious and individually-designed bungalows, suites and villas with terracotta-coloured exteriors blend in perfectly with the magnificent landscaped gardens. Guests will find the luxurious Spa Elixir 007 a great aid in recharging run-down batteries – an octagonal building with mirrored-glass walls and all the feel of a lagoon. The most wonderful bathing experience can also be had in the sheltered bays along the two beaches belonging to the hotel. The excellent Cape cuisine, which can be enjoyed either in the gourmet restaurant in the main building or on the spacious terrace, is truly befitting of the gods. Greek and international delicacies are offered alongside incredibly delicious seafood – a feast for all tastes.

Grecotel Cape Sounio
67 km Athens – Sounio Road
19 500 Lavrion, Sounio
Phone:
00 30 / 2 29 20 / 6 97 00
Fax:
00 30 / 2 29 20 / 6 97 70
E-mail:
hideaways@grecotel.gr
Internet:
www.grecotel.gr

149 bungalows, suites and villas from Euro 320 inclusive breakfeast. All accommodation units can be booked through airtours. More information about wedding arrangements, events and incentive is available on request.

Distance from airport:
40 minutes

Membership:
Preferred Hotels & Resorts

Schwungvoll im Design als Hommage an die Rundungen der Kykladen und überflutet vom Sonnenlicht Griechenlands schwelgen Reisende im Mykonos Blu im uneingeschränkten Luxus. Blau und Türkis, eingerahmt von einer hellen geschwungenen Bucht, leuchtet die Ägäis herauf zu dem weißen Haus hoch oben über dem Psarou-Strand. Die hundert Bungalows schmiegen sich in kleinen Gruppen terrassenförmig in einen herrlichen Mittelmeergarten. Ein zusätzliches Optimum an Luxus und Serviceleistungen bieten insbesondere die Mykonos Blu Villen, die 2006 zur Verfügung stehen werden und mit privatem Pool inklusive herrlichen Meerblick ausgestattet sind. Diskret lesen die dienstbaren Geister geradezu jeden Wunsch von den Augen ab. Die Raum-Highlights sind unbestritten die Deluxe Junior Bungalow Suiten, deren große Terrasse mit privatem Pool auch den weit gereisten Luxus-Traveller überzeugen. Genuss auf höchster Ebene verheißt ein Besuch im Toprestaurant „Aegean Poet". Hier treffen sich nicht nur die Hotelgäste, sondern auch die Gourmets aus aller Welt, deren Yachten unten im Hafen liegen, um die preisgekrönte Küche zu gustieren. Vitalität und Wohlgefühl durchströmt den Körper nach einem Besuch in der Elixir Fitness Gallery. Individuell abgestimmte Therapien, entspannende Massagen, Sauna und Hamam sowie modernste Trainingsgeräte im Fitnessraum lassen keine Wünsche offen.

Just imagine indulging yourself in sumptuous luxury, enjoying the rounded design that pays homage to the curves of the Cyclades and bathing in the marvellous sunlight of Greece at the Mykonos Blu hotel. Framed by a bright curved bay, the blue and turquoise shades of the Aegean Sea radiate upwards to the white buildings high above Psarou Beach. One hundred bungalows have been nestled in small terraced groups into a beautiful Mediterranean garden landscape. The ultimate in luxury and service offering especially the Mykonos Blu Villas, which will be available from 2006 complete with private pool and breathtaking views of the sea. Its almost invisible staff has the comforting ability to know what you want before you ask. When it comes to accommodation, the highlight is without any doubt the Deluxe Junior Bungalow Suites boasting a large patio area with private pool. Indeed, these are guaranteed to please the most discerning of luxury travellers. Dining out in the "Aegean Poet" restaurant promises uncompromising pleasure. While it's a favourite meeting place for the hotel's guests, it's also a magnet for gourmets from across the world, who make their way up from their yachts moored down in the harbour below to sample its award-winning cuisine. Visit the Elixir Fitness Gallery and your body will be brimming with vitality and well-being. With therapies tailored to your individual needs, relaxing massages, sauna and Hamam and the latest training equipment in the gym, all your fitness and well-being needs are taken care of.

Grecotel Mykonos Blu
Psarou Beach
Platis Gialos, Platis Yalos
GR-84600 Mykonos
Phone:
00 30 / 2 28 90 / 2 79 00
Fax:
00 30 / 2 28 90 / 2 77 83
E-mail:
hideaways@grecotel.gr
Internet:
www.grecotel.gr

102 bungalows
Double rooms from Euro 230 inclusive breakfeast.
All accommodation units can be booked through airtours.
More information about wedding arrangements, events and incentive is available on request.

Distance from airport:
15 minutes

Membership:
Preferred Hotels & Resorts

SANI ASTERIAS SUITES, SANI RESORT, GREECE

Das Sani Resort auf der griechischen Halbinsel Kassandra hat sich in den letzten Jahren von einem charmanten Insidertipp zu einem ungewöhnlichen Resort entwickelt. Pinienwälder, Olivenbäume und traumhafte Strände machen das 400 Hektar große ökologische Resort zu einer Urlaubsoase. Die luxuriöseste Möglichkeit, das Angebot des Sani Resorts zu genießen, ist das elegante Fünf-Sterne-All-Suite-Boutique-Hotel Sani Asterias Suites. Es ist das einzige Hotel Griechenlands, das auf der einen Seite an einem Privatstrand und auf der anderen Seite an einer privaten Yacht-Marina liegt. Eine exponierte Location, die durch die luxuriöse Gestaltung der 50 Suiten (18 Junior-Suiten, 26 Standard-Suiten, 4 Seafront-Deluxe-Suiten und 2 Marinafront-Executive-Suiten) noch getoppt wird. Die Komposition aus großzügigen Räumlichkeiten, edlen Interieurs und sämtlichen Errungenschaften modernsten Komforts bilden eine ganz private Wohlfühlinsel. Ein Luxushotel, in dem die professionell geschulten Servicemitarbeiter alles daransetzen, um den wohlverdienten Urlaub zu der schönsten Zeit des Jahres zu machen. Mit einem Rundum-Verwöhnprogramm, an dem es wahrlich nichts auszusetzen gibt. Dazu gehören natürlich auch die kulinarischen Genüsse. Das elegante Water Restaurant öffnet sich mit einmaligem Blick auf den Hafen und den großen Pool und ergänzt die Kulinarik des Resorts mit exzellent zubereiteten Spezialitäten aus der mediterranen und griechischen Küche, die man auch als romantisches Dinner im eigenen Garten oder auf der privaten Terrasse genießen kann.

Over the past few years, the Sani Resort on the Greek peninsula of Kassandra has developed from being a charming insider tip into something truly remarkable. Pine forests, olive trees and impossibly beautiful beaches make this ecological resort over 1,000 acres into a true holiday oasis. The most luxurious way of enjoying all that the Sani Resort has to offer is in its elegant Sani Asterias five-star-all-suite-boutique-hotel suite. It's the only hotel in Greece to have a private beach at one side and a private yachting marina at the other. It boasts a prominent location that is only surpassed by its 50 luxuriously designed suites (18 Junior Suites, 26 Standard Suites, 4 Seafront Deluxe Suites and 2 Marina-Front Executive Suites). A combination of generously-proportioned rooms, elegant interiors and all the latest modern conveniences conspire to create a wonderful feeling of wellbeing and contentment. Indeed, guests to this luxury hotel can look forward to enjoying the very best in care and attention by a professionally trained service team whose mission is to make sure that your hard-earned holiday is the highlight of the year. The hotel offers a perfectly-coordinated unadulterated pampering program. And it goes without saying, of course, that this includes its delicious culinary delights. Its elegant Water Restaurant opens onto and boasts fantastic views of the harbour and the large pool and complements the resort's culinary dishes with excellently prepared Mediterranean and Greek specialities. Just image enjoying a romantic dinner in the restaurant's garden or on its private patio.

Sani Resort
Sani Asterias Suites
GR-63077 Kassandra
Chalkidiki, Greece
Phone:
0030 / 2 37 40 / 9 94 00
Fax:
0030 / 2 37 40 / 9 95 08
E-mail:
info@saniresort.gr
Internet:
www.saniresort.gr
Reservations:
Phone:
0030 / 2 37 40 / 9 95 00
Fax:
0030 / 2 37 40 / 9 95 09

50 suites
from Euro 174 to 784

Distance from airport:
60 minutes

Das Porto Sani Village als weiteres mediterranes Schmuckstück der Sani Resorts ist ein in sich geschlossenes Dorf, das wie auch die Sani Asterias Suiten all jenen Urlaubsglück beschert, die Ruhe und Abgeschiedenheit suchen. Mittelpunkt des Fünf-Sterne-Hauses ist der wunderschöne Garten mit einer riesigen Poolanlage, die nicht nur bei den lieben Kleinen hoch im Kurs steht. Von den Balkonen und Terrassen der 113 eleganten Suiten mit modernstem Komfort und allen Fünf-Sterne-Serviceleistungen bietet sich besonders am Abend ein wunderschöner Blick auf die illuminierte Poollandschaft oder den Hafen. Wohn-Highlights im Porto Sani Village sind die individuell dekorierten Deluxe Suiten, deren Gäste das hervorragende Frühstück im stilvollen Gourmetrestaurant Byblos genießen können. Natürlich können die zahlreichen Stammgäste des Porto Sani Village genau wie das anspruchsvolle Klientel der Sani Asterias Suites die kulinarischen Möglichkeiten des „Dine-Around"-Programms nutzen. Dafür stehen 31 verschiedene Restaurants und Bars zur Verfügung, die allesamt auf die hochgesteckte Sani-Qualitätsphilosophie eingeschworen sind. Die Sani Marina Piazza lockt mit ihren Restaurants, darunter ein neues Gourmetrestaurant, Cafés, Bars und einer Kunstgalerie zu ausgedehnten Schlemmerfreuden und Shopping-Touren. Was will man mehr? Erholung und Entspannung garantiert das Beauty & Wellness Center mit einem neueröffneten Spa, The Spa Suite im Porto Sani Village. Der nächste Golfplatz ist in gut 45 Minuten erreichbar.

Porto Sani Village is a self-contained village and one of the Sani Resort's sparkling Mediterranean jewels. Indeed, just like the Sani Asterias Suites, it offers a wonderful holiday retreat for all those looking for peace and tranquillity. Its wonderful gardens with a huge pool complex is a firm favourite for adults and children alike and forms the centrepiece of this five-star establishment. Just image enjoying the views of the illuminated pool complex or harbour at night as you look out from your balcony or patio. The resort offers 113 suites boasting all the very latest comforts and a fine five-star service. For the very finest in accommodation it has to be the resort's individually decorated Deluxe Suites. Here guests can look forward to enjoying the delights of Porto Sani Village's outstanding breakfasts in the Byblos gourmet restaurant. It goes without saying, of course, that Porto Sani Village's large number of regular guests can join up with the discerning residents of the Sani Asterias Suites to delight in all the culinary possibilities offered by its Dine-Around program. This program prides itself in letting guests choose from 31 restaurants and bars, which all meet Sani's exceptionally high quality requirements. The Sani Marina Piazza is a place to go shopping and to indulge culinary fantasies in its restaurants, including a gourmet restaurant, cafés and bars. What more could you want? Porto Sani Village also has its own beauty and wellness centre with a new opening Spa, The Spa Suite, for rest and relaxation; the nearest golf course is only 45 minutes away.

Sani Resort
Porto Sani Village
GR-63077 Kassandra
Chalkidiki, Greece
Phone: 00 30 / 2 37 40 / 9 94 00
Fax: 00 30 / 2 37 40 / 9 95 08
E-mail:
info@saniresort.gr
Internet:
www.saniresort.gr
Reservations:
Phone: 00 30 / 2 37 40 / 9 95 00
Fax: 00 30 / 2 37 40 / 9 95 09

113 suites
from Euro 155 to 474

Distance from airport:
60 minutes

Zwischen kristallklarem Meer und steil aufragenden weißen Klippen liegt das Columbia Beach Resort versteckt in der Bucht von Pissouri an der Südküste Zyperns. Die Ruhe am Strand von Pissouri, in einer der schönsten naturbelassenen Buchten Zyperns, wird allenfalls durch das sanfte Meeresrauschen durchbrochen. Traditionelle Elemente der zypriotischen Architektur, gepaart mit höchstem zeitgemäßen Komfort machen das Domizil, das ausschließlich Suiten unterschiedlicher Größe und Ausstattung anbietet, so einzigartig wie die drittgrößte Insel des Mittelmeers selbst. Herrlich geht der Blick von vielen Zimmern auf das Meer. Die meisten von ihnen überblicken außerdem den 80 Meter langen Lagunen-Pool, Zentrum der Anlage mit ihren schattenspendenden hochragenden Palmen. In einem der besten Resorts auf Zypern kommen natürlich auch Feinschmecker mit einer fantasievollen mediterranen Frischeküche auf ihre Kosten. Derart gestärkt widmen sich die Gäste im „Health Club" dem Squash-Sport, besuchen den perfekt ausgestatteten Fitnessraum, den Aerobicraum oder den Tennisplatz mit Panoramablick. Zur Entspannung und Revitalisierung lädt dann das „Columbia Spa" mit vielfältigen Anwendungen für Schönheit und Gesundheit ein. Ein Erlebnis der besonderen Art sind die drei 18-Loch-Golfanlagen.

The Columbia Beach Resort lies hidden between crystal-clear sea and the steep ascent of white cliffs in the bay of Pissouri on the south coast of Cyprus. The only thing interrupting the tranquillity of Pissouri Beach, in one of Cyprus' most beautiful, unspoilt bays, is the gentle whooshing of the sea. Traditional Cypriot architecture, the ultimate in modern comforts and individualised suites, all of different sizes and design, all combine to create an environment as unique as the island itself, the third-largest in the Mediterranean. Most of the rooms offer wonderful views of the sea. Indeed, the majority also offer views of the 80-metre-long lagoon pool at the heart of the hotel with its shady palm trees. Of course, it goes without saying that, in one of the best resorts in Cyprus, gourmets will certainly not be disappointed with the imaginative mediterranean cuisine, all from the freshest of ingredients. Thus sustained, guests can then devote their energies to other things, such as a squash game, a workout in our fully-equipped fitness or aerobics studios or a round of tennis on our tennis court with panoramic views, all available in our Health Club. Finally, to relax and reenergise, the "Columbia Spa" offers a wide range of beauty and health treatments. And last, but not least, three 18-hole golf courses nearby offer golfers an unforgettable experience.

Columbia Beach Resort
Pissouri
General Manager:
Detlef Winter
P.O. Box 54042
CY-3779 Limassol / Cyprus
Phone: 0 03 57 / 25 / 83 30 00
Fax: 0 03 57 / 25 / 83 36 88
E-mail: columbia@
columbia-hotels.com
Internet:
www.columbia-hotels.com

94 suites
from CYP 195 to 495

Distance from airport:
75 minutes

Membership:
Great Hotels of the World

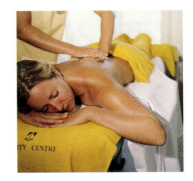

HOTEL BALTSCHUG KEMPINSKI MOSCOW, MOSCOW

Als Kempinski im Jahr 1992 nach einer 86 Millionen Dollar teuren Renovierung das Baltschug eröffnete, brachte die Gruppe eine der renommiertesten Hoteladressen Moskaus wieder zum Blühen: Das Hotel Baltschug Kempinski Moscow gehörte als erstes Domizil der russischen Hauptstadt zur Vereinigung der „Leading Hotels of the World"; das Restaurant Baltschug wurde von TTG & ITE als bestes Hotel-Restaurant Moskaus ausgezeichnet, das Baltschug selbst als bestes Hotel Russlands etc. Im Herzen Moskaus stehend und doch etwas entfernt vom Trubel jenseits der Moskwa, eröffnet das Hotel Baltschug Kempinski Moscow von den meisten seiner 232 Zimmer und Suiten einen Blick, der nicht zu schlagen ist: über den Fluss hinüber direkt zum Roten Platz, rechts davon liegt das Wahrzeichen Moskaus, die berühmte St.-Basil-Kathedrale, links der Kreml mit seinen fabelhaften Sehenswürdigkeiten. Das ist aber längst nicht alles, was Hausherr Gianni van Daahlen, vormals langjähriger Direktor des Berliner Adlon, zu bieten hat. Mit dem Restaurant Shogun rundet er sein vielfältiges kulinarisches Angebot echt japanisch ab, es gibt topmoderne Konferenzeinrichtungen, ein Fitness-Center, und in der Atmosphäre des Hotels Baltschug Kempinski Moscow schlägt authentisch der Puls Moskaus.

By re-opening the Baltschug in 1992 following an 86-million-dollar investment, the Kempinski Group has successfully rekindled one of Moscow's most famous hotels back into a thriving establishment. The Baltschug Kempinski was Moscow's first hotel to be included in the "Leading Hotels of the World". TTG & ITE declared its Baltschug Restaurant the capital's best hotel restaurant, and the hotel itself as the best in Russia etc. Located in the heart of Moscow, yet slightly set back from the hustle and bustle on the opposite side of the Moskwa, the Hotel Baltschug Kempinski Moscow offers unbeatable views from the majority of its 232 rooms and suites. Its guests can look forward to looking out across the River to Red Square, to the right of which stands one of Moscow's most famous landmarks, its famous St. Basil Cathedral, and to the left the Kremlin with its fantastic attractions. And that's just the beginning of what Gianni van Daahlen, who spent many years as the Director of the Adlon in Berlin, has to offer. The hotel's wide variety of culinary delights is rounded off by its Shogun Restaurant, serving authentic Japanese food. The Hotel Baltschug Kempinski Moscow also boasts cutting-edge conference facilities, a fitness centre and an atmosphere in which the authentic pulse of Moscow beats.

Hotel Baltschug Kempinski
Moscow
Direktor: Gianni van Daahlen
ul. Balchug, 1
RU-115035 Moscow
Phone:
0 07 / (0) 95 / 2 30 65 00
Fax:
0 07 / (0) 95 / 2 30 65 02
E-mail: reservations.
baltschug@kempinski.com
Internet:
www.kempinski-moscow.com

199 rooms, 33 suites
rates from Euro 330 to 3,500

Distance from airport:
35 kilometres

Membership:
The Leading Hotels
of the World

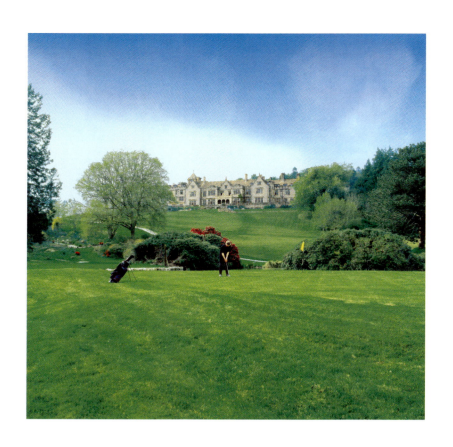

Das Country-House-Hotel Bovey Castle und sein Golf-kurs, das ist Devon wie im Bilderbuch. Der Golfplatz stammt aus dem Jahr 1926. 2004 wurde er nach einer kompletten Überarbeitung wiedereröffnet – mit Championship-Format und einer perfekten Harmonie von Kurs und Landschaft. Eine Renovierung wie aus einem Guss glückte auch mit Bovey Castle selbst. Besitzer Peter de Savary ließ die Atmosphäre der Gol-denen Zwanziger einziehen. Zugleich legte er Wert darauf, die klassischen Schlossinterieurs in detail-genauer Stiltreue zu rekonstruieren. So entstanden Wohnlandschaften (mit vielen Salons, mit Bibliothek, Pianobar, einem Billardzimmer, das sich in eine fest-liche Bankett-Ambiance verwandeln lässt, mit 65 Zim-mern, Suiten, Gartenlodges etc.), in denen sich das Flair des Art Déco reizvoll mit einem urbehaglichen englischen Landhausstil mischt. Küchenchef David Berry führt seine versierte Kreativität und die be-rühmten Produkte von Devon vor. Die topmodernen Konferenz- und Tagungsfaszilitäten sind in einem se-paraten Trakt untergebracht. Dazu gibt es ein Kino; ein Paradies für Kinder, ein erstklassiges Spa – und über-all den Blick auf die hinreißende Landschaft im Her-zen des Dartmoor-Nationalparks.

Bovey Castle offers a truly picture-book setting in the Heart of Dartmoor National Park, Devon. The Championship Old Course dates back to 1926, it was reopened in 2004 following a complete restoration and blends perfectly into the surrounding landscape. The Castle and Estate has also undergone a full re-furbishment with proprietor Peter de Savary deco-rating the Castle with the feel of the golden era of the 1920s. Importance has also been placed on recon-structing the traditional interior of the castle in keeping with the original style paying attention to every detail. The result is unique reception rooms which charmingly combine the flair of Art Déco with the traditional cosiness of English country living. Bo-vey Castle offers 65 luxuriously appointed bedrooms, staterooms and suites, a piano bar, a billiards room, spectacular Cathedral Room and Minstrel's Gallery and casual Clubhouse bar and dining room. Head chef David Berry; a master of his art makes his cre-ations using local ingredients which Devon has be-come famous for in the exquisite Palm Court Dining Room. The new, specially designed holistic spa of-fers fabulous relaxation and is complimented by our spectacular pool, sauna and Jacuzzi. The estate also offers numerous sporting pursuits including fly fish-ing, archery, falconry and horse riding. The state-of-the-art conference and events facilities are housed in the Mews building, along with a private cinema and children's play barn.

Bovey Castle
Owner: Peter de Savary
Club Director:
Henrietta Fergusson
North Bovey, Dartmoor
National Park, Devon TQ13
8RE, England
Phone: 00 44 / 16 47 / 44 50 00
Fax:　　00 44 / 16 47 / 44 09 61
E-mail:
enquiries@boveycastle.com
Internet:
www.boveycastle.com

65 rooms and suites
Double rooms from £ 180 to 345, State rooms from £ 450 to 650, Gate Lodge from £ 950, Suites from £ 550 to 1,500
(Value Added Tax at a rate of 17.5 % will be added to all room and dining)

Distance from airport:
2 hours

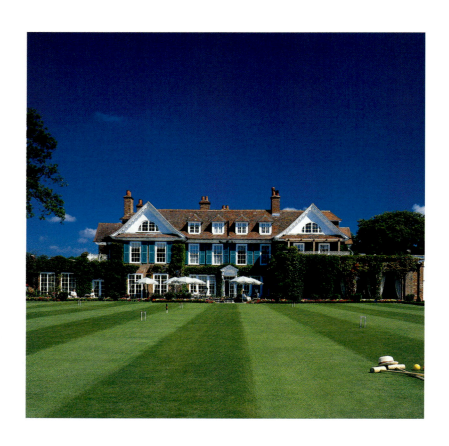

Im Süden Englands steht ein Country-House-Hotel, wie es sich Liebhaber eleganter ländlicher Gastlichkeit träumen: Chewton Glen. Es wurde zum Maßstab seines Genres. Die Besitzer, Martin Skan und seine Schweizer Gattin Brigitte, haben an der Grenze zwischen Hampshire und Dorset eine Residenz geschaffen, die sich Privatgästen ebenso attraktiv präsentiert wie dem Business- und Meetingpublikum (Räumlichkeiten für bis zu 120 Teilnehmer, jeder einzelne wird als VIP-Gast behandelt). Hinreißend die Lage: Zum Anwesen gehören weite malerische Parks und Gärten, Felder und Wälder. Gleich am Haus beginnt der eigene 9-Loch-Golfkurs. Die Croquet-Wiese liegt vor der Bar-Terrasse. Es gibt ein Tennis-Center mit zwei Indoor-Courts, dazu zwei Außenplätze mit Allwetterbelag. Die Attraktion für Wellnessfans: ein Spa der internationalen Spitzenkategorie. Eine Lehrstunde in luxuriösem Interior Design: die 35 Zimmer und 23 Suiten. Sie sind Brigitte Skans Domäne. Was sie an feinem, elegantem Country Style kreiert, ist einfach hinreißend. Versteht sich, dass ein Haus solcher Superlative auch kulinarisch reüssiert. Highlight: das Marryat-Restaurant. Chef Luke Matthews glänzt hier mit einem Michelin-Stern.

In the south of England lies the very kind of country house hotel that those with a passion for the elegance and hospitality of English country life can but dream of: Chewton Glen. Indeed, others in its league look to this country house hotel as a measure of excellence. The proprietors, Martin Skan and his wife Brigitte, have created a setting on the border between Hampshire and Dorset that appeals equally to private guests and those travelling for business or conference purposes (accommodating up to 120 participants, with each receiving VIP treatment). The grounds include expansive, scenic parks and gardens, fields and woodland. The hotel's own 9-hole golf course begins directly when you step outside. The croquet lawn is situated in front of the bar terrace. There is a tennis centre with two indoor courts, plus two all-weather outdoor courts. And for wellness enthusiasts, there is a world-class spa. On top of this, the 35 rooms and 23 suites offer the ultimate in luxury interior design, which is Brigitte Skan's speciality. Her elegant creations reflecting the finest in country living are simply bewitching. It of course goes without saying that an establishment of such superlative quality also triumphs in the culinary arena. Head chef Luke Matthews shines here in the Michelin-star crowned Marryat restaurant.

Chewton Glen Hotel
Spa and Country Club
Owner:
Martin and Brigitte Skan
Managing Director:
Andrew Stembridge
New Milton, Hampshire
England, BH25 6QS
Phone: 00 44 / 14 25 / 27 53 41
Fax: 00 44 / 14 25 / 27 23 10
E-mail: reservations@
chewtonglen.com
Internet:
www.chewtonglen.com

35 rooms and 23 suites,
double rooms from £ 280
to 435, junior suites from
£ 435, suites from £ 535,
Jacob Faithful Suite from
£ 665, Marryat Suite from
£ 775 (includes VAT and
Service Charge)

Distances:
from London Heathrow
1 hour 30 mins.
from Bournemouth 20 mins.
from Southampton 40 mins.

Membership:
Relais & Châteaux

The Capital ist ein exquisites Versteck mitten in London. David Levin, sein schottischer Besitzer, erfand dieses hinreißend englische Refugium im vornehmen Stadtteil Knightsbridge vor dreiunddreißig Jahren. Elegant und charmant die Atmosphäre. Das Hotel wird bis heute von der Familie geführt. Handverlesen die Möbel, jedes Kunstwerk (viele stammen aus der Sammlung der Levins). Mit der gleichen stilsicheren Sorgsamkeit wurde das Flair der 49 Zimmer und Suiten geschaffen (Topkomfort von der Klimaanlage bis zum drahtlosen Internetanschluss). Die Stoffe in vielen Räumen kommen aus der Ralph Lauren Collection, die Matratzen sind Handarbeit, das Bettzeug ist aus feinster ägyptischer Baumwolle. Luxuriös ausgestattet auch die schönen Marmorbäder. Fitness und Wellness bietet gleich um die Ecke The Peak Health Club & Spa mit Blick über die Dächer von London. Ebenfalls in nächster Nähe finden sich die königlichen Parks, die Nobelkaufhäuser Harrods, Harvey Nichols und die schicken Boutiquen der Sloane Street. Fürs Fine Dining freilich wird man The Capital nicht so leicht verlassen. Das Capital Restaurant ist eines der besten der Stadt: Chef Eric Crouillère Chavot kocht seine französische Gourmetcuisine unter zwei Michelin-Sternen.

The Capital is an exquisite hideaway in the heart of London. David Levin, the Scots proprietor established this fantastic English oasis in the fashionable area of Knightsbridge thirty-three years ago. The atmosphere is elegant and charming and to this day it is a family-run concern. Every piece of furniture and work of art (many have come from the Levins private collection) is hand-picked. The same stylish care is evident in the flair of the 49 rooms and suites. The highest level of comfort and convenience is achieved from the air-conditioning to the wireless internet connection. The textiles in the different rooms are by Ralph Lauren Collection, the mattresses are handmade while the bed linen is of finest Egyptian cotton. The marble bathrooms are also luxuriously furnished. Around the corner The Peak Health Club & Spa provides a fitness and wellness programme looking down over the roofs of London. Also close at hand are the royal parks, the leading department stores of Harrods and Harvey Nichols and the chic boutiques of Sloane Street. For fine dining there is no need to leave the Capital. The Capital Restaurant is one of the best in the city: The French gourmet cuisine created by Chef Eric Crouillère Chavot has won him two Michelin stars.

The Capital Hotel
General Manager:
Henrik Muehle
22 Basil Street
London SW3 1AT
United Kingdom
Phone: 00 44 / 20 / 75 89 51 71
Fax: 00 44 / 20 / 72 25 00 11
E-mail: reservations@
capitalhotel.co.uk
Internet:
www.capitalhotel.co.uk

49 rooms and suites
Executive Rooms from
£ 175 (weekend) to 275,
Deluxe Room from £ 325 to
355, Junior Suite from £ 385
to 425
+ 17,5 % VAT

Distance from airport:
London City Airport
10,9 miles, Heathrow International 15,8 miles, Gatwick
Airport 33,5 miles, Stansted
Airport 41,7 miles

Memberships:
Small Luxury Hotels
of the World,
Great Hotels of the World

Außer den eindrucksvollen Kirchen und Gebäuden sind es die imposanten Paläste, die von dem früheren Reichtum Venedigs zeugen. In einem der prächtigsten befindet sich das Bauer Il Palazzo. Direkt am Canale Grande spiegelt sich von der Fassade bis zum handgefertigten Kristalllüster die nostalgische Opulenz Venedigs wider. Der Palazzo ist Teil des traditionsreichen „Bauer Venezia", das seit seiner Eröffnung vor 125 Jahren immer zu den ersten Adressen der Lagunenstadt gehörte. Der Gast hat die Wahl zwischen zwei ganz eigenen Persönlichkeiten, das Fünf-Sterne-Bauer-Hotel im modernen Flügel am Campo San Moise mit 115 elegant ausgestatteten Zimmern und das überaus opulente Boutique-Hotel Bauer Il Palazzo in den historischen Palasträumen aus dem 18. Jahrhundert. Hier schuf man mit viel Stilgefühl 36 Zimmer und 40 individuelle Suiten mit einzigartigem Ausblick, die keinerlei Komfort vermissen lassen und sich als wahre Schmuckkästchen traditioneller venezianischer Handwerkskunst entpuppen. Von Venedigs höchster Dachterrasse, die schon seit ihrer Eröffnung nicht ohne Grund „Settimo Cielo" (siebter Himmel) genannt wird, präsentiert sich ein hinreißendes Panorama. Entspannung bietet das hauseigene Fitnesscenter mit Sauna, Dampfbad und Außen-Whirlpool. Unbedingt reservieren sollte man sich einen Tisch im erstklassigen Gourmetrestaurant De Pisis, denn die Aussicht von der Terrasse über den Canale Grande und die erstklassige mediterrane und venezianische Küche beeindrucken auch den anspruchsvollsten Reisenden.

Its impressive churches and buildings apart, it is Venice's collection of magnificent palaces that testify to its once affluence. One of the most splendid of these palaces is home to the Bauer Il Palazzo hotel. Right on the Grand Canal, from the façade to the hand-made crystal chandeliers, the Bauer Il Palazzo is a reflection of the opulence of Venice in former times. The Palazzo is part of the traditional "Bauer Venezia", which has been one of the leading addresses in the lagoon city since it first opened 125 years ago. The guest has the choice between two different hotel cultures; the five-star Bauer Hotel in the modern wing at "Campo San Moise" with 115 elegantly decorated rooms, and the absolutely opulent Boutique Hotel Bauer Il Palazzo in the historical part dating back to the 18th century. Here 36 rooms and 40 individual suites have been created with great flair. With every comfort and a wonderful view, you will soon discover that these quarters are veritable treasure troves of traditional Venetian craftsmanship. From the highest roof terrace in Venice, known since its opening as "Settimo Cielo" (seventh heaven) a vast panorama can be seen. For relaxation there is the hotel gym with sauna, steam bath and outdoor Jacuzzi. Given that the view from the terrace above the Grand Canal and the top quality Mediterranean and Venetian cuisine on offer is guaranteed to impress even the most demanding of travellers, reserving a table in the first class gourmet restaurant De Pisis is an absolute must.

Bauer Il Palazzo
President:
Francesca Bortolotto Possati
San Marco 1413/d
I-30124 Venezia
Phone: 00 39/0 41/5 20 70 22
Fax: 00 39/0 41/5 20 75 57
E-mail:
marketing@bauervenezia.com
Internet:
www. bauerhotels.com

36 rooms
from Euro 430 to 1,200
40 suites
from Euro 560 to 5,000

Distance from airport:
25 minutes

Membership:
The Leading Small Hotels
of the World

Sardiniens Costa Smeralda ist seit vier Jahrzehnten ein Hot-Spot für den internationalen Jetset. Zu den Top-Unterkünften der Region zählt seit seiner Erbauung 1963 das Hotel Cala di Volpe an der gleichnamigen Bucht. Dieses Paradebeispiel extravaganter Architektur – sie ist verschachtelt und pittoresk wie ein organisch gewachsenes Mittelmeerdorf – sucht ihresgleichen. Den Gästen stehen 125 traumhaft schöne Zimmer und Suiten zur Wahl, z.T. mit Tromp-l'Œil-Wandmalereien, eingerichtet im typisch sardischen Stil mit allem erdenklichen Komfort. Weltweite Bekanntheit erreichte das Hotel übrigens 1977, als dort Teile des James-Bond-Films „Der Spion, der mich liebte" mit Roger Moore gedreht wurden. Zur weitläufigen Anlage gehören u. a. ein eigener Yachthafen mit Marinasarda-Bootsverleih, ein riesiger Meerwasserpool, ein hoteleigener Sandstrand, Boutiquen sowie Beauty- und Friseursalon und Fitness-Center. Die beiden Restaurants des Cala di Volpe (internationale, mediterrane und original sardische Küche) zählen zu den besten der Insel. Für unvergessliche Stunden sorgen die stimmungsvollen Bars im Hause, allen voran die zauberhafte „Pontile"-Bar. Anspruchsvolle Golfer treffen sich im berühmten Pevero Golf Club Costa Smeralda.

Sardinia's Costa Smeralda has been the hot spot for the international jet set for 40 years. One of the leading lights in the region since its construction in 1963 is the Hotel Cala di Volpe located at the Costa Smeralda Bay. This prime example of extravagant architecture is pretty unique. It spreads out around the Bay like a picturesque Mediterranean village just as if it had grown over time. The guests have a choice of 125 heavenly rooms and suites, all of which are furnished in typical Sardinian style with every imaginable comfort. Some are decorated with tromp-l'Œil murals. Note: the hotel became internationally famous in 1977 when it was used as the backdrop to part of the James Bond film "The Spy Who Loved Me" with Roger Moore. The enormous complex contains a private marina with boats for rent, a huge salt-water pool, a private beach, boutiques, beauty and hairdressing salons and a gym. The two Cala di Volpe restaurants are among the best on the island for international, Mediterranean and original Sardinian cuisine. You can look forward to enjoying some unforgettable moments in the lively hotel bars especially in the "Pontile". Experienced golfers meet in the famous Pevero Golf Club Costa Smeralda.

Cala di Volpe
General Manager:
Hermann Gatti
I-07020 Porto Cervo (SS)
Costa Smeralda (Italia)
Phone: 00 39 / 07 89 / 97 61 11
Fax: 00 39 / 07 89 / 97 66 17
E-mail: res059.caladivolpe@
starwoodhotels.com
Internet: www.luxury
collection.com/caladivolpe

125 spacious, individually appointed guest rooms and suites offer a balcony overlooking the scenic panorama and are decorated with a unique selection of traditional furnishings and art

Distance from airport:
40 minutes drive by car

Membership:
Starwood Hotels
"The Luxury Collection"

Die Welt der Castel-Kulinarik wird von Gerhard Wiesers Gourmetküche bestimmt, die den Gästen sowohl in den stimmungsvollen Trenkerstuben als auch auf der großen Restaurantterrasse mit grandiosem Rundumblick über Meran und die umliegende Bergwelt mundet. Die hochdekorierte Kulinarik ist jedoch nur eine Facette im Reigen der Genießervielfalt, die Südtirols einziges inhabergeführtes Fünf-Sterne-Hotel zu bieten hat. Der Logenplatz auf der Sonnenseite der Alpen kultiviert die „Kunst des Wohlbefindens" und pflegt niveauvolle Lebensart. Die architektonische Gestaltung schafft Räumlichkeiten, welche die Sehnsucht nach Ruhe und Behaglichkeit erfüllen. Gäste logieren in 42 Zimmern und Suiten, die im Hinblick auf absolute Privatsphäre konzipiert wurden. Ihr luxuriöses Interieur gehört im Castel zum Wohlfühlstandard. Ebenso dazu gehören hochklassige Events sowie ein adäquates Sport- und Freizeitangebot, das von Wandern bis Golfspielen reicht. Das Beauty- und Wellnessreich „Carpe Diem" zählt zu den schönsten Refugien seiner Art und schafft mit seiner sonnendurchfluteten Großzügigkeit und exklusiven Treatments den Rahmen für ganzheitliches Wohlbefinden.

Gerhard Wieser's gourmet cuisine plays a large role in influencing the atmosphere of the Castel's fine food and drink setting. It's served in the Castel's atmospheric Trenker rooms, as well as on the restaurant's large patio with fantastic all-round views of Merano and the surrounding mountains. Yet for all this, its highly renowned cuisine is only one aspect of what this, South Tyrol's only family-run five-star hotel, has to offer for those who love the good life. Boasting a breathtakingly lovely position on the sunny side of the Alps, the Castel prides itself on having mastered the art of wellbeing and sophisticated lifestyle. Its architecture has been designed to create rooms that satisfy the desire for peace, tranquillity and comfort. Its guests reside in 42 rooms and suites conceived to create areas of unadulterated privacy. Its luxurious interiors are all part of the Castel's desire to create the ultimate in wellbeing. It also offers high-class events and an appropriate range of sport and leisure activities stretching from hiking to golf. When it comes to finding a truly wonderful retreat, you would have to go a long way to top its "Carpe Diem" beauty and wellness facilities. Indeed, its generously proportioned sunbathed facilities and exclusive treatments conspire to create the ultimate setting for holistic wellbeing.

Hotel Castel
Owner: Dobitsch family
I-39019 Tirol near Merano
South Tyrol
Phone: 00 39 / 04 73 / 92 36 93
Fax: 00 39 / 04 73 / 92 31 13
E-mail:
info@hotel-castel.com
Internet:
www.hotel-castel.com

17 rooms, 17 apartments, 11 suites
Double rooms from Euro 128, apartments from Euro 144, suites from Euro 149

Distance from airport:
30 minutes

Membership:
L'Art de Vivre

Der Meraner Bauherr Ulrich Ladurner hatte den Mut, auf dem autofreien Vigiljoch, in 1500 Meter Höhe, ein Luxusresort im Design von Matteo Thun entstehen zu lassen. Es pflanzt sich der Bergwelt mit so leiser wie erlesener Ästhetik ein: Das Vigilius Mountain Resort ist komplett mit Holz verkleidet, zwei Etagen hoch, und auf seinem flachen Dach blühen Blumen und Kräuter. Matteo Thuns Motto wurde Wirklichkeit: „With Nature in Architecture." Urgemütlich die „Stube" mit ihrer authentischen Südtiroler Küche. Fürs Gourmetrestaurant wurde ein kompletter, dreihundert Jahre alter Getreidestadel aufs Vigiljoch transferiert. Avantgardistisch das Design sonst, vom erstklassig geführten Spa bis zu den 35 Zimmern und sechs Suiten. Der Wohnraum (Möbel von B & B) und der Badbereich gehen offen ineinander über, nur durch eine (im Winter geheizte) Lehmwand getrennt. Die Außenwand zur Bergwelt ist ganz aus Glas. Das Interior Design von Matteo Thun ist puristisch und minimalistisch bis zur Perfektion. Seine leise Ästhetik tut wohl, gibt Raum für den Menschen, seine Gedanken, seine Träume, hält eine raffinierte Balance zwischen Tradition und Moderne. Überzeugend ist auch das Konzept des Vigilius Mountain Spa. Sämtliche Anwendungen bilden einen elementaren Kreislauf, beflügeln die Lebensquellen. Unterstützt wird das durch Aktivitäten wie Nordic Walking, Bogenschießen, Yoga oder Pilates.

Once upon a time the developer Ulrich Ladurner from Merano hat the vision and courage to create a luxury resort in the design of Matteo Thun on the Vigiljoch at a height of 1,500 metres. Fitting into the mountainous world with its gentle yet exquisite aesthetics, The Vigilius Mountain Resort is completely panelled with wood, two stories high and on its flat roof grow flowers and herbs. Thus Matteo Thun's motto "With nature in architecture" became reality. The "Stube" offering authentic dishes of South Tyrol is very cosy. To create the gourmet restaurant an entire three hundred year old grain barn was transported up to the Vigiljoch. Otherwise the design is avant-garde, from the first class spa to the 35 rooms and suites. The living area (furniture by B & B) and the bathing area are interconnected, only separated by a clay door, which is heated in winter. The outer wall to the mountains is made completely of glass. The interior design of Matteo Thun is purist and minimalist to perfection. Its gentle aesthetics are good for the soul giving people space for their thoughts and their dreams while maintaining a sophisticated balance between tradition and modernity. The Vigilius Mountain Spa concept is also very convincing. All its treatments have been designed to form an elemental cycle for inspiring the inner stream of life. Activities such as Nordic Walking, archery, yoga and pilates add to the health theme.

Vigilius Mountain Resort
Direction: Ulrich Ladurner
Vigiljoch
I-39011 Lana / South Tyrol
Phone: 00 39 / 04 73 / 55 66 00
Fax: 00 39 / 04 73 / 55 66 99
E-mail:
info@vigilius.it.
Internet:
www.vigilius.it

35 rooms and 6 suites
Off season (22. 4. – 30. 6.,
16. 9. – 13. 11., 16. 12. – 22.
12.): Suite Euro 535, Deluxe
Euro 310, Superior Euro 290,
Single Euro 210
In season (1. 7. – 15. 9.,
23. 12. – 8. 1. 2006): Suite
Euro 565, Deluxe Euro 330,
Superior Euro 310, Single
Euro 225

Distance from airport:
Bolzano 20 minutes

Kein Geringerer als César Ritz, der „Hotelier der Könige und König der Hoteliers", eröffnete 1894 Roms erstes Luxushotel, das St. Regis Grand Hotel, Rome. Nach einer aufwändigen Komplettrenovierung füllt die „Grande Dame" der römischen Hotellerie seit der Jahrtausendwende die glamourösen Visionen des César Ritz wieder mit Leben. Nicht als nostalgische Vision, sondern als eine reale Wiederherstellung des Glamours einer vergangenen Epoche mit dem Komfort von heute. Besondere Highlights der authentischen Rekonstruktionen sind die glamouröse Halle mit der „Le Grand Bar", der großartige Ballsaal und die 23 Suiten, in denen man auf Wunsch einen privaten Butlerdienst in Anspruch nehmen kann. Wie die anderen individuell gestalteten Zimmer fungieren sie als Fenster zur Geschichte Roms. Wer noch tiefer in die Geschichte der Ewigen Stadt eindringen möchte hat es nicht weit. Fast alle wichtigen Sehenswürdigkeiten sind zu Fuß zu erreichen. Und auch Gourmets zieht es nicht in die Ferne. Das hochdekorierte Gourmetrestaurant „Vivendo" und die Schätze des Weinkellers sind allein schon eine Reise wert.

He and only him or no less a person than César Ritz, the "Hotelier of kings and king of hoteliers", who opened Rome's first luxury hotel in 1894, the St. Regis Grand Hotel, Rome. Since thorough renovation at the turn of the millennium, this grande dame of Roman hotels has been bringing the glamorous visions of César Ritz to life again. Not simply a nostalgic tribute, but a real revival of the glamour of a bygone era, with the addition of modern comfort. Among the special attractions in the wake of the authentic renovation work are the glamorous foyer with "Le Grand Bar", the lavishly decorated ballroom and the 23 suites that include the option of a private butler service. As with the individually designed rooms, they serve as a window onto the history of Rome. Visitors wishing to delve more deeply into the past of the Eternal City need not look far. Almost every important attraction can be reached on foot. Culinary delights are never far away either. The top-award winning gourmet restaurant, "Vivendo" and the treasures of the wine cellar alone are worth a visit.

St. Regis Grand Hotel, Rome
Managing Director:
Michele Frignani
Via Vittorio Emanuele
Orlando 3, I-00185 Rom
Phone: 00 39 / (0) 64 70 91
Fax: 00 39 / (0) 64 74 73 07
E-mail: stregisgrandrome@
stregis.com
Internet: www.stregis.com/
GrandRome

138 rooms and 23 suites
Double rooms from Euro 270
Suites from Euro 937

Distance from airport:
30 minutes

Membership:
St. Regis Hotels & Resorts

Das Erfolgsgeheimnis dieser auf Topniveau umfassend renovierten Hotellegende zu ergründen, erweist sich als überaus knifflige Angelegenheit. Liegt es an der zentralen Lage unweit der Sehenswürdigkeiten der Stadt? An dem herrschaftlichen Ambiente, das den einzigartigen Charme der Jahrhundertwende einfängt? An den außergewöhnlichen Westin-typischen Serviceleistungen? An der hervorragenden Kulinarik? An der trendigen Bar „hclub→doney" – einer der In-Treffpunkte der Stadt? Am Health Club mit Schwimmbad, Sauna, Fitnessraum, Massagen und exklusiven Beautytreatments? Oder vielleicht an den stets freundlichen Mitarbeitern? Fragen, die nicht leicht zu beantworten sind – jede für sich bietet schon genug Grund, das The Westin Excelsior, Rome als komfortablen Stützpunkt für die nächste Rom-Reise zu wählen. Alles in allem sind es Gründe, die in dieser Kombination fast unschlagbar sind, denn das Luxusdomizil zeigt auf eindrucksvolle Art und Weise, dass sich die Tradition eines Hauses und moderner Lifestyle nicht widersprechen, sondern im Zusammenspiel eine lebendige Wohlfühlatmosphäre schaffen. Staatsoberhäupter oder Wirtschaftsbosse finden in der 1100 Quadratmeter großen Suite Villa La Cupola einen Wohntraum der Superlative.

This hotel legend has been comprehensively renovated to meet the very highest of standards. Yet for all this, putting your finger on the secret of its success is rather tricky. Could it be its central location close to the city's major attractions? Or perhaps it's its stately ambience that manages to capture the unique charm of the turn of the century? Or the remarkable way in which its services cater for your every need? Its outstanding cuisine? Its fashionable "hclub→doney" bar, which is the place to be? Its health club with swimming pool, sauna, gym, massages and exclusive beauty treatments? Or could it be something as simple as its ever-friendly staff? While providing a concrete answer to these questions is not easy, one thing's for sure. Each and every aspect of the hotel provides reason enough on its own for you to seriously consider the The Westin Excelsior as a comfortable base the next time you're in Rome. Put them together, however, and there's hardly an alternative. Indeed, this luxury residence provides a powerful demonstration that tradition and modern lifestyle are no contradiction and that when put together they can create a vibrant atmosphere of contentment and wellbeing. At 1,100 square metres, the Villa La Cupola offers Heads of state and senior executives accommodation of superlative proportions.

The Westin Excelsior Rome
General Manager:
Paolo Lorenzoni
Via Vittorio Veneto 125
I- 00187 Rome
Phone: 00 39 / 06 / 4 70 81
Fax: 00 39 / 06 / 4 82 62 05
E-mail:
ExcelsiorRome@westin.com
Internet: www.westin.com/
excelsiorrome

284 rooms and 31 suites
Double rooms from Euro 270
Suites from Euro 1,315

Distance from airport:
35 km / airport Fiumicino
30 km / airport Ciampino

Membership:
Starwood Hotels & Resorts

„If this isn't the most beautiful house in the world, it comes dangerously close", schrieb ein italienischer Connaisseur in das Gästebuch des Relais-&-Châteaux-Hauses in Ladispoli, einem beliebten Küstenort, nur fünfundvierzig Autominuten von Rom entfernt. Ein kleiner Satz, der den einzigartigen Charme dieses Highlights der italienischen Hotellerie überaus treffend auf den Punkt bringt. Denn das historische Anwesen über dem Tyrrhenischen Meer, dessen Ursprünge bis in die Antike zurückreichen, ist Anfang der 60er Jahre vom Multimillionär Paul Getty in einen wahren Tempel der Kunst und der Lebenslust verwandelt worden. Als der Ölmulti die Lust an dem Anwesen verlor, fand sich zum Glück ein kunstsinniger Liebhaber, der das Haus mitsamt dem Interieur und den Kunstschätzen kaufte und die auf der Welt wohl einmalige Kombination aus historischem Ambiente, wunderschöner Lage, märchenhaftem Garten, vorchristlichen Zeugnissen und kunstbeflissener Atmosphäre in Form eines kleinen Luxushotels der Öffentlichkeit zugänglich machte. Ein ungewöhnliches Domizil, das wohl allen Visionen von Reisenden mit hohen Ansprüchen entspricht – in punkto Ambiente und Lage genauso wie bei den innovativen Serviceleistungen und der exzellenten Kulinarik.

"If this isn't the most beautiful house in the world, it comes dangerously close", wrote an Italian connoisseur in the visitors' book of the Relais & Châteaux villa in Ladispoli, a popular coastal resort only forty-five minutes' drive from Rome. This single sentence captures perfectly the unique charm of this jewel among Italian hotels. In the early 1960s, this historic residence, which overlooks the Tyrrhenian Sea and dates back to ancient times, was transformed into a veritable temple of art and joie de vivre by multimillionaire Paul Getty. When the oil baron's interest in the residence waned, it was fortunately taken over by an art lover, who bought the villa together with its interior décor and art treasures. This unique combination of testimony to pre-Christian times, the beautiful location, the fabulous gardens, and the aesthetically sublime was then opened to the public as a small luxury hotel. This is certainly an unusual residence that lives up to all expectations of the sophisticated traveller, whether in terms of atmosphere, location, imaginative service or excellent cuisine.

Relais & Châteaux Hotel
La Posta Vecchia
President and owner:
Roberto Scio
Director of Sales
& Marketing: Lucia Garau
Hotel Resident Manager:
Barbara Panzera
Palo Laziale
I-00055 Ladispoli / Rome
Phone: 00 39 / 06 / 9 94 95 01
Fax: 00 39 / 06 / 9 94 95 07
E-mail:
info@lapostavecchia.com
Internet:
www.lapostavecchia.com

11 rooms, 5 Junior Suites
and 3 Master Suites
Double rooms Euro 580 Euro,
Junior Suites from Euro 930,
Master Suites Euro 1,410
Heated in house-pool, beauty
center, restaurant, in-house
roman museum, park,
small black sandy beach

Distance from Rome
city center: 45 minutes

Membership:
Relais & Châteaux

In Porto Ercole, auf der Halbinsel Argentario, befindet sich eines der luxuriösesten Hotels Italiens mit einem endlosen Blick aufs Meer. Ein zentrales Gebäude und mehrere kleine Villen liegen eingebettet in einen großzügigen mediterranen Park. Von terrassenförmig angelegten Patios schlängeln sich Wege zum Pool und zum Privatstrand. Die sehr geschmackvollen und individuell gestalteten Zimmer und Suiten sind in den verschiedenen Villen untergebracht und bestechen mit ganz eigenem Charme und spektakulären Aussichten auf das türkisfarbene Meer – genau wie die stilvolle Seeterrasse und der großzügige Meerwasserpool. Die Schönheiten dieses einzigartigen kleinen Privathotels, des Gartens und der Umgebung sind genauso unwiderstehlich wie die hohe Kunst des Gourmetrestaurants und des bestens bestückten Weinkellers. Das bestätigt nicht nur die prominente Stammkundschaft, sondern zeigen auch zahlreiche hochkarätige Auszeichnungen der Fachwelt, für die das Il Pellicano zu den besten Hotels der Welt gehört. Das Beauty & Spa gibt die Möglichkeit, eine umfassende Regeneration der Körperenergien durch Seetherapie und Phytomer-Produkte zu erreichen.

In Porto Ercole, on the peninsula of Argentario, you will find one of Italy's most luxurious hotels with a view stretching seemingly endlessly over the sea. It comprises a central building and several small villas, nestled in a generous expanse of Mediterranean gardens. The way to the pool and the private beach leads effortlessly from the stepped patios. The unique charm of each of the villas delights, each with its own stylish, individual design and spectacular views over the turquoise waters of the sea. Likewise the elegant sea terrace and the generous seawater pool. The beauty of this one-of-a-kind, small private hotel, its gardens and the surroundings are just as irresistible as the haute cuisine of the gourmet restaurant and its finely-stocked wine cellar. This opinion is not only shared by the hotel's prominent clientele, indeed it has also been the recipient of many top industry awards, judging Il Pellicano as one of the best hotels in the world. The beauty and spa facilities offer the guest the opportunity of an all-round reenergising experience with sea therapy and Phytomer products.

Il Pellicano
President and owner:
Roberto Scio
General Manager:
Cinzia Fanciulli
Director of Sales
& Marketing: Lucia Garau
Sbarcatello
I-58018 Porto Ercole
Phone: 00 39 / 05 64 / 85 81 11
Fax: 00 39 / 05 64 / 83 34 18
E-mail:
info@pellicanohotel.com
Internet:
www.pellicanohotel.com

31 rooms, 9 Junior Suites and 10 De Luxe Suites Double rooms from Euro 328, Junior Suites from Euro 489, De Luxe Suites from Euro 787 Privare rocky beach, seawater heated pool, beauty & spa, fitness center, tennis court, garage, 1 star Michelin Restaurant, bar

Distance from airport: (Rome Fiumicino) 150 km

Membership:
Relais & Châteaux

Wer die Renaissancemetropole Florenz wirklich entdecken will, sollte unbedingt im Palazzo Magnani Feroni mitten in der Altstadt Quartier nehmen. Der Palast aus dem 15. Jahrhundert bietet eines der geschichtsträchtigsten und individuellsten Logis im Umfeld der berühmten Sehenswürdigkeiten Ponte Vecchia, Uffizien und Dom. Ausgestattet mit antiken Möbeln, Muranoleuchtern und Gemälden, auf die so manches Museum stolz wäre, kunstvoll geschnitzten Holzvertäfelungen und liebevoll restaurierten original Wandmalereien, wandelt man hier auf den Spuren der florentinischen Aristokratie. Trotz aller nostalgischer Pracht muss man in den zwölf Suiten, die allesamt 100 Quadratmeter groß sind und über eine Deckenhöhe von sechs Metern verfügen, keineswegs auf die Annehmlichkeiten modernsten Komforts verzichten. Und auch Serviceleistungen wie 24-Stunden-Roomservice, Garage, Fitnessraum, Massage- und Beautyservice, Museum- oder Shoppingguides, die man eigentlich nur von großen Hotels kennt, gehören im Palazzo Magnani Feroni zu den Selbstverständlichkeiten – genau wie der lauschige Innenhof und die Dachterrasse mit Blick über die Dächer der Stadt.

If you really wish to explore the Renaissance metropolis of Florence, you absolutely must stay at the Palazzo Magnani Feroni in the old part of the city. This 15th century palace offers one of the most historical and individual settings surrounded by famous attractions like Ponte Vecchia, the Uffizi Museum and Cathedral. Decorated with antique furniture, artistically carved wooden panelling, original, lovingly restored murals, Murano candlesticks and paintings that many a museum would be glad to possess, you will soon find yourself following the trail of the Florentine aristocracy. In spite of all this historical resplendence there is no need to do without the most up to date comforts in the twelve suites, each of which is over 100 square metres and has ceilings six-metres high. Facilities that are normally only found in large hotels like 24 hour room service, a garage, gym, massage and beauty parlour, guides for museum visits and shopping are taken for granted at Palazzo Magnani Feroni, as are the cosy courtyard and the roof garden with a view above the roofs of the city.

Palazzo Magnani Feroni
Borgo San Frediano 5
I-50124 Firenze
Phone: 00 39 / 0 55 / 2 39 95 44
Fax: 00 39 / 0 55 / 2 60 89 08
E-mail:
info@florencepalace.it
Internet:
www.florencepalace.it

12 suites from Euro 210 to 750 depending on size and season

Distance from airport:
15 minutes

Im Herzen von Oberlech – dem „Logenplatz am Arlberg" – liegt das Burg Vital Hotel, dessen herzliche Gastgeber Hannelore und Thomas Lucian immer darauf bedacht sind, ihren Gästen sozusagen die Wünsche von den Augen abzulesen. Verwöhnt wird mit exzellentem Komfort, superber Kulinarik, umfassendem Service und einem Top-Beauty- & Wellness-Angebot. Neben Wellness liegt der Schwerpunkt im Bereich Gesundheit und Natur in luxuriösem Ambiente. Das alpine Schmuckkästchen beherbergt achtzig Zimmer im gemütlichen Wohnstil. Wer einmal davon träumt, alle Alltagszwänge abzustreifen, um in die heitere und ungezwungene Ambiance eines kleinen, feinen Hotels abzutauchen, der wird sich im Burg Vital Hotel sichtbar wohl fühlen. Die Inneneinrichtungen sind geprägt durch das Holz der Bergfichte, die hellen Farben der Stoffe und große Fenster. Alles zusammen entfaltet eine beschwingende Leichtigkeit. Für den hohen kulinarischen Standard garantiert die „Hauben-und-Sterne-Küche" mit vorwiegend heimischen Produkten aus der Region. Der Gast hat die Wahl zwischen feinster Cuisine, Vollwertkost und herzhaften Schmankerln. Umfassend ist das Weinangebot mit dem Schwerpunkt Österreich, das heute in der obersten Liga der Spitzenweine mitmischt.

Burg Vital Hotel is located in the heart of Oberlech and boasts a fantastic position on the Arlberg Mountain. Its warm-hearted hosts, Hannelore and Thomas Lucian, pride themselves on providing a second- to-none service for their guests. Just imagine being pampered with wonderful comforts, superb cuisine and the very best in comprehensive beauty and wellness facilities. In addition to its wellness area, the hotel also sets great store by providing a mix of health and nature in a luxurious ambience. This delightful alpine treasure houses 80 rooms, boasting a cosy and homely feel. If you've ever dreamed of getting away from it all, of enjoying the cheerful and relaxed atmosphere of a small and elegant hotel and of submerging yourself in a world of wellbeing, the Burg Vital Hotel has all the ingredients. Inside, the wood of the mountain pine has been used throughout and you are struck by the bright colours of the material and the large windows. All in all, you cannot fail but to feel at ease with yourself and the world. Its cuisine carries forward its high standards. You can look forward to enjoying "Star" cuisine made from local produce. Guests are free to choose between fine cuisine, healthy food and hearty delicacies. It offers a comprehensive selection of wines with an emphasis on Austria, which can today claim to be among the world's very best.

Burg Vital Hotel
Lucian family
A-6764 Lech am Arlberg
Phone: 00 43 / 55 83 / 31 40
Fax: 00 43 / 55 83 / 31 40-16
E-mail:
vitalhotel@lech.at
Internet:
www.burgvitalhotel.com

40 rooms and suites
from Euro 168 to 956

Distance from airport:
1 hour 40 minutes

Membership:
Relax Guide

Mitten im Herzen des sonnenverwöhnten Ötztales, das seit jeher als Skiparadies gilt, verzaubert das Central Spa Hotel Sölden seine Besucher mit exklusivem Luxus, einer erstklassigen Küche, der märchenhaft anmutenden Wasserwelt „Venezia" und Verwöhnprogrammen in der Wellness- und Beautyoase. Insgesamt laden 1500 Quadratmeter im neuen Central Spa Hotel Sölden mit seinen Arkadengängen und Wandmalereien zum Entspannen und Relaxen ein. Ob Bio-Sauna, Finnische Sauna, Osmanisches Dampfbad, Tepidarium, Eukalyptus-Grotte, Whirlpool, Hamam, vitale Wasserwelt mit Kaltwasserturm, Eisgrotte oder Floatarium – das Angebot an therapeutischen, kosmetischen und stressreduzierenden Maßnahmen ist riesengroß. Mit der gleichen Liebe zum Detail und Aufmerksamkeit, mit der das neue Spa und die Wasserwelt gestaltet sind, sind auch die Zimmer und Suiten eingerichtet. Jeder Raum ist einzigartig und besitzt seinen eigenen Stil. In allen Räumen gehen Luxus und Komfort, Geräumigkeit und Atmosphäre Hand in Hand, egal ob man lieber im mediterranen, im englischen oder im rustikalen Stil wohnt. Abendlicher Höhepunkt ist das exklusive Fünf-Gänge-Menü aus der Zwei-Hauben-Küche. Einheimische Spezialitäten sind ebenso Highlights der kulinarischen Reise wie internationale Zubereitungen der Spitzengastronomie. Adäquat umschmeichelt werden die feinen Genüsse von formidablen Kreszenzen aus dem hoteleigenen Weinkeller.

Situated in the heart of the sun-drenched Ötztal Vally and located in a spot renowned as a skiing paradise, the Central Spa Hotel Sölden prides itself on offering its visitors exclusive luxury, first-class cuisine, a fairytale-like "Venezia" Water World, and second-to-none pampering in its wellness and beauty oasis. All in all, the new Central Spa Hotel Sölden with its arcades and murals invites you to unwind and relax in an area covering 1,500 square metres. Be it the bio-sauna, Finnish Sauna, Ottoman steam bath, tepidarium, Eucalyptus Grotto, whirlpool, Hamam or its vitality Water World with cold-water tower, Ice Grotto and Floatarium, the hotel offers an incredibly large variety of therapeutic, cosmetic and stress-reducing treatments. And if a great deal of attention has been paid to detail in creating its new Spa and Water World, its rooms and suites boast the same qualities. Every room is unique and individually designed. From luxury and comfort to spaciousness and atmosphere, its rooms have it all in abundance, regardless of whether you want a Mediterranean, English or rustic feel. An exclusive 5-course meal from its 2 Gault-Millau-awarded cuisine forms the highlight of the evening. You can look forward to enjoying local specialties and international dishes of the very highest standard. All enveloped by fine Kreszenzen from the hotel's own wine cellar.

Central Spa Hotel Sölden
Direction: Waschl family
A-6450 Sölden (Ötztal / Tirol)
Phone:
00 43 / 52 54 / 2 26 00
Fax:
00 43 / 52 54 / 2 26 05 11
E-mail:
info@central-soelden.at
Internet:
www.central-soelden.at

120 rooms and suites
from Euro 134 to 314

Distance from airport
Innsbruck: 60 minutes

Membership:
Best Wellness Hotels Austria

Dem Himmel ganz nah ist man im schneesichersten Wintersportort der Alpen, Hochgurgl. Von Mitte November bis in den Mai hinein erlebt man hier zwischen 1800 und 3 080 Metern Skivergnügen pur. Sowohl für die breiten Pisten, für die urigen Hütten, die moderne Ski-Infrastruktur als auch für die Hotellerie gilt: Qualität geht vor Quantität. Den beeindruckenden Beweis dafür tritt das Top Hotel Hochgurgl an. In 2 150 Metern Höhe direkt an der Liftstation Hochgurgl offeriert das höchstgelegene Fünf-Sterne-Hotel der Alpen exklusive Winterfreuden von der ersten bis zur letzten Minute. Alle Wünsche frei hat der Gast bei der Wahl der Zimmer und Suiten. So unterschiedlich ihr Interieur auch ist, zwei Dinge haben sie gemeinsam: viel Platz für Privatsphäre und luxuriösen Fünf-Sterne-Komfort. Nach einem anstrengenden Skitag ist das wohldimensionierte Hotel-Wellnessreich genau die richtige Adresse, um seine strapazierten Muskeln zu pflegen. Daneben sorgen die Expertinnen der Beautyfarm für einen strahlenden Auftritt beim Après-Ski. Nomen est omen! Das gilt im Top Hotel Hochgurgl insbesondere für das Niveau der Kulinarik in den authentischen Tiroler Jagdstuben. Die familiäre Gastlichkeit, ein vorbildlich agierendes Serviceteam und unzählige Details machen das Hochgurgler Winterglück perfekt.

Just imagine enjoying some of the finest skiing conditions that the Alpine region has to offer in Hochgurgl. From mid November until well into May, you can look forward to enjoying unadulterated thrills and excitement from 1,800 to 3,038 metres. Whether it's the wide pistes, its wonderfully cosy lodges, its modern skiing infrastructure or its hotels, here quality comes before quantity. And nowhere else is this more evident than the Top Hotel Hochgurgl. Located at 2,150 metres and situated right next to the Hochgurgl ski lifts, the Alpine region's highest 5-star hotel offers unadulterated winter luxury from beginning to end. It also offers guests a variety of room and suites to meet every taste. As different as the interior designs of the rooms might be, however, they all have two things in common: plenty of room for privacy and luxurious five-star refinement. And after working hard on the slopes what could be better than to relax in the hotel's generously proportioned wellness facilities and give your tired muscles some tender loving care. There are also beauty farm professionals on hand to make sure that you look your very best for the après-ski. Nomen est omen! Indeed, this is especially true of hotel's very high standard cuisine in its authentic Tyrolean hunting lodges. Its warm hospitality, its exemplary service team and numerous other delightful features all conspire to make Hochgurgl your very own winter wonderland.

Top Hotel Hochgurgl
Owner: Scheiber family
General Manager:
Daniel Vogler
A-6456 Hochgurgl, Ötztal /
Tirol, Austria
Phone: 00 43 / 52 56 / 62 65
Fax: 00 43 / 52 56 / 62 65 10
E-mail:
tophotel@hochgurgl.com
Internet:
www.tophotelhochgurgl.com

28 rooms and 36 suites
Double rooms from Euro 113,
suites from Euro 198,
Presidential Suite from
Euro 430 (rates depending on
season incl. breakfast)

Distance from airport:
Innsbruck 100 km

Membership:
Relais & Châteaux

THURNHERS ALPENHOF, ZÜRS/ARLBERG

FACILITIES

Inmitten der atemberaubenden Schönheit der Arlberger Bergwelt im mondänen Wintersportort Zürs finden anspruchsvolle Traveller alles, was ein weißes Urlaubsglück perfekt macht: Schneesicherheit von Ende November bis Ende April, traumhafte Abfahrtmöglichkeiten in Höhen zwischen 1450 und 2800 Metern, eine exklusive Gastronomie und – nur ein paar Schritte vom Lift und der Zürser Skischule entfernt – dieses charmante Fünf-Sterne-Refugium, eine der ersten Adressen im alpenländischen Raum. Hochkarätige Auszeichnungen wie der schon mehrfach verliehene „Five-Star Diamond Award" der American Academy of Hospitality Sciences und zahlreiche Stammgäste sind eine Bestätigung dafür, dass die besondere Servicebereitschaft der Mitarbeiter und die persönliche Ansprache durch die Gastgeberfamilie besonders geschätzt werden. Die komfortablen Zimmer und Suiten, die teilweise mit eigener Whirlpoolwanne oder offenem Kamin ausgestattet sind, bieten für jeden Geschmack genau das Richtige, mal mediterran inspiriert, mal zurückhaltend-elegant, mal romantisch-verspielt. Neben dem überaus luxuriös behaglichen Ambiente, einem vorbildlichen Service und einem traumhaften Skigebiet am Arlberg sorgt die hervorragende Gastronomie dafür, dass in Thurnhers Alpenhof weiße Urlaubsträume in Erfüllung gehen.

The Thurnhers Alpenhof, a member of the Leading Hotels of the World, is a luxurious hotel surrounded by beautiful mountain scenery and located in one of the most prestigious European ski domains. It has received first-class distinctions such as the "Five-Star Diamond Award", granted on several occasions by the American Academy of Hospitality Sciences. You need look no further than to the many loyal customers as proof of the special service provided by the staff and the personal welcome given by the hosts. The comfortable rooms and suites, with optional private whirlpool bath or open fireplace, can perfectly accommodate all tastes, whether you are looking for a Mediterranean feeling, traditional reserve and elegance or a romantic ambience. The hotel successfully combines modern comfort and alpine charm to create an elegant yet cosy mountain hideaway. The famous Thurnhers Alpenhof restaurant serves exquisite culinary delights enabling you to sample local specialities or gourmet cuisine. Ski from the doorstep of the hotel and take advantage of the ski guide who will show you the quietest pistes, the most enchanting scenery and the best mountain restaurants.

Thurnhers Alpenhof
Owner: Elfi Thurnher
and Dr. Beatrice Zarges-Thurnher
A-6763 Zürs / Arlberg
Phone: 00 43 / 55 83 / 21 91
Fax:　　00 43 / 55 83 / 33 30
E-mail: mail@thurnhers-alpenhof.com
Internet: www.thurnhers-alpenhof.com

13 rooms and 26 suites
Double rooms from Euro 510,
Junior Suites from Euro 580,
Suites from Euro 720 (all prices per room/per night) inclusive: Gourmet-breakfast-buffet, afternoon snack, exquisite 5–8 courses dinner in the gourmet restaurant, service, VAT, taxes. Activities with ski instructor.

Distance from airport:
Innsbruck, Friedrichshafen –
100 km, Zürich – 220 km.
A private transfer by taxi, helicopter or Maybach limousine which will ensure your save arrival at Thurnhers Alpenhof can be arranged

Membership: The Leading Hotels of the World

Das im Herzen von Ischgl, direkt an der Ski-Talabfahrt und nur einen Katzensprung von der Silvretta-Bahn zur Idalp, gelegene Fünf-Sterne-Domizil zählt zu den führenden Hotels im gesamten Alpenraum. Vielfach schon wurde das Trofana Royal der Familie von der Thannen für seine hohe Qualität von internationalen Magazinen ausgezeichnet. Die engagierten Gastgeber haben das Haus zu einem einzigartigen Gourmet- und Relaxtempel, zu einem Wellness-, Fitness-, Beauty- und Gesundheitsresort etabliert. Tirolerische Handwerkskunst, stilvolle Eleganz und First-Class-Service geben sich hier ein gelungenes Stelldichein. Die 82 Zimmer und Suiten sind einheitlich besonders hochwertig ausgestattet und vermitteln höchsten Wohnkomfort. Martin Sieberers berühmte 3-Hauben- und 1-Michelin-Stern-Küche ist ein Versprechen für tägliche kulinarische Hochgenüsse und wird harmonisch umrahmt von 5-Sterne-Service, erlesenen Weinen, sorgfältig gewählten Edeldestillaten sowie einem exklusiven Zigarrensortiment. Im „Royal" erwarten den Gast klassische Beauty- und Wellnessangebote und viele alternative Methoden. Von Reiki, Massagen über die 5 Tibeter, Qi Gong bis hin zu Anti-Aging-Konzepten und Royal-Med reicht der Reigen der attraktiven Angebote rund um Schönheit und gesundes Wohlbefinden.

This five star domicile, located in the heart of Ischgl at the edge of the downhill ski slopes and just a stones throw from the Silvretta way to Idalp is one of the leading hotels in the entire alpine region. The Trofana Royal, belonging to the von der Thannen family has already received many awards from international magazines for its high quality. The highly motivated hoteliers have turned the facility into a unique temple of relaxation and gourmet pleasure and have thus established a resort for wellness, fitness, beauty and health. Tyrolean craftsmanship, stylish elegance and first class service all combine to create the perfect place to come together. The 82 rooms and suites are uniformly decorated to the highest level and offer the best comforts. Martin Sieberer's famous restaurant boasts three Gault Millau toques and one Michelin star. It promises daily culinary delights rounded off by five star service, select wines, carefully chosen liquors of the highest quality and an exclusive range of cigars. Guests are treated to classical wellness and beauty treatments as well as many alternative practices in the "Royal". Reiki, massage, 5 Tibetans, Qi Gong, anti-aging concepts and Royal-Med are some of the services on offer for the enhancement of beauty and the natural "feel good" factor.

Trofana Royal
Gourmet- & Relaxhotel
Owner:
von der Thannen family
A-6561 Ischgl / Tirol
Phone: 00 43 / 54 44 / 6 00
Fax: 00 43 / 54 44 / 6 00 90
E-mail: office@trofana.at
Internet: www.trofana:at

82 rooms and suites
from Euro 150 to 380

Distance from airport:
60 minutes

Membership:
Premier Hotels & Resorts

Märchenhaft klingt der Name des rosaroten Luxushotels im Tannheimer Tal, das die Gastgeberfamilie Huber seit den 70er Jahren mit visionären Ideen zu einem einzigartigen Relax- und Genussrefugium inszeniert hat: 101 äußerst großzügig gestaltete und mit traumhaftem Komfort ausgestattete Zimmer, Junior-Suiten und Luxus-Suiten, verteilt auf drei miteinander verbundene Häuser. Jedes Zimmer und jede Suite widmet sich einem anderen Wohnthema. Überdurchschnittlich einfallsreich präsentiert sich die Gastronomie mit dem Restaurant „Via-Mala", das einem rätoromanischen Bergdorf originalgetreu nachempfunden wurde. Im Rahmen der Rund-um-die-Uhr-Gourmetpension „Lukullus" wählen die Gäste außerdem zwischen dem Grillrestaurant „Loch Ness" sowie der Haubenküche des „La Cascata nobile". Das bayerische Schloss Neuschwanstein stand Pate, als im Februar 2003 das grandiose Cinderella Castle eröffnet wurde – ein Wellnesstempel wie im Märchen, dessen Angebote von den verschiedensten Saunen und Dampfbädern über Thalassoanwendungen und Ayurvedakuren bis hin zu den umfangreichen Programmen des Beautysalons und Vitaltempels reichen. Weltweit einzigartig: der ganzjährig beheizte Außenpool mit Energiewasser.

The name of the pink-coloured, luxury hotel in Tannheimer Valley ("Lovely Red Flüh") sounds like something out of a fairytale. Here the Huber family, with visionary ideas, has created a unique place of relaxation and pleasure. There are 101 extremely large rooms, junior suites and luxury suites spread over three connected buildings, all offering fantastic comfort. Each room and suite is dedicated to an individual theme. The "Via-Mala" Restaurant was built as an exact replica of a Rhaetian mountain village and is well known for its above average gastronomic creativity. In the gourmet restaurant "Lukullus", which is open 24 hours a day, guests can choose between the prize-winning cuisine of the "La Cascata nobile" restaurant and barbequed food at "Loch Ness". The Bavarian castle Neuschwanstein was the inspiration for the fabulous Cinderella Castle, a fairy tale wellness temple built in 2003 where you can use different saunas and steam baths, receive Thalasso and Ayurveda treatments, as well as a broad range of programmes from the Beauty Salon and Vitality Temple. One special feature you won't find anywhere else in the world is the outdoor pool containing energy water and heated all year round

Liebes Rot-Flüh
General Management:
Huber family
Seestraße 26
A-6673 Haldensee / Tirol
Phone: 00 43 / 56 75 / 64 31
Fax: 00 43 / 56 75 / 64 31 46
E-mail:
traumhotel@rothflueh.com
Internet:
www.rotflueh.com

101 rooms, junior suites and luxury suites depending on category and saison from Euro 115 to 329 per person, including "Lukullus" gourmetboard

Distance from airport:
Innsbruck Airport 105 km,
Munich Airport 195 km,
Zurich Airport 220 km

In der einst so riesigen österreichisch-ungarischen Monarchie gab es nur eine Herberge, wo gekrönte Häupter zu residieren pflegten: das „Imperial" am Kärntner Ring. Erbaut wurde es 1863 als herrschaftliches Privatpalais des Fürsten Württemberg und anlässlich der Weltausstellung 1873 in das Hotel Imperial umgewandelt. Seitdem gingen hier offizielle Staatsgäste ein und aus, wie Otto von Bismarck als Gast Kaiser Franz Josef I. Eine Tradition, die das Hotel zu einem Stück Wiener Geschichte gemacht hat. Und das nicht nur, weil Staatsmänner hier ein und aus gingen, sondern weil die unvergleichliche Melange aus herrschaftlichem Ambiente und Wiener Charme viele große Namen in ihren Bann zog. Und daran hat sich in all den Jahrzehnten nichts geändert. Gekrönte und ungekrönte Häupter treffen sich bis heute in dem prächtigen Deluxe-Hotel. Doch von den technischen Finessen, den luxuriösen Marmorbädern, dem Fitnessstudio mit Sauna oder einer eigenen Terrasse hätten selbst Gäste wie Richard Wagner oder Thomas Mann nicht einmal zu träumen gewagt. Das „Imperial" führte auch als erstes Haus im deutschsprachigen Raum den Butlerservice ein. Besondere Wohn-Highlights sind die Maisonette-Suiten und natürlich die Royal Suiten auf der Beletage, welche zusammen eine wahrhaft kaiserliche Residenz auf über 500 Quadratmetern bieten. Wie in allen Zimmern und Suiten fügen sich modernste Technik und internationale Sicherheitseinrichtungen harmonisch in die Möblierung und Dekorationselemente der Zimmer im kaiserlichen Stile ein.

In the days when the Austro-Hungarian monarchy reigned supreme, only one establishment was good enough for royalty, the Imperial on the Viennese Kärntner Ring. It was built in 1863 as a stately home for the Prince of Württemberg and transformed into the Hotel Imperial to mark the World Fair in 1873. Official state guests such as Otto von Bismarck, who was the guest of Kaiser Franz Josef I, have been gracing the establishment ever since and have helped to establish the hotel as part of Vienna's history. And not only because it has been frequented by statesmen, but also because it manages to combine its stately atmosphere with the charm of Vienna. Indeed, a large number of prominent names have been captivated by its special character. And over the decades nothing has changed. Crowned and uncrowned heads of state still meet up in this magnificent deluxe hotel. Yet even prominent guests of the past such as Richard Wagner or Thomas Mann could hardly have imagined the technological advances, the luxurious marble bathrooms, the gym with sauna and your own patio available today. The "Imperial" was the first German-speaking hotel to introduce a butler service. The most exclusive accommodation on offer is the Maisonette Suites and the Royal Suites on the first floor, which offer a truly royal residence covering 500 sq. metres. All its rooms feature the very latest technology and international security facilities. These have been tastefully blended in to match the furnishings and decorations in rooms that are fit for royalty.

Hotel Imperial
General Manager:
Thomas Schön
Kärntner Ring 16
A-1015 Wien
Phone:
00 43 / (1) / 5 01 10-0
Fax:
00 43 / (1) / 5 01 10-4 10
E-mail: hotel.imperial@ luxurycollection.com
Internet: www.luxury-collection.com/imperial

138 rooms and suites
Double rooms from Euro 563
Suites from Euro 972 to 4,815

Distance from airport:
15 minutes

Memberships:
The Luxury Collection,
Starwood Hotels & Resorts

Das Palais Coburg im Herzen Wiens ist das derzeit spektakulärste Ereignis der österreichischen Hotelszene, ein aufsehenerregendes Highlight zugleich auf dem europäischen Luxuslevel. Brillant ausgelegt das Spannungsfeld zwischen historischer Bausubstanz, modernem Design und visionärer Technik. Kernstück ist das prachtvoll restaurierte ehemalige Palais der herzoglichen Familie von Sachsen-Coburg und Gotha. Generös der Raum, der den Gästen zur Verfügung steht. Sie wohnen in nicht mehr als 35 Suiten (Zimmer sind nicht vorhanden) in der Größe zwischen 65 und 165 m², welche sich meist über zwei Geschosse erstrecken, allesamt individuell eingerichtet, keine gleicht der anderen. Egal ob City Suiten mit Blick zur Innenstadt, Palais Suiten mit Blick auf Stadtpark und Ringstraße (darunter die drei Imperialen Palais Suiten welche die oberste Kategorie bilden) oder moderne Suiten wie zum Beispiel das Loft, exklusivste Ausstattungen zeigen sie alle. Sensationell der Veranstaltungsbereich von den historischen Prunkräumen zu den einzigartigen Kasematten, den ehemaligen Befestigungsanlagen der Stadt Wien. Auf Spitzenniveau bewegt man sich auch im Gourmetbereich des Palais Coburg mit Sternekoch Christian Petz und Sommelier Karl Seiser, der für das Weinarchiv mit dem besten Keller Europas verantwortlich zeichnet. Außergewöhnlich auch die Leitung des Hauses mit den beiden Geschäftsführern Johann A. Sommerer und Jan Hendrik van Dillen, die den Servicelevel innerhalb kürzester Zeit auf höchstes Niveau brachten.

Located in the heart of Vienna, the Palais Coburg is a spectacular residence commanding a position at the very top of Austria's and, indeed, Europe's list of fine luxury hotels. It strikes a wonderful balance between historical architecture, modern design and cutting-edge technology. Piéce de résistance is the magnificently renovated Palais, which formally belonged to the ducal family of Sachsen-Coburg and Gotha. The amount of space available to guests is very generous indeed. The hotel has 35 suites (there are no rooms) offering between 65 and 165 m² of space. Most suites have two floors, they all individually furnished and no two suites are the same. Regardless of whether it's a City Suite with views of the city centre, a Palais Suite with views of the circular road and city park (this category includes its three highest-standard Imperial Suites) or one of its modern suites such as the Loft, they are all finished to the most exclusive of standards. Its events facilities are absolutely sensational. From its magnificent historical rooms to its unique casemates, which were formally part of Vienna's city defences. With its Star Chef Christian Petz and its expert Sommelier Karl Seiser, who is responsible for Europe's very best wine cellar, the Palais Coburg is also one of the very finest culinary addresses. Even the way in which the hotel is managed is remarkable, having two Directors, Johann A. Sommerer and Jan Hendrik van Dillen, who have managed to bring its standard of service up to the very highest within an incredibly short period of time.

Palais Coburg
Hotel Directors:
Jan Hendrik van Dillen,
Johann A. Sommerer
Coburgbastei 4, A-1010 Wien
Phone: 00 43 / 1 / 51 81 80
Fax: 00 43 / 1 / 51 81 81
E-mail: hotel.residenz@
palais-coburg.com
Internet:
www.palais-coburg.com

35 suites
City Suites from Euro 460 to
730, Modern Suites from
Euro 810 to 1,430, Palais
Suites from Euro 840 to
1,890, Imperial Suites from
Euro 1,760 to 1,920

Distance from airport:
45 minutes

Membership:
Relais & Châteaux

Es gibt sie noch ... die kleinen Fluchten für Städter, für Gourmets, Golfer, Skifahrer, für Gäste, die das Besondere suchen. Schloss Prielau mit Hotel und Restaurants ist ein Kleinod ganz besonderer Art. Ein intimes Hotel der Luxusklasse mit Antiquitäten, Kachelöfen und Holzvertäfelungen, aber auch dem modernen Komfort eines internationalen Domizils. Umgeben von einem großen Park mit uralten Bäumen, eigener Rotwildzucht und Fischteichen wirkt dieses Schloss wie ein Märchen aus alten Zeiten. Zwei Restaurants bieten die Gastgeber an: die Schlossküche mit österreichischen Spezialitäten und hausgemachtem Kuchen tagsüber. Am Abend wird die hohe Kunst der Küche im „Mayer's" zelebriert. Ausgezeichnet mit einem Michelin-Stern und Chef eines der Top-Ten-Restaurants in Österreich, hat sich Andreas Mayer rasch einen festen Platz im Herzen seiner Gäste erkocht. Die 6 Doppel- und 2 Einzelzimmer sind liebevoll eingerichtet. In der ersten Etage die Hugo-von-Hofmannsthal-Suite mit eleganten Bädern und Antiquitäten auf über 250 Quadratmetern. Ergänzt wird das Wohlfühlangebot durch das Badehaus mit Sauna, Dampfbad und Massagen, im Sommer mit dem Privatstrand am 200 Meter entfernten See. Zell am See bietet zwei 18-Loch-Golfplätze. Gäste Schloss Prielaus erhalten 30 % Ermäßigung auf das Green und beste Abschlagzeiten. Im Winter lädt die Europa-Sportregion mit Schmittenhöhe, Kitzsteinhorn und den Skigebieten Saalbach-Hinterglemm und Leogang zum Skivergnügen.

They still exist ... the little places for city people to escape to, for gourmets, golfers and skiers. In short, for guests who are looking for something special and in this sense Schloss Prielau is a very special treasure. This is an intimate hotel of the luxurious kind with antiques, tiled ovens and wood panelling. However it is also the modern comfort of an international domicile that makes Schloss Prielau unique. Surrounded by large grounds with ancient trees, fishponds, and a herd of red deer bred on the estate, this castle feels as if it belongs in a medieval fairy tale. Two restaurants will appeal to the palate of the guests: the castle's own restaurant for Austrian specialities and home-baked cakes during the day. In the evening the high art of fine dining is celebrated in "Mayer's". Conferred with a Michelin star and as the chef of one of Austria's top ten restaurants, Andreas Mayer has cooked his way into hearts of his guests in a very short period of time. With regard to accommodation, the six double and single rooms have been lovingly decorated. On the first floor there is the Hugo-von-Hofmannsthal-Suite with its elegant bathrooms and antique furniture in an area of 250 square metres. The "feel good" factor is enhanced by the spa with sauna, steam bath and massage, not to mention the private beach and lake just 200 metres away from the hotel for use in the summertime. In Zell am See there are two 18-hole golf courses. There, the guests of Schloss Prielau receive a 30 % reduction off green fees and are given the best times for teeing off. In winter the local area is famous for winter sports.

Hotel Restaurant
Schloss Prielau
Owner: Anette Müller
and Andreas Mayer
A-5700 Zell am See
Phone:
00 43 / 65 42 / 72 91 10
Fax:
00 43 / 65 42 / 7 29 11 11
E-mail:
info@schloss-prielau.at
Internet:
www.schloss-prielau.at

6 double rooms
and 2 single rooms:
double room Euro 110,
single room Euro 130,
suite (2 double rooms and
1 single room) Euro 620,
rates per day / per person
incl. breakfast

Distance from airport:
60 minutes

Wildromantische Bergszenerien, idyllische Parkanlagen, ein Schloss, umweht von seiner 900 Jahre alten Geschichte und verwandelt in eine Fünf-Sterne-Residenz mit bezaubernden Atmosphären, das ist Hotel Schloss Pichlarn – und noch vieles mehr. Gäste erleben die naturverwöhnte First-Class-Adresse in der Steiermark als ein Refugium mit vielen Facetten, als eine stilvolle Zuflucht, die ihre traumhafte Lage im Ennstal harmonisch mit reizvollen Urlaubsangeboten verbindet. Wie schön, hier zu wandern, zu Fuß oder mit dem Fahrrad, und danach erlesene Wohnambiancen zu genießen, von den komfortablen Doppelzimmern bis zu den luxuriösen Golf-, Turm- oder Schlosssuiten; eine Küche, die – vielfach ausgezeichnet – Genießer nicht nur mit kulinarischer Qualität verwöhnt, sondern auch mit kultiviertem Ambiente, mit behaglicher Ländlichkeit hier, mit historischer Festlichkeit dort, ganz nach Raum und Anlass. Golfer finden eine der schönsten Meisterschaftsanlagen Europas direkt vorm Haus, malerisch ins Landschaftsbild gefügt; Wellnessfans ein Beauty- und Regenerationsangebot von Ayurveda bis Anti-Aging, und das alles, auch die perfekten Meeting- und Kongressfaszilitäten, präsentiert man mit einer Gastlichkeit, deren Wärme spürbar von Herzen kommt.

Think of an incredibly romantic mountain setting, idyllic gardens and a château, which, with its 900-year-old history, has been transformed into a five-star residence with a really special atmosphere and what you have is Hotel Schloss Pichlarn. Nestled in a wonderful country location, this first-class hotel in the Steiermark region offers its guests supreme variety and all the ingredients for combining its impossibly beautiful location in Ennstal with a large number of exciting holiday activities. Just imagine hiking or mountain biking in this breathtakingly beautiful region before returning to enjoy all of the hotel's fine elegance. And then there are its well-appointed double rooms and its luxurious Golf, Tower and Schloss Suites and its award-winning cuisine, which, as well as offering connoisseurs the very best in gourmet food also boasts a very cultivated setting. Indeed, whether it's something cosy and rustic you're looking for or whether you're looking for something a little more traditional with atmosphere, you will find it all here. And if golf is your passion, you can look forward to finding one of Europe's most beautiful championship courses right in front of the hotel. And when it comes to wellness facilities, the hotel offers a range of beauty and regeneration treatments from Ayurveda to anti-aging, which, along with the perfect meeting and congress facilities and everything else in the hotel, are served with a genuine sense of hospitality that comes right from the heart.

Hotel Schloss Pichlarn
Host: Frenzel family
A-8952 Irdning / Steiermark
Phone: 00 43 / 36 82 / 22 84 10
Fax: 00 43 / 36 82 / 22 84 16
E-mail:
reservierung@pichlarn.at
Internet:
www.pichlarn.at

Rooms from Euro 113 to 345

Distance from
Salzburg / Maxglan airport:
130 kilometre,
helicopter service

HOTEL SCHLOSS SEEFELS, PÖRTSCHACH/WÖRTHERSEE

In privilegierter Lage direkt am malerischen Wörthersee eröffnet sich dem Schloss-Connaisseur ein europäisches Spitzenhotel, das wahren Lebens-Genuss verspricht und feinste Facetten eines stimmungsvollen Aufenthaltes ganzjährig erlebbar macht. Wer im Hotel Schloss Seefels logiert, der ist den kulinarischen Genüssen, der legendären Gastfreundschaft eines Relais & Châteaux-Hotels und grenzenlosem Golfvergnügen ein Stück näher gerückt, Kärntner Lebensart ebenso wie stilvoller Wohnkultur. Dem anspruchsvollen Gast vermitteln die 71 großzügigen Zimmer und Suiten Luxus und Behaglichkeit in höchstem Maße. Einen entscheidenden Beitrag zum Rundum-Wohlgefühl leistet auch die feine Cuisine. Im Hauben-Restaurant „La Terrasse" läuft die Küchen-Crew allabendlich zur Höchstform auf, um ihre Gäste bei Kerzenschein und Seeblick mit neuen lukullischen Hochgenüssen zu begeistern. Neben dem kulinarischen Herzstück hat der Feinschmecker noch die Wahl zwischen den Restaurants „Orangerie" mit internationaler Küche und dem Strandrestaurant „Porto Bello". Im 1100 Quadratmeter großen Seefels Felsen Spa rückt der Alltag rasch in weite Ferne. Nicht nur die hoteleigene Marina macht das Hotel Schloss Seefels zu einer begehrten Adresse: Liebhaber des Golfsportes haben die Auswahl zwischen acht hochklassigen Golfplätzen und Tennisspieler bevorzugen die drei hoteleigenen Sand-Tennisplätze.

At an exclusive location directly on Lake Wörth, castle connoisseurs can enjoy a top European hotel offering the good things in life and a pleasurable stay right down to the finest nuance, twelve months of the year. Those choosing a stay at Hotel Schloss Seefels will certainly be closer to their goal of partaking of the culinary pleasure and famous hospitality of a "Relais & Châteaux" hotel, along with limitless golfing opportunities, Carinthian savoir-vivre and stylish living. The ultimate in luxury and easy comfort is afforded even the most discerning guest by the 71 generously-proportioned rooms and suites. The fine cuisine is also pivotal in generating an all-round feeling of well-being. In the Gault Millau "La Terrasse" restaurant, the culinary team gives their all every single evening to bowl the guests over with new Epicurean delights to be enjoyed along with candlelight and a view over the lake. The culinary centrepiece apart, gourmets can also choose from the "Orangerie" restaurant, offering international cuisine, and the "Porto Bello" beach restaurant. At the 1,100 square metres "Felsen Spa", everyday problems quickly disappear. And not only does the hotel's private marina makes the Hotel Schloss Seefels a sought-after address, but golf lovers too can choose from eight top-class golf courses, while tennis enthusiasts can avail themselves of the hotel's three sand tennis courts.

Hotel Schloss Seefels
Director: Egon Haupt
Töschling 1
A-9210 Pörtschach /
Wörthersee
Phone: 00 43 / 42 72 / 23 77
Fax: 00 43 / 42 72 / 37 04
E-mail:
office@seefels.at
Internet:
www.seefels.com

71 rooms and suites
from Euro 100 to 540
per person / day

Distance from airport:
23 kilometre

Membership:
Relais & Châteaux

Auf einem der sieben Hügel, auf denen Lissabon erbaut wurde, erhebt sich das Lapa Quartier, einst bevorzugter Platz der Reichen und Einflussreichen, heute Diplomatenviertel. In einer der prächtigen Villen des Stadtteils empfängt das Hotel Lapa Palace sein internationales Publikum, pflegt die kultivierte Lebensart in einem einzigartigen Ambiente aus Neo-Klassizismus des 18. Jahrhunderts, mediterraner Leichtigkeit und den modernen Annehmlichkeiten unserer Zeit. Das historische Herrenhaus sowie ein Garten- und ein Villenflügel beherbergen insgesamt 109 luxuriöse Zimmer und Suiten. Edelste Materialien wie verschiedenfarbiger Marmor, portugiesische „Azulejo"-Fliesen, unterschiedliche Hölzer, handgearbeiteter Stuck, wertvolle Stoffe von Rubelli und eigens für das Hotel angefertigte Möbel machen den Charme und die Eleganz des Lapa Palace aus. Unterstrichen wird diese Atmosphäre von einem terrassenförmigen Traumgarten mit kleinen Teichen, Wasserspielen, verschlungenen Spazierwegen und einem herrlichen Pool. Höchste Erwartungen erfüllt auch die exzellente Cuisine des „Ristorante Hotel Cipriani", dessen feinste Zubereitungen italienisch-venezianische Tradition mit portugiesischem Einfluss bekunden. Für die nötige Entspannung von Körper und Geist sorgen das Lapa Wellness Center und der Schönheitssalon „La Prairie Art of Beauty".

The Lapa Quarter rises up majestically on one of the seven hills on which Lisbon was founded. Once the favourite place of the rich and influential, it is known today as Lisbon's diplomatic district. In one of its splendid Palaces, the Hotel Lapa Palace welcomes guests from around the world. The Property prides itself on its cultivated lifestyle and offers an ambience that is a special mix between 18th century neo-classicism and Portuguese light-heartedness – all supported by every modern comfort required. The historical stately palace with two new wings presents 109 luxurious rooms and suites. Finest materials such as different coloured marble, Portuguese "Azulejo" tiles, different types of carved wood, handmade plasterwork, rich textiles and specially made furniture are all part of the charm and elegance of the Lapa Palace. Another feature of the special atmosphere here is the terraced, fairytale garden containing little streams, fountains, intertwining paths and a beautiful heated outdoor pool. The highest expectations are fulfilled by the excellent cuisine of the "Ristorante Hotel Cipriani", whose finest dishes testify to an Italian-Venetian tradition with Portuguese influences and suggestions. A visit to the Lapa Wellness Centre and "La Prairie Art of Beauty" Salon will ensure relaxation for body and soul.

Lapa Palace
General Manager:
Sandro Fabris
Rua do Pau de Bandeira n° 4
P-1249-021 Lisboa
Portugal
Phone:
0 03 51 / 21 / 3 94 94 94
Fax:
0 03 51 / 21 / 3 95 06 65
E-mail:
info@lapa-palace.com
Internet:
www.lapa-palace.com

109 guest rooms and suites, all are fully equipped, all with magnificent views over the river Tagus and Lisbon or over the oasis like gardens. Room rates depending on category and season Euro 350 to 2,500 incl. breakfast

Distance from airport:
15 – 20 minutes drive by car

Memberships:
Leading Hotels of the World
Owned by Orient-Express Hotels, Trains and Cruises

Umgeben von einer traumhaften Landschaft und dem idyllischen Naturschutzgebiet der Ria Formosa liegt das Hotel Quinta do Lago in einem der größten Golfresorts Europas mit 72 Löchern auf vier Plätzen. Der Aufenthalt im 5-Sterne-Domizil ist wie der Eintritt in eine Welt voller Luxus und Lebensart. Gediegene Eleganz mischt sich gekonnt mit der Leichtigkeit eines portugiesischen Sommers, mit den fröhlichen Farben südlicher Sphären. Und es sind nicht ausschließlich die Golfer Europas, die sich von dieser Atmosphäre angezogen fühlen. Auch Gourmets, Tennisspieler, Reiter, Naturfreunde, Wassersportfans und andere Sportenthusiasten fühlen sich im Quinta do Lago bestens umsorgt. Das im Stil eines Terrassenhauses konzipierte Gebäude öffnet sich weit zum Garten, der bis zur Lagune des Nationalparks hinunterreicht. Und von fast jedem der 141 Zimmer und Suiten mit allem Komfort genießt man diesen herrlichen Ausblick, der über die Lagune über die weißen Sanddünen bis zu den Fluten des an endlos scheinende Strände brandenden Atlantiks reicht. Zwei Restaurants locken mit hervorragenden Zubereitungen: das Gourmetrestaurant „Cá d'Oro" mit seiner italienischen Cucina – und nicht weniger köstlich sind die internationalen und portugiesischen Gerichte im Restaurant „Brisa do Mar".

Surrounded by a breathtaking scenary and the idyllic Ria Formosa nature reserve, the Hotel Quinta do Lago is situated in one of the biggest golf resorts in Europe with a total of 72 holes in its four courses. A stay at this 5-star establishment means stepping into a world of utter luxury and savoir-vivre. Easy elegance mixes effortlessly with the airiness of a Portuguese summer and the merry colours of the south. And it is other than the European who find the ambience here charming. Gourmets, tennis players, horse-riders, nature lovers, water sports enthusiasts and many others all feel in the best of hands in Quinta do Lago. The building design is that of an apartment house on a terraced slope, looking far out onto the gardens that stretch all the way down to the National Park's lagoon. Almost every one of the 141 fully-equipped rooms and suites offers this splendid view, stretching across the lagoon and the white sand dunes to the waters of seemingly endless Atlantic breaking against the beaches. Two restaurants beckon with excellent cuisine: the "Cá d'Oro" gourmet restaurant offers Italian delights whilst the dishes served in the "Brisa do Mar" restaurant, Portuguese and international, are equally as delicious.

Quinta do Lago
8135-024 Almancil / Algarve
Portugal
Phone: 0 03 51 / 2 89 / 35 03 50
Fax: 0 03 51 / 2 89 / 39 63 93
E-mail:
info@quintadoloagohotel.com
Internet:
www.quintadolagohotel.com

141 rooms and suites
from Euro 235 to 1,827

Distance from airport:
30 minutes

Membership:
The Leading Hotels
of the World

Es gab eine Zeit, als portugiesische Seefahrer die Welt entdeckten. Jetzt ist es an der Zeit, Portugal zu entdecken – und mit ihm Vila Vita Parc, eine der außergewöhnlichsten und eindrucksvollsten Luxus-Hotelanlagen an der atlantischen Algarve. Insgesamt sechs verschiedene Luxuswohneinheiten mit 182 Zimmern und Suiten sowie zwölf Apartments verteilen sich auf spektakuläre 22 Hektar gestaltete subtropische Parklandschaft. Man sieht die Gebäude kaum zwischen all der herrlichen Vegetation. Jedes Logis hat seine ganz eigenen Reize und Vorzüge, die dem Gast die Wahlmöglichkeit lassen. Sämtliche Interieurs dieses einzigartigen Privathotels wurden von stilsicherer Hand ausgewählt – orientiert an Land und Landschaft, ergänzt durch traditionelle Keramik, kostbare Teppiche und originale Kunstwerke. Feinschmecker werden von der großartigen Restaurantauswahl – dem verwöhnten Publikum stehen bis zu acht Locations zur Wahl – und der Vielfalt auf den Speisekarten hellauf begeistert sein. Kulinarisches Flaggschiff ist das „Ocean-Restaurant" mit feinster Gourmet-Cuisine auf klassischer Basis und mediterranem Touch. Zu den weiteren Highlights von Vila Vita Parc gehören: Vila Vita Vital Beauty- und Gesundheitszentrum, 9-Loch-Pitch-and-Puttig-Golfanlage, Tenniscourts, Gewölbeweinkeller sowie eine 22-Meter-Luxusyacht.

In the bygone era, Portuguese seafarers set out to discover the world. Now it is time to discover Portugal – and on your journey Vila Vita Parc. One of the most distinctive, impressive luxury hotel resorts on the Algarve's steep Atlantic coast. A total of six different luxury residence categories offering 182 rooms and suites and 12 apartments are to be found in this spectacular subtropical landscape, stretching across 22 hectares. The buildings themthelves are hardly noticeable among all the splendid vegetation. Each residence has its very own charm and special merits, so much so that it is sometimes difficult for the guests to choose between them. All the interiors of this unique hotel have been carefully selected by experts in matters of style. They reflect the country and its landscape and are complemented by traditional ceramics, sumptuous carpets and original works of art. Gourmets will be utterly inspired by the fabulous selection of restaurants and the range of Epicurean offerings, with eight possible eateries to choose from. The culinary flagship is the "Ocean Restaurant" with the finest traditional gourmet delights with the Mediterranean accent. Other high points of any sojourn at Vila Vita are: the Vila Vita Vital Beauty and Health Centre, 9-hole pitch & putting green, tennis courts, Cave de Vinhos and a luxury 22-metre yacht.

Vila Vita Parc
General Manager:
Rüdiger C. Hollweg
Alporchinhos
P-8400-450 Porches
Algarve / Portugal
Phone: 0 03 51 / 2 82 / 31 01 00
Fax: 0 03 51 / 2 82 / 32 03 33
E-mail: reservas@
vilavitaparc.com
Internet: www.vilavita.com
vilavitahotels.com

182 rooms, suites and apartments in six different, luxurious, individually-designed complexes. Depending on chosen accommodation and saison from Euro 134 to 1,449 per room per night including breakfast

Distance from airport:
35 minutes drive by car

Membership:
The Leading Hotels
of the World

Die portugiesische Felsalgarve gehört zu den faszinierendsten Küsten Europas. 140 weiße Sandstrände und rund dreitausend Sonnenstunden pro Jahr prägen diese attraktive Urlaubs- und Golfregion. Nur sechs Kilometer westlich von der Touristenhochburg Albufeira thront die romantische Vila Joya über den malerischen Stränden der Praia de Galé. Dieses Luxusrefugium im maurischen Stil mit elegantem Ambiente verwöhnt seine Gäste mit exquisiter Gourmetküche, die mit zwei Michelin-Sternen ausgezeichnet ist. Vom ersten Augenblick an spürt man hier die Zwanglosigkeit, die diesen wundervollen Palazzo umfängt. „Zu Hause bei Freunden", lautet denn auch die Philosophie des privat geführten Domizils. Bei nur zwölf Zimmern und fünf Suiten (alle natürlich mit Meerblick) bleibt eine familiäre Atmosphäre natürlich auch nicht aus. Die Interieurs werden geprägt durch liebevoll zusammengetragene Details, durch feinste Stoffe und High-Tech-Komfort wie Stereoanlagen von Bang & Olufsen und luxuriöse Bäder, wunderschön gefliest mit original portugiesischen „Azulejos". Der weitläufige Swimmingpool wird umgeben von einem wahren Garten Eden mit unzähligen Bougainvilleen, Hibiskus und vielem mehr. Ganz neu ist die geschmackvolle Wellnessabteilung.

The Portuguese rocky coast of Algarve belongs to one of Europe's most fascinating coasts. This attractive holiday- and golfing region is characterized by 140 sandy beaches and three-thousand hours of sunshine every year. Only six kilometres west of the lively tourist centre of Albufeira, enthroned over the picturesque beaches of the Praia de Galé, lies the romantic Vila Joya, a Moorish-style private luxury refuge with an elegant ambience and exquisite gourmet cuisine which has been awarded two Michelin stars. From the beginning you can feel the informality which surrounds this wonderful domicile. It is like being at home with friends. With only 12 rooms and five suites (all of course with sea view) a familiar atmosphere is also not absent. The fact, why all the guests feel so at ease here, is about the tasteful interiors with all the little details put together with great love, the fine fabrics, the pretty cushions, the Bang & Olufsen stereo systems, the wonderful baths tiled with original "Azulejos". The huge swimming-pool is surrounded by a Garden of Eden, a flowering paradise with bougainvilleas, hibiscus and much much more. Brandnew is the wonderful spa- and wellness-area.

Vila Joya
General Manager: Joy Jung
Praia de Galé
P.O. Box 120
P-8200 Albufeira
Portugal
Phone:
0 03 51 / 2 89 / 59 17 95
Fax:
0 03 51 / 2 89 / 59 12 01
Reservation Office Germany:
Phone:
00 49 / 89 / 649 33 37
E-mail: info@vilajoya.de
Internet: www.vilajoya.de

12 Deluxe Rooms,
rates depending on
category and season
from Euro 370 to 580,
5 Suites, rates depending
on category and season
from Euro 510 to 1,030
All prices for two person
including breakfast and
dinner in the two-star-
restaurant

Opening hours restaurant:
daily from
1.00 pm – 3.30 pm and
7.30 pm – 10.00 pm

HOTEL EDEN ROC, ASCONA

Das HOTEL EDEN ROC in traumhafter Lage am Lago Maggiore verfügt über einen Privatstrand, einen eigenen Bootssteg sowie eine wunderschöne Gartenanlage. Bis zur Piazza von Ascona sind es nur wenige Gehminuten. Das luxuriöse Haus wurde von dem herausragenden Tessiner Innenarchitekten Carlo Rampazzi im Stil eines majestätischen Palazzos renoviert. Gäste verfallen leicht dem mediterranen Charme der 82 klimatisierten Deluxe-Zimmer und Deluxe-Suiten, die alle einen atemberaubenden Blick auf den See oder die Berge bieten. Der Wellnessbereich mit Innen- und Außenpool, Sauna, Finarium und Whirlpool sowie das Eden Roc SPA by Clarins mit Coiffeur, Massage, Solarium und vielfältigen Beautyanwendungen sorgen für Erholung und Entspannung. Die hoteleigene Wasserskischule sowie die freie Benutzung der Fahrräder lassen Sportlerherzen höher schlagen. In den drei Restaurants mit großer Sonnenterrasse wird man kulinarisch verwöhnt. Das EDEN ROC Restaurant (14 Punkte Gault Millau) ist bekannt für seine französischen Gaumenfreuden; das Restaurant LA BREZZA BAR & LOUNGE (15 Punkte Gault Millau) begeistert mit seiner kreativ-vielfältigen mediterranen Küche, die auch „Il piacere del Sud" genannt wird; und LA CASETTA, das kleine Paradies direkt am See, bezaubert mit seinem südlichen Charme und frisch zubereiteten Pastagerichten, Grillspezialitäten und Süßspeisen. In der EDEN BAR erlebt man Lifestyle mit Livemusik! Seminar- und Banketträumlichkeiten bis zu 150 Personen stehen das ganze Jahr zur Verfügung.

You will find The HOTEL EDEN ROC in a beautiful place on Lake Maggiore with a private beach and jetty as well as wonderful gardens. It is only a few minutes walk to the Piazza of Ascona. The luxurious stately house was decorated by the excellent Ticino interior designer Carlo Rampazzi in the majestic style of a palazzo. You will soon succumb to the Mediterranean charm of the 82 air-conditioned deluxe rooms and deluxe suites, all of which have a breathtaking view of the lake and the mountain range. The wellness area with indoor and outdoor pool, sauna, dry finish sauna and Jacuzzi as well as the Eden Roc SPA by Clarins with hair styling, massage, solarium and various beauty treatments provide the right ambience for rest and relaxation. The more sporty types will find their pulses racing at sight of the water-ski school and the freely available bicycles. In the three restaurants with large sun terrace you will be spoilt with culinary pleasures. The EDEN ROC Restaurant (14 Gault Millau points) is well known for its French delicacies that delight the palate. The Restaurant LA BREZZA BAR & LOUNGE (15 Gault Millau points) enthuses the guests with its creative Mediterranean cuisine and is also known as "Il piacere del Sud" ("the pleasure of the south"). LA CASETTA, the little paradise on the edge of the lake will put you under its spell with its Italian charm and freshly made pasta dishes, grilled specialities and desserts. In the EDEN BAR you will be entertained by live music. Rooms for seminars and banquets are available for up to 150 people all year round.

Hotel Eden Roc
Director: Daniel J. Ziegler
Via Albarelle 16
CH-6612 Ascona
Phone: 00 41 / 91 / 7 85 71 71
Fax: 00 41 / 91 / 7 85 71 43
E-mail:
info@edenroc.ch
Internet:
www.edenroc.ch

82 rooms and suites – according to season and category at the following rate:
Deluxe double room for single occupancy from Euro 173 to 453, Deluxe double room from Euro 220 to 540, Junior Suites from Euro 480 to 707, Suites from Euro 433 to 893, Deluxe Suites from Euro 940 to 1,327

Distance from airport:
30 minutes

Memberships:
Swiss Deluxe Hotels,
The Leading Small Hotels of the World

GUARDA VAL, LENZERHEIDE

FACILITIES

So ein Romantik Hotel gibt es kein zweites Mal: Guarda Val ist Teil eines Maiensäss. Das ist ein Dorf auf der Schweizer Alp, wo die Bergbauern im Mai hinaufziehen, um über den Sommer das Vieh zu weiden. Ursprünglicher kann man nicht Urlaub machen; und dabei wird man verwöhnt mit allem, was Vier-Sterne-Komfort zu bieten hat. Der Maiensäss Sporz mit dem Romantik Hotel Guarda Val liegt oberhalb von Lenzerheide in Graubünden. Gäste wohnen romantisch in 34 Zimmern, Studios, Appartements und Suiten. Sie verteilen sich auf zehn schön restaurierte, teils bis zu dreihundert Jahre alte Bergbauernhäuser. Reizvoll die Idee für die Interieurs. Hier wohnt man unterm offenen Giebelgebälk, dort in einem ehemaligen Stall, spannend der Kontrast: Viele Einrichtungen sind modern, die Möbel oft Designerstücke. Beispielhaft dafür die beiden Suiten, die Maisonetta mit der Sauna unterm Giebeldach, die Stailetta, zu der sogar ein kleines privates Spa gehört. Ringsherum liegt ein herrliches Wandergebiet, aber manchmal reicht ja auch der kleine Spaziergang ins Haus Rischatsch, es birgt das Gourmetrestaurant (zwei Hauben, 16 Punkte im Gault Millau), oder ins Crap Naros, dort speist man herzhaft schweizerisch. Garant für die ganz persönliche Umsorgung: Besitzer und Direktor Erich Kurzen.

There is no other Romatik Hotel like this. Guarda Val is part of Maiensäss, a village in the Swiss Alps where the alpine farmers go in May every year to let their animals graze during the summer months. A holiday here could not be more rustic and yet you will be spoilt by everything that four star comfort has to offer. The Maiensäss Sporz with the Romantik Hotel Guarda Val lies above Lenzerheide in Graubünden. Guest accommodation is provided in the form of 34 romantic rooms, studios, appartements and suites. They are spread over ten beautifully restored alpine farm houses that are up to 300 years old. The concept for the interieurs is novel. In one room you will sleep under open gable beams, in another you will find yourself in a former stable. The contrast could not be more intriguing. Many furnishings are modern, some of the furniture made by designers. Both suites are examples of this as is the two-storey sauna under the roof – the Stailetta – which even has a small private mineral spring. All around lies a wonderful hill-walking area but sometimes a little walk to Haus Rischatsch is enough; This is a gourmet restaurant with torques and 16 points from the Gault Millau. Alternatively you may like a stroll to Crap Naros. There you can dine in the hearty Swiss tradition. Guarantor of the very individual service is owner and director Erich Kurzen.

Guarda Val
Managing Director
and Owner: Erich Kurzen
CH-7078 Lenzerheide
Phone:
00 41 / (0) 81 / 3 85 85 85
Fax:
00 41 / (0) 81 / 3 85 85 95
E-mail:
hotel@guardaval.ch
Internet:
www.guardaval.ch

32 rooms, 2 suites; single and double rooms according to season from Euro 127 to 220, "Giebelzimmer" and studio from Euro 227 to 254, apartments from Euro 300 to 360, suites from Euro 394 to 934

Distance from Airport:
2 hours

Membership:
Romantik Hotels

Kaum ein Hotel hat eine so begeisterte Fangemeinde – Liebhaber Asconas, die wohl nirgend woanders hinfahren würden, als an diesen Ort des hinreißenden Rundumgenusses. Ein Hideaway im Stil einer romantischen Villa mit südlicher Heiterkeit und umgeben von einem üppigen exotischen Garten. Mit Franz Reichholf führt ein Österreicher eines der schönsten und besten Hotels der Schweiz, der dem Gast das „Wohlfühlen" in all seinen Facetten näherbringt. 54 Zimmer, 16 Suiten und zwei Junior Suiten vermitteln Luxus und höchsten Komfort in südländischem Stil. Der vorbildlichen Gastlichkeit des Hauses entspricht die unkomplizierte mediterrane Frischeküche von Küchenchef Ulf Braunert. Der Gast hat die „kulinarische Freiheit" zwischen dem Gourmetrestaurant Aphrodite, der Osteria Giardino und dem Poolcafé. Entspannung im höchsten Maße verspricht das neue Giardino Spa mit römischem Badetempel und „Giardino di Bellezza". Ob Edelsteinsauna, Smaragd-Dampfbad oder Kräutersauna – auf einer Fläche von dreihundert Quadratmetern sorgt eine Saunawelt auf höchstem Niveau für erholsame Stunden. Ein romantisches Schwimmbad mit großer Liegewiese sowie zwei 18-Loch-Golfplätze bieten weitere Möglichkeiten für sportlich ambitionierte Gäste.

Hardly any other hotel can claim to have a more devoted set of fans. For lovers of Ascona there is only one place to be – this strikingly beautiful location and all the enjoyment it offers. Albergo Giardino is a romantic villa hideaway with southern serenity set in luxuriantly exotic gardens. An Austrian, Franz Reichholf, is responsible for managing one of Switzerland's best and most beautiful hotels. It's a place with only one ambition – to make sure that its guests experience the ultimate in wellbeing. 54 rooms, 16 suites and two Junior Suites offer unadulterated Mediterranean-style luxury, convenience and comfort. Master Chef Ulf Braunert prides himself on serving fresh and uncomplicated Mediterranean cuisine in line with the exemplary hospitality that the hotel offers. As far as the hotel's culinary delights are concerned, guests are free to choose between the Aphrodite gourmet restaurant, the Osteria Giardino and the pool café. The new Giardino Spa with its Roman bathing temple and "Giardino di Bellezza" offers unadulterated relaxation. Be it the precious-stone sauna, emerald steam bath or herb sauna – a generously proportioned 300 square metres sauna area to the highest standards has been designed to provide its guests with hours of relaxation and enjoyment. A romantic swimming pool with a large lawned area and two 18-hole golf courses are also available for the more sporting minded.

Albergo Giardino
Relais & Châteaux
Hotelier: Franz Reichholf
Via Segnale 10
CH-6612 Ascona
Phone: 00 41 / 91 / 7 85 88 88
Fax: 00 41 / 91 / 7 85 88 99
E-mail:
welcome@giardino.ch
Internet:
www.giardino.ch

54 rooms, 16 suites
and 2 junior suites
from Euro 363 to 643

Distance from airport:
Lugano / Agno
45 minutes
Milano / Malpensa
1 hour 30 minutes

Memberships:
Relais & Châteaux,
Swiss Golf Hotels,
Wellness Hotels Schweiz

Lenk ist das südlichste Dorf des Berner Oberlandes und liegt in einem Seitental von Gstaad. Die unberührte Natur dieses einmalig schönen Hochtals auf 1100 Metern, am Fuße des majestätischen Wildstrubels, ist das Ferienparadies par excellence für Naturliebhaber, Famlien, Sportler und Aktive. Der Lenkerhof ist zugleich das neueste und jugendlichste Fünf-Sterne-Hotel der Schweiz. Die Spannung von Nostalgie und Moderne ist allgegenwärtig, Farben und Formen prägen die Kulisse, welche sich stetig wandelt und ändert. Der Lenkerhof versteht sich als ganzheitliches Wellnesshotel, dessen Atmosphäre sich aus Schönheit, Entspannung und Spannung, Ausgewogenheit, Freude, Echtheit und Glücklichsein zusammensetzt. Lockerheit, gemeinsames Erleben, Natürlichkeit und die freundlichen Mitarbeiter lassen bei den Gästen schnell ein Gemeinschaftsgefühl entstehen. Wunderschöne Zimmer und Suiten sind private Oasen des Wohlgefühls, das „7 Sources Beauty & Spa" ist mit seinen 2000 Quadratmetern einer der größten und schönsten Wellness-Tempel der Schweiz. Die speziellen Aveda und Ligne St. Barth Treatments werden zelebriert von hervorragend qualifizierten Kosmetikerinnen und Therapeuten. Die Kulinarik balanciert gekonnt zwischen mediterraner Leichtigkeit, regionalen Schmankeln und ausgewogener Wellnesscuisine – und das auf internationalem Niveau.

Lenk is the most southerly village in the Bern Uplands and is situated in one of the side valleys of Gstaad. The untouched natural environment of this uniquely beautiful valley, lying 1,100 metres high at the foot of the majestic Wildstrubel is a holiday paradise for nature lovers, families, athletes and active people. Lenkerhof is both the newest and most youthful five star hotel in Switzerland. Here nostalgia and modernity, side by side, are everywhere to be seen. Colours and form characterise the backdrop, which adapts and changes constantly. Lenkerhof positions itself as a holistic wellness hotel with an atmosphere influenced by beauty, relaxation, excitement, balance, fun, authenticity and contentment. Friendly staff and the generally relaxed and natural atmosphere quickly lead to a feeling of togetherness among the guests. Beautiful rooms and suites are private oases to make you feel good. The "7 Sources Beauty & Spa" covering 2,000 square metres is one of the largest and loveliest wellness temples in Switzerland. The special Aveda and Ligne St. Barth Treatments are celebrated by excellently qualified beauticians and therapists. There is a culinary programme of light Mediterranean food, tasty regional specialities and balanced health food, at top international level.

Lenkerhof Alpine Resort
General Manager:
Philippe Frutiger
CH-3775 Lenk im Simmertal
Phone:
00 41/ (0) 33/ 7 36 36 36
Fax:
00 41/ (0) 33/ 7 36 36 37
E-mail:
welcome@lenkerhof.ch
Internet:
www.lenkerhof.ch

68 rooms und suites depending on category and saison from Euro 230 to 600 including halfboard and many activities

Distance from airport:
Bern 70 km

Award:
Gala Spa Award 2004

Im Herzen der Schweiz, direkt am Ufer des Vierwaldstättersees und am Fuße der Rigi gelegen, gilt das Park Hotel Vitznau als eines der schönsten Ziele Europas. Seine romantische Architektur und sein diskreter persönlicher Service haben das Hotel berühmt gemacht, ebenso die hervorragende Küche. Mit seiner Gartenterrasse am Seeufer ist das A-la-carte-Restaurant „Quatre Cantons" ein Ort, wo Liebe durch den Magen geht. Für ihre innovativen mediterranen Zubereitungen erhielt die Küche 15 Punkte vom Gault Millau. Komfort und Eleganz erwarten die Gäste in den 103 Zimmern und Suiten, die in sanften Pastellfarben gehalten sind und über geräumige Bäder in weißem und rosafarbenem Marmor verfügen. Ganz auf die Schönheit ihrer Gäste eingestellt sind die Fachfrauen des Beauty-Spas. In sechs privaten, harmonisch gestalteten Behandlungsräumen stehen traditionelle wie moderne Behandlungen auf dem Programm – mit Topprodukten von Kanebo, Clarins und Phytomer. Umfangreiche Sport- und Freizeitmöglichkeiten mit geheiztem Hallen- und Freibad, großer Liegewiese, Fitnessraum, Sauna, Solarium, Dampfbad, zwei Tennisplätzen, Tischtennis, Fahrrädern, Wasserski und Motorbooten runden das hoteleigene Angebot ab.

In the heart of Switzerland, right on the edge of Lake Vierwaldstatter and at the foot of the Rigi Mountain, the Park Hotel Vitznau is considered one of the loveliest hotels in Europe. Its romantic architecture and circumspect personal service have made the hotel renowned. This also applies to the hotel's excellent cuisine. With a garden terrace on the waterfront, the à la carte restaurant "Quatre Cantons" is a place that will win the heart of the most ardent gourmet. Innovative Mediterranean dishes have won the restaurant fifteen points from Gault Millau. Comfort and elegance greet the guests in the 103 rooms and suites that are decorated in pastel colours and contain roomy bathrooms in white and pink marble. Enhancing the attractiveness of the clients is the number one priority of the highly trained beauticians at the Beauty Spa. In six private, harmoniously decorated facilities, both traditional and modern treatments are open to the guests. Only top products such as Kanebo, Clarins and Phytomer are used. An extensive sports and leisure programme is on offer in the hotel. A heated indoor and outdoor pool, a large green area with loungers, a gym, sauna, solarium, steam bath, two tennis courts, table tennis facilities, bicycles, water-skis and motorboats are all available for use by the guests.

Park Hotel Vitznau
Managing Director:
Thomas Kleber
CH-6354 Vitznau / Luzern
Phone:
00 41/ (0) 41 / 3 99 60 60
Fax:
00 41/ (0) 41 / 3 99 60 70
info@parkhotel-vitznau.ch
www.parkhotel-vitznau.ch

103 luxurious rooms and suits, each of the highest standards, depending on category and saison from Euro 253 to 1,200 including breakfast and parking

Distance to airport:
Zurich-Kloten
1 hour drive by car

Memberships:
Swiss Deluxe Hotels,
Preferred Hotels & Resorts Worldwide, Virtuoso,
The Crown Collection

Eingebettet in den größten Hotelpark der Schweiz inmitten der grandiosen Alpenarena von Flims Laax Falera eröffnet sich dem Flimser Gast eine einzigartige, magische Berg-, Natur-, Luxus- und Lichtwelt. Das Park Hotel Waldhaus ist seit jeher geprägt von der Großzügigkeit der Parkanlage mit ihrer reichen Fauna und Flora und von der Eleganz und Grandezza der Belle Epoque. Kombiniert mit der neuen, im Juni 2004 eröffneten Bade- und Wellnesswelt „delight – spa & beauty" lässt das traditionelle und gleichzeitig moderne Hotel Freiheit und Geborgenheit, Raum, Zeit und Ruhe, aber auch Freude und Leichtigkeit aufkommen. Das Hotelensemble besteht aus insgesamt vier Gästehäusern (Grand Hotel Waldhaus, Hotel Belmont, Jugendstil-Villa Silvana und dem Pavillon), die durch ein unterirdisches Tunnelsystem alle miteinander verbunden sind. Insgesamt sechs Restaurants sorgen für eine unübertreffliche kulinarische Auswahl und Abwechslung. Der Gault Millau wählte das Park Hotel Waldhaus zum „Hotel des Jahres 2005". Damit wurde nicht nur die gelungene Gesamterneuerung mit dem extravaganten Wellnesszentrum als Glanzstück ausgezeichnet – gleichzeitig bewerteten die kritischen Tester die mediterrane Küche des Restaurants „La Cena" mit 15 Gault-Millau-Punkten.

The visitor to the largest Hotel Complex in Switzerland in the middle of the great alpine arena of Flims Laax Falera will find a unique and magical world of mountains, nature, luxury and light. Park Hotel Waldhaus has been characterised since time immemorial by the extensiveness of the grounds with its rich fauna and flora and by the elegance and grandeur of "La Belle Epoque". In June 2004 the traditional and yet modern Hotel joined with the newly constructed Bathing and Wellness World "delight spa and beauty" offering the guest a feeling of freedom and security, of space, time and peace as well as a chance to have fun and escape from the demands of everyday life. The Complex consists of a total of four hotel buildings (Grand Hotel Waldhaus, Hotel Belmont, Jugendstil Villa Silvana und the Pavillon) that are interconnected by an underground passage system. Six restaurants provide an unsurpassable choice and variety of culinary delights. The Gault Millau voted the Park Hotel Waldhaus the "Hotel of the Year 2005". Not only was the successful renovation and the extravagant Bathing and Wellness World honourably mentioned, the highly demanding critics also awarded the Mediterranean cuisine of the Restaurant "La Cena" 15 Gault Millau points.

Park Hotel Waldhaus
General Manager:
Ch. and S. Schlosser
CH-7018 Flims Waldhaus
Phone:
00 41 / (0) 81 / 9 28 48 48
Fax:
00 41 / (0) 81 / 9 28 48 58
E-mail:
info@parkhotel-waldhaus.ch
Internet:
www.parkhotel-waldhaus.ch

150 rooms and suites depending on category and saison from Euro 129 to 1,161 including breakfast

Distance from airport:
150 km

Das Victoria-Jungfrau pflegt eine schöne Tradition: Liebenswürdig und charmant werden in Interlaken schon seit 140 Jahren anspruchsvolle Reisende empfangen. Eine Legende der Schweizer Luxushotellerie, die modernsten Komfort mit Tradition und dem Charakter und Charme eines Grandhotels unter dem Dach der fünf Sterne vereint. Verwöhnszenarien der Extraklasse versprechen die 222 Zimmer, darunter 117 Doppelzimmer, 75 Junior Suiten, 20 Suiten, 9 Duplex Suiten und als luxuriöses Highlight die Tower Suite mit Kuppeldach. Dank des Victoria-Jungfrau Spa einem modernen und exklusiv ausgestatteten Health-, Fitness- und Beauty-Center (Clarins) verfügt das Hotel über einen Ort der Entspannung, Schönheit und Fitness. Eine ultimative Oase der Erholung ist das ESPA, das Gäste mit bedürfnisorientierten Programmen aus traditionellen und neuen Behandlungsmethoden in einem ausgesucht ästhetischen Ambiente verwöhnt. Mit Köstlichkeiten aus Küche und Keller verzaubern im Victoria-Jungfrau nicht nur die „Jungfrau Brasserie" mit Schweizer Spezialitäten, das „La Pastateca" mit internationalen Pastagerichten oder das Restaurant „La Terrasse" (16 Gault-Millau-Punkte), das Feinschmeckern mit seiner kalorienbewussten „Spa Cuisine" himmlische Genüsse ohne Reue verspricht.

The Victoria-Jungfrau is still continuing a wonderful tradition today that stretches back 140 years, providing the discerning guest with a warm, charming welcome to Interlaken. This establishment is a legend among Swiss hotels, bringing the ultimate in modern comfort and the tradition, character and charm of a Grand Hotel together under its five-star roof. Indulgence beckons in all of the 222 rooms and suites, comprising 117 double rooms, 75 junior suites, 20 suites and 9 duplex suites, and the crowning glory, the domed Tower Suite. The Victoria-Jungfrau Spa, a modern, exclusively equipped health, fitness and beauty centre, offering Clarins treatments, is a place for relaxation and gaining a sense of wellbeing. The ultimate oasis is the ESPA, where guests are pampered with an individualised programme of both traditional and new treatments, all tailored to their own particular needs and in select, elegant surroundings. Guests will also be bewitched by the fine wine and cuisine offered in the hotel, be it from the "Jungfrau Brasserie", offering Swiss specialities, "La Pastateca" with international pasta dishes, or "La Terrasse" with 16 Gault-Millau points and a low-calorie "spa cuisine" menu for guilt-free gourmet indulgence.

Victoria-Jungfrau
Grand Hotel & Spa
Direction: Rosmarie
and Emanuel Berger
Höheweg 41
CH-3800 Interlaken
Phone:
00 41 / (0) 33 / 8 28 28 28
Fax:
00 41 / (0) 33 / 8 28 28 80
E-mail: interlaken@
victoria-jungfrau.ch
Internet:
www.victoria-jungfrau.ch

117 rooms, 75 Junior Suites,
20 Suites, 9 Duplex Suites,
Tower Suite from Euro 293
to 1,463

Distance from Zurich airport:
2 hours
Distance from Bern airport:
45 minutes

Membership:
The Leading Hotels
of the World

Die ehemalige Ölmühle Ca's Xorc ist heute wohl einer der reizvollsten Zufluchtsorte in der Tramuntana, abgelegen von jedem Verkehr, keine touristische Atmosphäre dringt hier herauf, weit und breit nur Natur: idyllische Gärten, endlose Olivenhaine, ein Panorama über die Bergwelt bis hinab ins Tal von Sóller und zum Meer. Für das „Agroturismo"-Hotel Ca's Xorc wurden zwei Fincas, 250 bzw. 150 Jahre alt, behutsam restauriert und miteinander verbunden. Das ergab eine Wohnlandschaft, die nicht nur Platz für zwölf schmucke, von der Klimaanlage bis zum Internet-Anschluss topkomfortable Zimmer hat, sondern auch für viele charmante Ecken, Winkel und Patios – ideal, um sich zurückzuziehen oder zusammenzufinden, fürs Gespräch, zum Arbeiten, zum Träumen. Idyllisch die Gärten, schön angelegt der Überlaufpool, man schwimmt buchstäblich ins Tal hinaus. Über der Kaskade ein Jacuzzi: vor diesem Bergpanorama wirklich kein alltägliches Angebot. Fein die Cuisine: Küchenchef Victor Garcia (28) hat bei Gourmets mit ambitionierten mediterranen Menüs Erfolg. Schön aber auch, dass er in seiner Crew einen Kollegen wie Jaime Butanó hat: Die Paellas von Jaime sind nicht zu schlagen.

The former oil mill Ca's Xorc is one of the most attractive places to escape to in the Tramuntana, far away from the hubbub of daily life. This is not the normal tourist fare. From this hotel, nature unfolds far and wide with idyllic gardens, endless olive groves, a mountain panorama extending down into the valley of Sóller and in the distance you can even see the sea. Under the heading of "Agrotourism" Ca's Xorc comprises of two Fincas, 250 and 150 years old that have been carefully restored and joined together. The living space offers not only twelve chic rooms with every top comfort from air-conditioning to internet connections but also many corners, bends and patios; ideal places to be alone or to meet, to converse, to work or to dream. The gardens are idyllic, the waterfall pool is beautifully conceived allowing you to swim literally down into the valley. Above the waterfall is a Jacuzzi: sitting there watching the mountain panorama unfold is a very unique pleasure. The cuisine is particularly fine. Chef Victor Garcia (28) pleases gourmets with his ambitious Mediterranean dishes. It is also worth nothing that the paelleas of colleague Jaime Butanó are unbeatable.

Ca's Xorc
Carretera de Deià, Km 56,1
E-07100 Sóller
Phone: 00 34 / 9 71 / 63 82 80
Fax: 00 34 / 9 71 / 63 29 49
E-mail:
stay@casxorc.com
Internet:
www.casxorc.com

12 rooms
Interior Room Euro 160,
Vista Room Euro 180,
Superior Room Euro 220,
Deluxe Room (with terrasse)
Euro 290
Meeting facilities
for up to 38 persons
Opening hours restaurant:
daily from 1.00 pm to 3.30 pm
and 8.00 pm to 10.30 pm
Closed from
14. 11. 05 to 15. 02. 06

Distance from airport:
35 minutes

Im Süden Mallorcas, nur gut eine halbe Autostunde von Palma entfernt, empfängt die luxuriöse Finca ihre Besucher inmitten eines 75 000 Quadratmeter großen Naturgrundstücks. Wer ein individuelles Domizil sucht, das die Atmosphäre eines stilvollen Privathauses mit dem Komfort eines luxuriösen kleinen Hotels mischt, ist bei Nicole Bibard und Jörg Hertzner bestens aufgehoben. In den zwölf großzügigen Doppelzimmern und Suiten bestimmt nicht agrotouristische Rustikalität die Atmosphäre, sondern warme Farben und natürliche Materialien verleihen jedem Zimmer mediterrane Leichtigkeit. Dabei sind der eigene Garten, Balkon oder die eigene Terrasse genauso selbstverständlich wie die Errungenschaften modernsten Komforts, etwa ein DVD-CD-Player (für den 160 kostenlose Leih-DVDs bereitstehen). Besonders großer Beliebtheit erfreuen sich die Suiten Amapola (82 Quadratmeter) und Rosa (55 Quadratmeter), die jeweils in einem separaten Haus untergebracht sind, sowie die Casa Bomba; sie alle haben einen eigenen Pool. Familien finden in den beiden Family-Suiten Girasol und Margarita optimalen Freiraum. Ein üppiges Frühstücksbuffet (bis 12.00 Uhr) ist genauso selbstverständlich wie entspannende Wellnesstage und eine hervorragende mediterrane Küche. Sportlich aktiven Gästen bieten sich eine Joggingbahn (800 Meter), ein Beach-Soccer-Volleyballplatz, eine Boule-Bahn und ein Hauptpool, der 10 x 20 Meter misst; eigene Driving-Range (240 Meter) mit sieben Abschlagplätzen und Bunkerübungsanlage.

In the south of Majorca and only 30 minutes' drive from Palma, Amapola Finca is a luxurious residence set in a 75,000 square metre natural plot of land. If you're looking for somewhere individual that combines the stylish luxury of a private house with all the comforts of a small hotel, then you will feel at home with Nicole Bibard and Jörg Hertzner. Rather than the rustic feel of ecological tourism dominating the atmosphere of the rooms, it's their warm colours and natural materials that give each and every room its light Mediterranean feel. Indeed, it also goes without saying that all its rooms come with their own balcony or patio area and all the latest conveniences, incl. a DVD-CD player (the hotel has 160 free DVDs for you to watch). Its Amapola (82 square metres) and Rosa (55 square metres) suites enjoy particular popularity. Each of these suites is located in a separate house, as, too, is the Casa Bomba; all of these have their own pool. Families can look forward to enjoying all the space offered by the Finca's Girasol and Margarita family rooms. Just imagine waking up to a sumptuous breakfast buffet (till 12 pm), enjoying a relaxing wellness program and sampling some absolutely fantastic Mediterranean cuisine. The more sporting minded have also been catered for with a jogging track (800 metres), a beach-soccer volleyball pitch, a Boule area, a swimming pool measuring 10 x 20 metres, a driving range (240 metres) with seven tees and bunker practice area.

Amapola, Die Finca
Owner: Nicole Bibard
and Jörg Hertzner
Ctra. Sa Rapita km 2,3
E-07630 Campos / Majorca
Phone: 00 34 / 9 71 / 65 02 44
E-mail:
info@finca-amapola.com

12 rooms and suites
from Euro 150 to 320

Distance from airport:
20 minutes

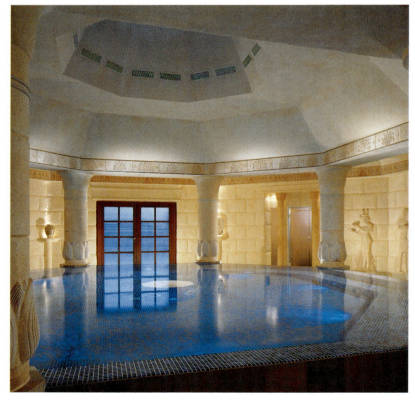

Brillante, großzügigste Ambiancen im maurisch-mediterranen Stil; 133 Zimmer und Suiten, deren luxuriöses Interieur Gäste mit ungewöhnlich viel Raum (Terrassen inklusive) verwöhnt; erstklassige Lage auf dem Kliff an der Südwestküste; ein Spa mit Tiefendimensionen; ein Gourmetrestaurant mit elaborierter Cuisine – das sind nur die hervorstechendsten Highlights, die diese Urlaubs- und Meetingdestination schnell zu einer der attraktivsten Residenzen Mallorcas gemacht haben. Immer deutlicher wird dabei, dass Mardavalls Altira-Spa nicht nur alles bietet, was anspruchsvolle Beauty- und Wellness-Gäste gewöhnlich erwarten. Das Angebot reicht von der traditionellen chinesischen Medizin über Ayurveda bis hin zu Thalassotherapien. Wer in einem Spa – wie es seine klassische Definition vorsieht – auch medizinische Qualitäten sucht, findet im Altira Hilfe, Linderung und Heilung. Wie versiert Cuisinier Gerhard Berktold eine Küche beherrscht, die fit macht, zeigt die Karte des Restaurants „S'Aigua". Die meisten Positionen leiten sich aus dem neuen Konzept „functional eating" ab, über das Gerhard Berktold gerade ein Buch herausgebracht hat. Wie vitalisierend aber auch hochkreative Feinschmecker-Cuisine sein kann, erfahren Gäste allabendlich im Gourmetrestaurant „Es Fum". Hier zeigt Berktold eine exquisite, asiatisch inspirierte Mittelmeerküche.

Choosing the most striking highlights of a holiday and meeting destination in Majorca that has fast become one of the island's most attractive establishments is not easy. It offers lavish Moorish-Mediterranean splendour, 133 rooms and suites providing guests with an unexpectedly large amount of space (incl. patio), a first-class location on the cliff on the south-west coast, a thoroughly comprehensive health spa and a gourmet restaurant serving elaborate cuisine. And the closer you look, the more you come to realize that Mardavall's Altira Spa offers more than discerning beauty and wellness guests would usually expect. The range of treatments on offer stretches from traditional Chinese medicine, to Ayurveda to Thalasso therapies. Those looking for medicinal qualities in a health spa can look forward to finding help, alleviation and therapy in the Altira Spa facilities. And you only have to take a look at what's on offer in the "S'Aigua" Restaurant's menu to see just how experienced Cuisinier Gerhard Berktold is. Most of the menu items come from the new functional eating concept, about which Gerhard Berktold has just published a book. Indeed, you can look forward to finding out just how vitalizing and highly creative gourmet cuisine can be in the "Es Fum" gourmet restaurant every evening. Master Chef, Gerhard Berktold prides himself on serving exquisite Asian-inspired Mediterranean cuisine.

Mardavall Hotel & Spa
Hotel Manager:
Andreas Oberoi
Passeig Calvià, s/n
E-07181 Costa d'en Blanes / Calvià
Phone: 00 34 / 9 71 / 62 96 29
Fax: 00 34 / 9 71 / 62 96 30
E-mail: info@mardavall-hotel.com
Internet: www.mardavall-hotel.com

45 rooms and 88 suites
Rates from Euro 312 to 3,338

Distance from airport:
15 minutes by limousine

Memberships:
Luxury Collection of Starwood Hotels & Resorts, American Express Fine Hotels & Resorts

Wer unter Urlaub Sonne und Meer satt versteht, der ist hier schon einmal richtig: hinter Maricel, dem Namen der Fünf-Sterne-Adresse direkt an der Uferstraße, steckt der mallorquinische Ausdruck für Sonne und Meer. Die großzügig gestaltete Hallenlounge dieses Boutique-Hotels mit herrschaftlicher Architektur und unbeschwertem, minimalistischen Interior Design gibt schon beim Entree den Ton an: viel schwarzes Leder, viel dunkles Holz, Säulen und Bögen aus Stein – Architekt Xavier Claramunt hat es verstanden, der majestätischen Palazzo-Architektur aus den 40er Jahren eine unaufdringliche Ästhetik einzuhauchen. Die 29 Zimmer und Suiten nehmen die gestalterische Linie harmonisch auf. Man wohnt umgeben von perfektem Fünf-Sterne-Komfort, DSL-Internetanschluss, DVD-Player und kostenlose Minibar inklusive; die Räume haben teilweise Terrasse und überall überwältigt der Blick aufs Meer. Der Pool scheint hinauszufließen und schöne Steintreppen führen hinab zum Meer. Yachten machen am hoteleigenen Anleger fest. Viele von ihnen kommen, um die feine mediterran-mallorquinische Küche zu genießen oder ein weiteres Highlight des Hauses: „das beste Frühstück der Welt", eine Auszeichnung, die das Hotel auf einer Gastronomiemesse in Madrid erhielt. Es gibt ein eigenes Restaurant dafür (natürlich mit „Maricel-Blick"), und es wird à la carte serviert, mit unterschiedlichen Brotsorten, hausgemachten Marmeladen, Foie gras, Sobrasada und vielem mehr.

If holiday for you means sun and sea, then this is the right place for you: Maricel, the name of the five-star establishment right on the quayside, just happens to be the Majorcan word for sun and sea. The roomy hall and lounge area of this boutique hotel with stately architecture and light minimalist interior design sets the tone for the hotel right from the start: plenty of black leather, dark wood, pillars and arches of stone. Architect Xavier Claramunt knew how to complement the majestic Palazzo architecture of the 1940s with simple aesthetics. The 29 rooms and suites take up the design theme in a harmonious way. Here one is surrounded by every comfort the five stars have to offer – broadband internet connections, DVD player and free mini-bar. Some of the rooms have a terrace and everywhere there is an overpowering view of the sea. The pool appears to flow outwards and lovely stone steps lead down to the sea. Yachts are tied up at the hotel's own jetty. Many visitors arrive this way to enjoy either the fine Mediterranean, Majorcan cuisine or to sample a further highlight of the hotel, the "best breakfast in the world", an award presented to the hotel by a gastronomic fair in Madrid. There is even a special breakfast restaurant – with "Maricel view" of course. The menu is à la carte, with different types of bread, homemade jams, goose liver pâté and a lot more.

Hospes-Hotel Maricel
Ca's Català–
Carretera d'Andratx 11
E-07181 Calvià
Phone: 00 34 / 9 71 / 70 77 44
Fax: 00 34 / 9 71 / 70 77 45
E-mail: maricel@hospes.es
Internet: www.hospes.es

29 rooms and suites depending on category and season from Euro 250 to 640

Distance from airport:
45 minutes

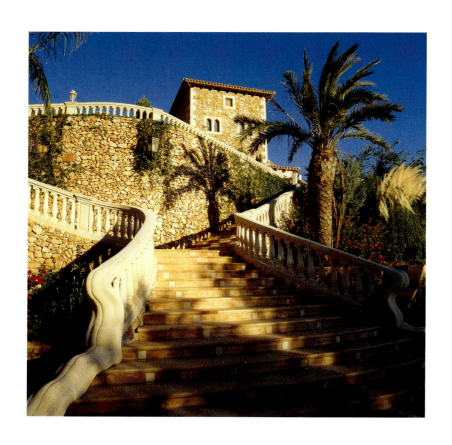

Die Lage der Villa Hermosa könnte nicht schöner sein: Malerisch an den Hang unter dem Santuario de Sant Salvador gesetzt – oben die Villa mit ihren zehn luxuriösen Zimmern und Suiten, im Stil eines eleganten mallorquinischen Herrenhauses erbaut, etwas unterhalb, durch eine prachtvolle Treppenarchitektur damit verbunden, das Restaurant Vista Hermosa – bietet die 5-Sterne-Destination ihren Gästen spektakuläre Blicke übers Land und hinaus aufs Meer. Im Frühling und Sommer lockt natürlich der Open-Air-Pool im XXL-Format zu ausgiebigen Sonnenstunden. Von ihm führt die Freitreppe hinauf zur Vista Hermosa und damit zu einer der schönsten Speiseterrassen der Gegend. Feinschmecker freuen sich über die Kreativität einer mediterranen, leicht asiatisch akzentuierten Cuisine. Die Lektüre der Karte macht Lust auf formidable Kreszenzen der bedeutendsten Anbaugebiete Spaniens. Gerne arrangiert die Direktion Abschlagzeiten auf allen fünfzehn Plätzen Mallorcas. Mit dem nahen Club Val d'Or (fünf Autominuten entfernt) sind auch individuelle Arrangements möglich, ob es um die gezielte Verbesserung des Handicaps geht oder auch nur darum, einfach mal in den Sport hineinzuschnuppern. Ein breitgefächertes Wellnessprogramm bietet für Körper und Seele viele angenehme Anregungen.

Villa Hermosa's location could hardly be more lovely. Commanding a picturesque position on the sloping hillside below the Santuario de Sant Salvador, this five-star establishment offers its guests spectacular views across the land to the sea. The villa, which resembles an elegant Majorcan mansion, has ten luxurious rooms and suites and enjoys a raised position. Slightly lower down and connected by splendid steps is the Vista Hermosa restaurant. In the spring and summer what could be better than enjoying the delights of the generously proportioned open-air pool in the sunshine. Outdoor steps climb up from the pool to the Vista Hermosa restaurant, which undoubtedly offers one of the most delightful dining patios around. Gourmets can look forward to enjoying creative Mediterranean cuisine with a slightly Asian accent. The wine list reads like a who's who of fine Kreszenzen from Spain's most important winegrowing areas. The management can also arrange tee-off times at all of Majorca's fifteen golf courses. Villa Hermosa also has contacts with the nearby club of Val d'Or (five minutes' drive) and can organise individual arrangements regardless of whether you want to work on your handicap or just give golf a try. A comprehensive wellness program has been designed to pamper with wonderful treatments for the body and soul.

Villa Hermosa
Direction: Annelore and
Ralf zur Brügge
Ctra. Felanitx – Portocolom,
Km. 6
E-07200 Felanitx
Phone: 00 34 / 9 71 / 82 49 60
Fax: 00 34 / 9 71 / 82 45 92
E-mail:
vhermosa@baleares.com
Internet:
www.hotel-villahermosa.com

10 rooms and suites
from Euro 153 to 325

Distance from airport:
40 minutes

Als Freund der Architektur und Landschaftsgestaltung erfüllte Prinz Alfonso von Hohenlohe 1954 seinen Traum von einem exklusiven Club, heute bekannt als ganzjährig geöffnetes Marbella Club Hotel · Golf Resort & Spa. Spektakulär schon immer die Gärten des der Vereinigung „Leading Small Hotels of the World" angehörenden Beach Hideaways. Das prachtvolle Naturreservat steht bis heute in schönster Blüte. Es fasst ein Urlaubsrefugium ein, das eher einem andalusischen Dorf gleicht als einem herkömmlichen Hotel. Man wohnt in 121 luxuriösen Zimmern und Suiten. Sie sind über das Resort verstreut. Wer es absolut privat haben will, der zieht in eine der sechzehn privaten Pool Villen. Über die Hälfte haben einen eigenen Pool. Einzigartig an der Costa del Sol: das 800 Quadratmeter große Marbella Club Thalasso Spa mit direktem Blick auf das Element, aus dem die entspannenden, revitalisierenden, verjüngenden, schlankmachenden Elixire kommen, aufs Meer. Aber nicht nur die Lage ist exponiert, sondern auch das Angebot. Modernste Installationen, therapeutischer Innen-Meerwasserpool, Sauna, Solarium, osmanisches Hammam und zwölf Anwendungsräume. Sportlich ambitionierten Gästen steht mit dem Marbella Club Golf Resort ein wunderschöner, hoteleigener 18-Loch-Golfplatz in den Bergen von Benahavis, der von Dave Thomas entworfen wurde, zur Verfügung. Im näheren und weiteren Umkreis können zahlreiche attraktive Courses gespielt werden.

As an avid landscape designer, Prince Alfonso von Hohenlohe fulfilled his dream in 1954 in creating a club known today as the Marbella Club Hotel · Golf Resort & Spa, which is open all year round. The gardens of this Beachfront Hideaway have always been singularly beautiful and the hotel is one of the "Leading Small Hotels of the World". Today the gorgeous resort is still in full bloom not just literally but also metaphorically. It encompasses a place of rest and relaxation that looks more like an Andalusian village than a conventional hotel. Guests stay in 121 luxurious rooms and suites distributed throughout the fragrant flowered gardens. Those looking for an atmosphere of absolute privacy will choose to occupy one of the 16 villas with private garden and private heated pool. Unique on the Costa del Sol is the large Marbella Club Thalasso Spa covering 800 square metres with an undisturbed view of the element from where the hotel's invigorating, rejuvenating, slimming elixirs have their origin, the sea. However it is not just the location that is in a league of its own but also the health and wellness programme using modern equipment, a dynamic therapeutic indoor seawater pool, sauna, solarium, osmanic hammams and twelve treatment rooms. The hotel's very own 18-hole golf course in the foothills of Benahavis, designed by Dave Thomas, is available for use by guests. Greens provide endless pleasure for golf enthusiasts.

Marbella Club Hotel ·
Golf Resort & Spa
Bulevar Príncipe Alfonso
von Hohenlohe
E-29600 Marbella / Malaga /
España
Phone:
00 34 / 95 / 2 82 22 11
Fax:
00 34 / 95 / 2 82 98 84
Internet:
www.marbellaclub.com
E-mail:
hotel@marbellaclub.com

84 rooms, 37 suites and
16 private pool villas
from Euro 250 to 3,750 per
night, exclusive breakfast
and VAT, currently 7 %

Distance from airport:
35 minutes / 62 km

Memberships:
The Leading Small Hotels
of the World,
Leading Spa of the World

Schon zu Beginn des 20. Jahrhunderts zog die Costa Brava Reisende magisch an. Leider hat der Massentourismus auch hier seine Blüten getrieben, doch bezeugen jede Menge prächtige Villen, dass die Küste mehr zu bieten hat als Party und Bettenburgen. Seit letztem Jahr ist die Grandezza auch in die Luxushotellerie der Küste zurückgekehrt. In dem zentral gelegenen Örtchen Playa de Fenals verwöhnt das Alva Park Resort & Spa mit exklusiven Interieurs und einer Servicephilosophie, die nicht nur an der Costa Brava neue Maßstäbe setzt. Nur wenige Meter vom Strand entfernt präsentiert sich das gesamte Resort wie eine luxuriöse Privatresidenz. Das fängt bei der Größe der 88 Junior Suiten und Suiten – mindestens siebzig Quadratmeter – an und hört bei den modernsten technischen Komfortraffinessen noch längst nicht auf. Die überaus luxuriöse und komfortable Ausstattung der Suiten weckt bei Luxustravellern hohe Erwartungen – Erwartungen, die das Resort bis ins kleinste Detail erfüllt; im Service und im Veranstaltungsbereich genauso wie im „Molton Brown Spa" und erst recht auf der kulinarischen Seite. Für das Küchenkonzept des Gourmetrestaurants „A Flor D'aigua" konnte man den bekannten menorquinischen Küchenchef Damia Coll gewinnen und für die Authentizität des japanischen Spezialitätenrestaurants „Minamo" bürgt ein japanischer Spitzenkoch.

Ever since the beginning of the 20th century, the Costa Brava has had a magical attraction for travellers. Unfortunately, the region has also been a popular mass tourism destination. Yet for all this, a large number of magnificent villas clearly demonstrate that the Costa Brava has much more to offer than just nightlife and large tourist developments. And last year the grandeur returned to the coast's luxury hospitality sector. The small town of Playa de Fenals boasts a central location. Here the Alva Park Resort & Spa promises exclusive interiors and a service mentality that is setting new standards in the Costa Brava and beyond. Located just a few metres from the beach, the entire complex resembles a luxurious private residence. Starting with its 88 generously-proportioned Junior Suites and Suites (at least 70 square metres) and certainly not ending with all its modern conveniences, this is a luxurious resort. Its incredibly luxurious and comfortable suites certainly have the wherewithal to raise the expectations of the discerning traveller. Expectations that are met down to the very last detail. Be it its service standards or events, its "Molton Brown Spa" or its delightful cuisine, quality shines through. The resort was also successful in tempting the well-known Menorcan Chef, Damia Coll, to preside over its "A Flor D'aigua" gourmet restaurant and culinary concept. A top Japanese Chef has also been recruited for its "Minamo" Japanese speciality restaurant.

Alva Park Resort & Spa
Francesc Layret 3–5
E-17310 Platja de Fenals /
Lloret de Mar (Girona)
Spain
Phone: 00 34 / 9 72 / 36 85 81
Fax: 00 34 / 9 72 / 36 44 67
E-mail:
mail@alvapark.com
Internet:
www.alvapark.com

88 Junior Suites and suites
Junior Suite from Euro 450
to 570, Deluxe Junior Suite
from Euro 510 to 630, Premier Seaview Junior Suite
from Euro 660 to 780,
Top Suites from Euro 1,650
to 5,100

Distance from Barcelona
airport: 60 minutes

EINE REISE VON TAUSEND MEILEN
BEGINNT MIT EINEM EINZIGEN SCHRITT ...
Even a journey of a thousand miles begins with a single step ...

Mit einem Abonnement von HIDEAWAYS reisen Sie viermal im Jahr zu den schönsten Hotels der Welt – und Sie erhalten von uns zusätzlich 2 000 Prämienmeilen für Ihr Miles & More Konto!

Subscribe to HIDEAWAYS and you will discover four times a year the most beautiful hotels and destinations of the World – and you will receive additional 2.000 miles from us for your Miles & More account.

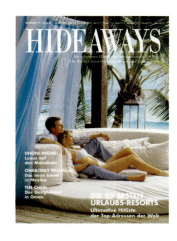

Das exklusive Reisemagazin HIDEAWAYS präsentiert Ihnen viermal im Jahr zweisprachig in Deutsch/Englisch die besten Hotels und die atemberaubendsten Destinationen. Erstklassige Fotografie, ein großzügiges Layout und wertvolle Tipps unterstreichen den Anspruch, eines der führenden Reisemagazine der Welt zu sein.

First class photography, a generous layout, bilingual text in German/English and valuable insider's tips lay claim to HIDEAWAYS to be one of the leading travel magazines of the World.

Unsere **Classic Edition** mit traumhaften Urlaubshotels erscheint jeweils im März und September, im Juli laden wir Sie jedes Jahr mit dem **Golf Special** zu „fairways to heaven" ein und im Oktober dreht sich alles in unserem umfangreichen **Beauty Special** rund um die schönsten Wellness- und Beauty-Hotels.

*The **Classic Edition** with dreamlike holiday hotels and resorts appears every year in March and September, in July we will whisk you with the **Golf Special** to really "fairways to heaven" and in October you will discover in the **Beauty Special** breathtaking Wellness- and Spa-Hotels.*

Das Abonnement mit vier Ausgaben pro Jahr kostet nur 30,– Euro (inkl. Portokosten im Inland, im Ausland zzgl. Porto). Bestellen Sie Ihr Abonnement einfach auf unserer Homepage **www.hideaways.de**

*The price for a subscription with 4 issues a year is only 30,– Euro (including postage in Germany, plus postage abroad). You can order your subscription at our website **www.hideaways.de***

Oder rufen Sie uns an: gebührenfreie Abo-Hotline 08 00 / 9 11 11-10 (Inland) oder 00 49 521 / 9 11 11-0 (Ausland).

Or call us: 08 00 / 9 11 11-10 (toll-free from Germany) or 00 49 521 / 9 11 11-0.

Partner of
Miles & More ®
✈ Lufthansa

KLOCKE VERLAG GMBH, HÖFEWEG 40, D-33619 BIELEFELD, PHONE 00 49 521 / 9 11 11-0, FAX 00 49 521 / 9 11 11-12, INFO@KLOCKE-VERLAG.DE, WWW.KLOCKE-VERLAG.DE